P9-CEU-978

Lonesome Traveler

Lonesome Traveler

THE LIFE OF

LEE HAYS

Doris Willens

W. W. NORTON & COMPANY

New York · London

Copyright © 1988 by Doris Willens
All rights reserved.
Published simultaneously in Canada by Penguin Books Canada Ltd.,
2801 John Street, Markham, Ontario L3R 1B4.
Printed in the United States of America.

The text of this book is composed in Trump Medieval, with
display type set in Brush Script.
Composition and manufacturing by Arcata Graphics.
Book design by Lynn Fischer.

FIRST EDITION

Library of Congress Cataloging-in-Publication Data

Willens, Doris.
Lonesome traveler : the life of Lee Hays / Doris Willens.
p.   cm.
Includes index.
1. Hays, Lee, 1914–1981.
2. Folk singers—United States—Biography.   I. Title.
ML420.H28W5   1988
784.4'92'4—dc19   87–26933
[B]

ISBN 0-393-02564-0

W. W. Norton & Company, Inc.
500 Fifth Avenue, New York, N.Y. 10110
W. W. Norton & Company Ltd.
37 Great Russell Street, London WC1B 3NU

1 2 3 4 5 6 7 8 9 0

Song Permissions for "Lonesome Traveler: The Life of Lee Hays"

"The State of Arkansas," by Lee Hays, Fred Hellerman, & Ronnie Gilbert. Copyright © 1960 by SANGA MUSIC INC. All Rights Reserved. Used by Permission.

"Raggedy," by Lee Hays & John Handcox. Copyright © 1967, 1982 by SANGA MUSIC INC. All Rights Reserved. Used by Permission.

"Organize, Organize," by Claude Williams. Copyright © 1947 by Claude Williams. All Rights Reserved.

"Union Train," by Lee Hays, Pete Seeger, & Millard Lampell. Copyright © 1947 by STORMKING MUSIC INC. All Rights Reserved. Used by Permission.

"Roll the Union On," by Lee Hays & John Handcox. Copyright © 1947 by STORMKING MUSIC INC. All Rights Reserved. Used by Permission.

"Talking Union," by Lee Hays, Pete Seeger, & Millard Lampell. Copyright © 1947 by STORMKING MUSIC INC. All Rights Reserved. Used by Permission.

"Harry Bridges," by Woody Guthrie. Copyright © 1966 by STORMKING MUSIC INC. All Rights Reserved. Used by Permission.

"Pittsburgh," by Woody Guthrie. Copyright © 1957 by WOODY GUTHRIE PUBLICA-TIONS. All Rights Reserved. Used by Permission.

"Walk Along Together," by Lee Hays. Copyright © 1947 by Lee Hays. All Rights Reserved. Used by Permission.

"Pineville," by Lee Hays. Copyright © 1946 by Lee Hays. All Rights Reserved. Used by Permission.

"The Rankin Tree," by Lee Hays & Walter Lowenfels. Copyright © 1946 by STORM-KING MUSIC INC. All Rights Reserved. Used by Permission.

"Ballad for Un-American Blues," by Lee Hays & Walter Lowenfels. Copyright © 1947 by STORMKING MUSIC INC. All Rights Reserved. Used by Permission.

"I've Got a Ballot," by Yip Harburg, based on "I've Got Sixpence." Copyright © 1948 by Mutual Music Society. All Rights Reserved.

"Friendly Henry Wallace," words by Yip Harburg, music by Milton Agar. Copyright © 1948 by Yip Harburg & Milton Agar. All Rights Reserved.

"Banks of the Ohio," by Lee Hays. Copyright © 1962 by SANGA MUSIC INC. All Rights Reserved. Used by Permission.

"Weaver Theme Song," by Woody Gurthrie. Copyright © 1988 by WOODY GUTHRIE PUBLICATIONS INC. All Rights Reserved. Used by Permission.

"Goodnight Irene," Words and Music by Huddie Ledbetter and John A. Lomax. TRO—Copyright © 1936 (renewed 1964) and 1950 (renewed 1978) Ludlow Music, Inc., New York, N.Y. Used by Permission.

"If I Had a Hammer," (The Hammer Song), Words and Music by Lee Hays and Pete Seeger. TRO— Copyright © 1958 (renewed 1986) and 1962 Ludlow Music, Inc., New York, N.Y. Used by Permission.

"Lonesome Traveler," Words and Music by Lee Hays. TRO—Copyright © 1950 (renewed 1978) and 1951 (renewed 1979) Folkways Music Publishers, Inc., New York, N.Y. Used by Permission.

"The Butterfly and the Bird," by Lee Hays & Sue Brown Hays. Copyright © 1966 by SANGA MUSIC INC. All Rights Reserved. Used by Permission.

"Get Up and Go," Words collected and adapted and set to original music by Pete Seeger. TRO— Copyright © 1964 Melody Trails, Inc., New York, N.Y. Used by Permission.

"Farewell Little Toe," by Lee Hays. Copyright © 1988 by SANGA MUSIC INC. All Rights Reserved. Used by Permission.

"In Dead Earnest," by Lee Hays. Copyright © 1981 by SANGA MUSIC INC. All Rights Reserved. Used by Permission.

For Jeff, Pete, and Dan, who made my heart sing.

"We felt that if we sang loud enough and strong enough and hopefully enough, somehow it would make a difference."

—RONNIE GILBERT, of the WEAVERS

Contents

Preface

Lee Hays should, of course, have written his own book. He talked about it often. He even had the title: "My Posthumous Memoirs." But writing a book is a long and lonely business, and Lee preferred working with people. The times he got really serious about a book, he'd immediately enlist one of his "young people" to help.

I became one of Lee's "young people" in 1955. My husband and I, back from five years of journalism in London, had moved into the third-floor apartment of a Brooklyn Heights brownstone. Lee lived on the second floor. He and I had plenty of time to share during the day—I was home with my year-old baby, and Lee was blacklisted.

Lee was always on the lookout for raw material, undeveloped talent in the young people who came his way. He soon had me writing and singing songs for Baby Jeff. With two more of his young people—Alan Arkin and his wife—Lee turned us into a quartet, the Babysitters. We recorded four albums on the Vanguard label. Children, parents, and critics loved them.

The Babysitters were among Lee's happier experiences, unfraught with the political tensions of his earlier life. We'd worked well together on the albums. Lee had watched me go on to write a five-days-a-week column for the business pages of the *New York Journal-American*. I guess he figured I got things done.

So, in the 1960s, he talked to me about helping him assemble a "Lee Hays Commonplace Book"—a collection of songs, stories, recipes, whatnot. He sent me a baby photograph of himself, and then nothing else. I felt relieved; I'd said yes out of friendship rather than enthusiasm for a paste-up book. In 1976, he asked me to work with him on his memoirs. The logistics of my life by then precluded my taking on so large an assignment. But at the least I could guide him through a kind of oral history. We began taping in September 1976.

Unhappily, the memories of old conflicts dredged up by the process "murdered sleep," grumbled Lee, in a shattering message recorded in the middle of a night in March 1977. He signed off on the project forever. I could do whatever I wished with his material after his death.

In the years of his life that remained, he must have brushed off questions about his book with the response "Doris is working on it," because at his memorial service, the other Weavers and their manager, Harold Leventhal, all seemed to take for granted that the book was in my hands.

How could I say it wasn't?

Acknowledgments

$\mathcal{M}$y abiding thanks:

To Lee Hays, for believing in me. To Harold Leventhal, Pete Seeger, Fred Hellerman, and Ronnie Gilbert, for assuming Lee knew what he was doing and helping me make it through. To the members of Lee's family, who opened their homes and their files to me.

To a half century of Lee's co-workers and friends and neighbors, whose memories filled in so much that Lee, for whatever reasons, had forgotten.

To a young woman—Arlene Carmen of Judson Church—who felt strongly about the project, although she'd never met Lee, for tracking down key people and archival information and, most astonishingly, Lee's long-missing documentary film on sharecroppers.

To Irene Allong and Joy Graeme of Harold Leventhal's staff—Irene, for graciously handling so many spin-off chores my frequent presence produced, and Joy, for gathering the all-important song clearances from music publishers. Salaam.

To the archivists of the Highlander Folk School, and the Charlotte and Raymond Koch Collection in Wayne State University's Walter Reuther Archives, for their invaluable material on the radical South in the 1930s. And to Donald H. Grubbs, professor of history at the University of the Pacific, for generously sharing with me his rare collection of letters from the Reverend Claude Williams.

To those whose names are in neither the text nor the footnotes, but who provided important insights—among them Dr. Broadus Mitchell, Dr. Joseph Wortis, Zenaide Reiss, and the Murtagh family.

To Bernie Asbell, author and (truly extraordinary) professor of writing at Penn State College and old friend of Lee's, whom I came to call my "dramaturg" because of the encouragement and editorial guidance he so exuberantly gave me.

To Ronda Shaw, who wisely talked me through the conflicts that Lee's conflicts churned up in me.

To my agent, Gina Maccoby, for taking on a first-time author and giving the kind of care and attention that other agents expend only on potential "big packages." And to my editor, Jim Mairs, for lavishing love on my manuscript.

Lastly, because personally, to Roy Block, for being there when I need him, which is most of the time.

*C*arnegie Hall, November 28, 1980. The great old concert hall is filled to capacity and then some, with a noisy, excited audience. Tonight the Weavers will sing again, their first time in Carnegie since 1963. Their concert is billed as a thirtieth-anniversary re-union. No one expects a thirty-fifth, or even a thirty-first.

On the unadorned stage, four microphones have been set up—three free-standing, the fourth attached to a skirted dais no more than three feet high.

The hall darkens, the audience hushes, the stage lights up. From the wings come the Weavers, in an entrance unlike any from their past. Pete Seeger, whose long legs seem to stretch almost up to where his long neck begins, pushes a wheelchair that bears his old friend Lee Hays, who now has no legs at all. Ronnie Gilbert and Fred Hellerman flank Pete and Lee, lightly touching the wheel-chair as they start downstage.

At the sight of them, the audience rises and erupts in a torrent of emotion that hits the Weavers with visible force. They stop for one brief, confused moment, then quickly make for the micro-phones, holding on to the wheelchair for support. The audience sees the astonishment on their faces, and cheers and whistles and stomps the louder. It goes on and on. The Weavers blink hard, looking out on faces glistening with tears.

This is not ordinary show business sentimentality. The Weavers represent a triumph over a dark part of American history. They trigger memories of the bloody riot at Peekskill, of the sickening McCarthy years, of a rampant House Un-American Activities Committee, of boycotts and hate campaigns and blacklists. The Weavers had lived through it all. Rising unexpectedly from hoote-nannies to the peak of musical stardom in 1950, they'd been tar-geted by self-appointed loyalty experts, dogged by "patriotic" groups, accused in headlines, scorned by clubs that had once fought to book them, banned by broadcasters, struck from their recording company's catalog. They'd been forced to disband in 1952.

But in 1955 they'd returned to Carnegie for a Christmas concert, which relaunched their remarkable career. They built new audiences in concert halls and on college campuses. Although the major companies refused to record them (because the blacklist kept them off the air), a small company would find ways to make and sell their albums profitably. Never again would they be heard on jukeboxes, but their songs and the singers they influenced would change the course of mainstream American music.

With dignity and humor, the Weavers overcame the worst that America could give. From the 1955 concert through their final tour, in 1964, their every appearance filled auditoriums with excited young and old audiences that revered their music and their courage.

Any hope among their devotees that the Weavers would reunite after 1964 faded with time and reports of Lee's amputations.

But now, for one last, momentous time, the Weavers have come together. And the audience can't contain its feelings of joy and love, and vindication.

Lee, behind the skirted dais, welcomes the audience to the reunion concert. He confides that he'd "been fixin' to retire to the old folks home in Washington, D.C., only it was just taken." The audience laughs comfortably at the familiar Hays mix of self-deprecation and comment on current events. A Weavers concert isn't a Weaver's concert without Lee's humor.

He hasn't been on a stage since 1964, has not come to the city since 1972. But this concert is special in more ways than the audience realizes. It is being filmed as the climax of a documentary on the Weavers. Lee believes in the project as a summing up of the group's story and spirit, as perhaps his legacy, and he has willed himself to make it to Carnegie tonight.

Wasn't That a Time!, released after Lee's death in August of 1981, surpassed the filmmakers' hopes. The film was not only good but, like the Weavers themselves, good *and* commercial. In the big cities, long runs followed loving reviews. Then, worldwide distribution. Finally, repeated runs on public television across the country.

The filmmakers had centered the documentary on Lee and peppered it with his humor. Certainly, it buttressed Fred Hellerman's contention that the spirit of the Weavers, and their only irreplaceable member, was Lee. Posthumously, the film brought Lee stardom.

Only a few years earlier, after another in a long line of researchers bearing tape recorders had prospected his memories of Woody Guthrie, Pete Seeger, Leadbelly, Emma Dusenberry, and others, Lee mused that he was "destined to be a footnote to history." He was, in fact, a legend in the world of music.

Lee had come out of Arkansas in 1940 with a batch of songs that had lifted the hearts of sharecroppers and miners and CIO organizers in the South—songs that would roll the unions on throughout the nation.

Bunyanesque in size, he strode north and beguiled city folk with what seemed an exotic mix of Methodist parsonage upbringing, rural southern humor, prodigious book learning, foot-thumping folk singing, and politics that would land him before HUAC.

He was always ready to craft a song for a cause and to draw out the song-writing potential in others.

Through good times and bad, he could be found on the side of movements and ideas that supported the downtrodden, but not in a doctrinaire way. He questioned everything (often clear out of existence) and distrusted authority of every kind.

Lee's renown is linked to that of the two legendary singing groups he and Pete Seeger brought forth—the Weavers and the Almanacs. With the release of the film, old and new audiences wanted to know more about the remarkable man whose courage illuminated the screen.

I hope my work does justice to his story and spirit.

Lonesome Traveler

1

"The State of Arkansas"
1914–1930

I've travelled this wide world over,
And some ups and downs I've saw,
But I never knew what misery was
Till I came to Arkansas.

—From *"The State of Arkansas,"*
a ballad collected and arranged
by LEE HAYS

*N*owhere in Lee Hays's words does one find a description of a room or a house from his childhood. He calls no place his hometown. One soon learns why.

Before he was twelve years old, Lee had lived in five widely separated Arkansas towns. That's how it was for the family of a Methodist minister. The church believed in moving its ministers frequently, so they wouldn't become corrupt or lazy.

By the last move, to the dusty, foothill town of Booneville, Lee's brothers and sister had grown up and gone off. That left Lee alone with his mother and father. Mostly with his mother. His father, as presiding elder of the Booneville district, had a large rural area of parishioners to serve. He'd be gone for days or weeks, covering the hilly territory by train or in his open Ford.

One day, soon after he'd turned thirteen, Lee saw two men drive up to the parsonage, looking distraught. He sensed something awful had happened. He heard them tell his mother there'd been an accident over in Danville, about thirty miles up the road.

He would always remember the date—May 17, 1927. From the talk around Booneville he constructed an image he would see forever: his father's car overturning, his father's girth pressed against the steering wheel, keeping him from being thrown clear, his father's brains dashed on the roadway, his father dying instantly.

His mother took in the news, and within weeks suffered a nervous breakdown from which she never recovered.

Lee rarely spoke of his childhood in the years that followed. Few people remarked on that. His great size and burdened face overwhelmed the idea of his ever having *been* a child. He seemed instead to have stepped giantlike out of some frontier myth. Facts could only have gotten in the way. He was, simply, "from Arkansas." In most places, the laughter began with that statement. The name itself sounded funny, suggesting hillbillies and moonshine and circuit-riding preachers. A perfect state for the tall tales and satiric verses of a radical minstrel.

But for all Lee's silence, his actions revealed his hurt—the rejection of everything his father believed, the search for substitute fathers, the restless looking for a home, the identification with those who had nothing.

Then, decades after the accident, having achieved some fame, Lee began to look back with less anger. Now he wanted to know as much as possible about the parents he'd lost and about the child he had been. He found some of what he was looking for in letters from his siblings.

They sent Lee photos, and he framed them and hung them on his walls. It rather pleased him to see how much he looked like the Reverend William Benjamin Hays. In size—both around six foot three and weighed well over 250 pounds (usually over 300 pounds for Lee). In features—including the blue eyes and oversized ears. His sandy hair came from his mother, Ellen Reinhardt Hays, from whom he also got his middle name, Elhardt.

He shared more than physical traits with his father: a passion for books, a passion for food, a passion for gardening, a facility for writing, an ability to move an audience. These suggested environment rather than heredity. Some of them Lee developed early, some late. One thing he could be sure he inherited from his father: the diabetes that destroyed his own health.

* * *

The Hayses were all tall and big-boned, starting back with Grandfather Reuben Hays, born in the Mississippi territory in 1810. Reuben, a six-foot-tall farmer, fought in the Creek Indian wars. When he was thirty, he married fifteen-year-old Laura Ann McCary. Their first child was born in 1842; their tenth and last (who would be Lee's father), in 1868.

Much like Lee a century later, Reuben and Laura never had a place they called a hometown. With their growing family, they lived and farmed in Alabama, Mississippi, and Tennessee, moving on, looking for more-productive land. "The pioneer spirit," William Benjamin called it, and he felt that same spirit strongly in himself.

In 1880, the family moved one last time—to Cato, Arkansas— where Reuben died seven years later. By then, all the children but William Benjamin had gone off to make their own lives.

William Benjamin's ambitions went beyond farming, though he saw them as within the pioneer tradition. If he could get himself through college, he would become a minister. He knew as a Methodist that the church believed in an itinerant ministry. That was much of its appeal to the athletic young man. He loved the image of the Methodist minister on horseback, who from the earliest days of the Republic carried the word of God's grace to the frontier. The frontiers were disappearing, but Arkansas certainly was so sparsely settled, its struggling farmers often so far from churches, that itinerancy came with ordination.

Somehow William Benjamin put himself through Hendrix, a Methodist college in Arkansas, graduating in 1897, when he was twenty-nine. A few traces of his student days remain in the family archives. A propensity for practical jokes—one night he dragged a calf up into the school tower belfry. A journalistic ability—he served as editor of the school paper, the *Hendrix College Mirror.* A readiness to moralize—he led off his by-lined columns with such warnings as "The fear of the Lord is the beginning of wisdom."

After Hendrix, William Benjamin headed for Nashville, and a postgraduate course in theology at Vanderbilt University. "Brother Hays had to work hard for his education," a church publication later noted, "and graduated late, but he kept up his studies and became a strong preacher and a very successful presiding elder, giving unusual attention to the rural church."

"He sought out forgotten places and unknown people," another article said of him, "always hoping to serve his Master thereby. He certainly endeavored to carry the torch into the uttermost parts of his parish."

The Reverend Hays's first parish was in Missouri, where in 1898 he married Miss Loutie Bonner. She bore him a son, Reuben, in 1899, and then died, disappearing from history when the widower remarried and left Missouri for Arkansas, so that the child would not hear that the minister's wife was not his own mother.

His second wife, Ellen Reinhardt, had made feminist history of

Lee's mother, Ellen Reinhardt Hays (*center*, with friends), was one of the first two women court reporters in Arkansas history.

a sort in Arkansas—she and her friend Minnie Vernor working as the first two women court reporters in the state. Of course, she quit her job when she married the Reverend Hays. She named her first baby, born in 1903, after Minnie. For Minnie's middle name, Ellen followed a southern custom and chose one associated with the opposite sex. Thus, Minnie Frank Hays, a name her only daughter would always loathe.

A year later came Bill, Jr., and that seemed to be the end of that.

Minnie Frank told Lee their mother grew up "as such a sheltered little Southern girl, with a Mammy and silks and satins and wonderful books and music, and imported fans, and so on, and then when this preacher came along with his pioneer instinct, she very happily goes riding around on a buffalo." How the sheltered little girl became the self-supporting court reporter is a transformation lost in the past. But Mrs. Hays's secretarial skills were a boon to the family. She "took down" her husband's sermons in shorthand and typed them up for him. And she taught the children how to type before they learned penmanship at school.

Their father, said Minnie Frank, was a "roarer," not out of meanness, but rather in the custom of that day and age. He roared at the children, rather than at his wife, and chiefly at Reuben. Still, and despite the frequent reassignments to new districts, Lee's siblings had only happy memories of their childhoods.

"It seemed like an awfully safe and happy world," Minnie Frank wrote, ". . . One of my favorite memories of our father is of how he would discuss Malthus, Mendel and Kant with the more eminent of our Methodist bishops and then say, 'Excuse me, I have to go milk the cow.' "

"Our family was always happy," Reuben recalled. "The distinguishing characteristic of the family was an amused way of looking at things."

Bill sang out "The constipated cross-eyed bear" in church, and only later learned that everyone else was singing "The consecrated cross I bear."

The three children were one another's playmates; as a self-contained play group, they didn't much mind the moving in and out of parsonages. And despite his roaring, their father was rather like

Lee's parents, the Reverend William Benjamin Hays and Ellen Reinhardt Hays, evoking the pioneer spirit astride a photographer's buffalo during their honeymoon, in 1902.

their camp leader. They always lived near mountains and rivers and lakes. The Reverend Hays led Reuben and Bill, Jr., on camping, hiking, fishing, and swimming weekends, extolling the beneficial, self-improving effects of outdoor activities. He'd take Minnie Frank out hunting for mushrooms, teaching her to distinguish the edible from the deadly.

If they feared their father's roaring and occasional spanking, that didn't stop the boys from playing practical jokes. Reuben and Bill together ate up the ice cream in the freezer and refilled it with leftover mashed potatoes. They substituted a red sock for the white handkerchief in the Reverend Hays's frock coat, so that when he mopped his brow while "preaching to beat hell" (Bill's words), his congregation's eyes popped.

They laughed all day and into the night after executing the maneuver of wiring an old Ford spark coil and battery to the commode just before their father sat himself down, at which moment they pushed a button and delivered an electric jolt that brought him flying back up to his feet.

Minnie Frank remembered fishing with Bill, and playing in Confederate breastworks, digging out Yankee bullets to use for sinkers. And with Reuben when they lived in Batesville, prankishly taking over a railroad handcar and riding into the mountains in it. Luckily, they didn't meet an oncoming train.

Occasionally, the Reverend Hays would take Reuben along on a trip through the district. Reuben remembered his father sawing and splitting wood for his parishioners, and helping them with their hog killing, before preaching to them at night. The people came willingly to his sermons. He'd have them laughing one minute and crying the next. He'd move with his congregation, clearing his nose and wiping away a tear after a sad story. Reuben felt something like awe at his father's physical, spiritual, and dramatic performance.

Given his energy and abilities and education and devotion, the Reverend Hays was an obvious candidate for promotion to presiding elder. As 1914 began, he was invited to serve as editor of the *Arkansas Methodist,* published in Little Rock.

In that city, on March 14, 1914, Lee was born, just months after Reuben departed for Hendrix Preparatory Academy.

His siblings thought Lee was a beautiful baby. They'd look after him and brag about how smart he was. But, of course, he *was* a baby, hardly a playmate.

In 1915, the Reverend Hays asked for reassignment from editing the paper back to the rural church work he loved. Lee moved with his family from Little Rock to Newport; a few years later to Paragould; thence to Conway, home of Hendrix College. Happily, the Conway assignment coincided with Minnie Frank's and Bill's years at Hendrix College. Those were the years, too, when the family began to think Lee might become a writer. They saved one of his earliest poems:

THE SWEET LITTLE BABE

The sweet little babe in the manger,
The night was cold,
A perfect stranger—
The wise men saw His star they say,
And went to see Him on the hay.
Herod thought he would kill the child,
But his father and mother so quiet and mild,
Fled into Egypt,
The child to save.
He grew to a man,
And made us behave.
He died on the cross to save us from sin,
If we open our hearts,
And let Him in,
He will be true,
I hope He will take me with him too.

—by LEE ELHARDT HAYS
(9 years old)

Through all the moves, some things remained constant. The vital areas in every Hays parsonage were the library, the kitchen, and the garden.

The Reverend Hays had amassed books from his college days on. Books on philosophy and history and religion, books in Greek and Latin, books well thumbed, read and reread. The size of his library struck his contemporaries as remarkable, especially given his lack of financial resources. Moreover, books had somewhat limited appeal in that part of the world. Minnie Frank liked to tell Lee about a man of good family, arrested for murdering his brother. "Oh well, he always was queer," a neighbor said. "How do you mean queer?" someone asked the neighbor, who responded, "He always had his nose in books."

When he wasn't in his books, or on the road, the Reverend Hays might be found in his beloved garden. With each move, he went to work on the parsonage garden even before he unpacked his treasured books. He lectured his children about the glories of gardening.

Perhaps most of all he loved to eat. One of Reuben's most vivid memories, he told Lee, was, "of father's great love—delicious hot

At the time of Lee's birth, in 1914, the Reverend Hays
was editor of the *Arkansas Methodist*. Later, as a
presiding elder of the church, he returned to the rural
parishes he most enjoyed serving.

fluffy biscuits, melted butter and molasses; that, with spicy country
sausage, was heaven on earth, or almost."

That was Lee's kind of eating, too, when he had the means.
When he hadn't, he'd quote the sharecropper who said, "I've got
a thousand things to eat, and all of them are beans."

Reading his siblings' memories of his father, Lee thought how
different they were from his own. Years later, taping his own memo-

The earliest extant photo of Lee Hays, at five, straddling a squash in his father's vegetable garden.

ries, he mulled some of his negative feelings. The injustice he'd felt at his father's insistence that he do gardening chores, the shame he'd known when he couldn't keep up with his father on a hike (while his father sermonized on William James's concept of "the second wind"), the panic when his father deemed him ready enough, at the age of nine, to go to New York alone on a train to spend the summer at the YMCA camp where Reuben counseled.

He could remember seeing his father refilling a bottle of River Jordan holy water from the tap. He was sure he'd smelled old tobacco once when he'd helped his father unpack—after all the Reverend Hays's preaching against the evils of the foul weed (and of alcohol).

Lee had taken up smoking and drinking at an early age, and never given them up. He'd published funny stories about the Reverend Hays's vanities, real or imagined. Southern preachers were the source of much of his comic material. How much of that was anger at having been orphaned?

Now many things he learned about his father touched him. For

Lee's sister, Minnie Frank Hays, won her A.B. in literature from Hendrix College in 1923, the youngest member of her class. She told the yearbook editor she "ain't never done nothin' worth speakin' about," but her record proclaimed otherwise. She went on to graduate study at the University of Chicago.

one, the news (to Lee) that their father had, in Minnie Frank's words, "a very bad case of diabetes, when there was no known cure. Banting and Best discovered insulin just in the nick of time. . . . Dad finally managed to give the injections to himself, as he was traveling so much."

Touching also was the comment of a young minister on the death of the Reverend Hays: "We feel that we have lost a friend and a father." Young people looked to Lee, too, as "a friend and a father" throughout his adult life.

With a different kind of feeling, Lee read a line from his father's obituary onto the tape of his memoirs: "Devoted to his family, he had given his three older children the best educational advantages and they are all making places for themselves in the world."

Reuben, Bill, and Minnie Frank had prepped at church-founded academies, graduated from Hendrix College, and then attended great institutions of learning in the North for graduate work. Lee's brothers went on to Columbia University—Reuben in economics and Bill in journalism. Minnie Frank took a graduate degree in English literature at the University of Chicago.

They would all do well. Reuben would rise to chairmanship of a big city bank. Bill made a comfortable career in middle management of a Fortune 500 company. Minnie Frank married a North Carolina lawyer who later was elected to the state legislature.

"I was the young one," Lee continued on his tape, "thirteen when my father died, and while the other three were making places for themselves in the world, I was going to have to make my own 'educational advantages.'

"They weren't anything like those of my brothers and sister. And they led me to intensely different conclusions about the state of the world."

Everything changed at once after his father's accident. The parsonage had to be vacated to accommodate the Reverend Hays's successor. Reuben, recently married and living in Boston, immediately took charge, renting a house in Booneville for Mrs. Hays and Lee. Almost as immediately, Mrs. Hays lost touch with reality. A nervous breakdown, the family called it. They assumed her condition was temporary and curable. Reuben moved her to Little Rock for medical attention and sent Lee to summer camp in Fay-

Brother Bill, a year younger than
Minnie Frank, hitchhiked from
Conway, Arkansas, to New York
in 1923, to work as a counselor in
a YMCA camp. Hitting the road
came naturally to Hayses.

etteville. Minnie Frank's emotions began to show cracks. She'd
been teaching at Hendrix, but she needed care. Bill, freshly launched
on his first job in New York City, could hardly be expected to
tend to Minnie Frank. Reuben packed her up and took her back
to Boston.

The sequence of events bewildered young Lee. Father, mother,
brothers, sister—gone.

Misery then indeed was Arkansas.

Later, Lee's deliberate vagueness encouraged the romantic vision
of a very young boy hoboing around the country. Not a Woody
Guthrie image of riding the rails—Lee never looked the part of a
rod rider. But certainly of a kid without a home, without a family,
without formal education (and yet with more book learning than
most college graduates), who had lived many difficult and dangerous

years on the road. And indeed, years of traveling, of poverty, of danger lay ahead, but not just yet. His brothers watched over Lee until he ran off in 1934, after which he never saw his oldest brother again.

Pious young Lee, aged thirteen, to Reuben, in June of 1927, from Camp Markham in Fayetteville:

> "It is very hard on me to be in a place where my opinions differ from the rest of the people around me. No one here but me believes in a hereafter and nobody admits that they are infidels, which they are. I just got in from a long talk with Mr. Pratt. I had a good mind to get up and get a piece of paper and write down the things he said. He believes in evolution just as Darwin did. . . . When I told him everything he said disputed the Bible, to get around it he said that the Bible had gone through so many editions and had been translated so many times it wasn't true. . . . There is just one person beside me who says the blessing so he and I sit down a little before the rest of the bunch and have our blessing. . . ."

"Smite the infidels!" appended Lee, decades later.

As the summer progressed, neither Mrs. Hays nor Minnie Frank improved. A new arrangement might help. Bill arranged a transfer from his employer, B. F. Goodrich, to Atlanta, where he gathered all three of the homeless—mother, sister, Lee—under the roof of a small rented house on Candler Street. Lee enrolled in Bass High, the neighborhood public school.

"Lee and I manage to get along without an armistice," wrote Bill to Reuben in October. "He is getting along fine in school and as there is nothing else to do here but read I find time to help him with his studies. It would never have done to have separated him from Mother this year as the events of the summer had dazed him considerably. He is playing tennis and seems to be getting back more of the old pep and meanness."

Lee completed the ninth grade at Bass. In 1928, following the family tradition of prepping at church academies, Lee went off to Oxford, Georgia, to the Methodist-founded Emory Junior College Academy, which boasted "full secondary instruction for college entrance requirements."

"A decrepit school, where all the talk was about losing one's cherry," said Lee later.

And where he remembered losing his to a golden-haired girl in a nearby Confederate cemetery.

Emory's since-computerized records show Lee Elhardt Hays to have been in attendance from 1928 to 1930 and to have received a graduation certificate on May 23, 1930.

His mother by then was under institutional care. Bill and Minnie Frank had left Georgia. Lee made his way back to Arkansas, with a hope that was recorded by a Conway newspaper in the summer of 1930:

"Lee Hays, son of the late Rev. W. B. Hays and Mrs. Hays, was here yesterday arranging to enter Hendrix-Henderson College next session. [Hendrix had merged with Henderson in 1929.] He graduated last June from the academy of Emory Junior College at Oxford, Ga., and desires to take his bachelor's degree from Hendrix-Henderson, where his two brothers and a sister were graduated. . . ."

Lee never entered Hendrix-Henderson. When at last he did enroll in a college, four years later, he had shucked all the Hays family traditions. "Intensely different conclusions" had led him to socialism.

"Empty Pocket Blues"

1930–1934

I got most of my education reading books in the stacks of the
public library in Cleveland, where I was a page.
I started as a paragraph and worked my way up to page.

—LEE HAYS, *taped memoirs*, 1976

*L*ee may have wanted to take a bachelor's degree, but none of
his siblings could or would take on the burden of his tuition.
The stock market crash of 1929 and the nation's slide into depression threatened everyone's livelihood. Amid such calamity, college
seemed less than essential.

In March of 1930, President Hoover reassuringly announced that
the crisis would be over in thirty days. In May, he declared with
confidence that the country had "passed the worst."

The Great Depression was just beginning.

Whatever worries and belt-tightening they may have experienced, Lee's brothers and sister couldn't be counted among the
down and out during the Great Depression. Minnie Frank had
married an earnest, hardworking, conservative young lawyer; soon
afterward, he won appointment as city attorney for Greensboro,
North Carolina. B. F. Goodrich transferred Bill from Atlanta to
New Orleans, promoting him to credit manager. (The promotion
enabled him to split the cost with Reuben for their mother's institutional care, which they now knew would continue for her lifetime.)
Reuben began to make his mark in the world of finance as an
analyst for Continental Shares, a Cleveland investment fund.

Searching for companies to recommend for investment, Reuben

spent hours each week in the Cleveland Public Library's well-stocked business information department. His gallant southern manners and the high-stakes nature of his research intrigued Rose Vormelker, the energetic librarian who had built and now ran the department. No request by Reuben for material, whatever the effort required, was other than cheerfully attended to. Most satisfactory.

Perhaps Miss Vormelker could do him another favor? Could she talk to the library people about a job for his young brother Lee? Reuben worried about whether Lee was getting enough to eat in his summer wanderings.

She said she'd speak up, of course, but doubted anything would come of it. She underestimated the weight she carried at the library, whose prestige had been enhanced by her department.

The education division needed a morning-hours page. If it would please Miss Vormelker to have Reuben Hays's sixteen-year-old brother in that job, the library would most happily hire him. She couldn't wait to report her unexpected triumph to Reuben.

By general delivery to post offices along Lee's expected route, Reuben soon made contact. Lee hurried to Cleveland and moved into the third floor of his brother's house.

On September 15, 1930, about the time he had hoped to enter Hendrix-Henderson, Lee reported for work at the Cleveland Public Library. Starting pay: fifteen cents an hour. He stayed until May 24, 1934. He was never to hold a regular job longer in his life.

Lee's four years in Cleveland were a turning point in his life. Here the pious young minister's son was radicalized by a conjunction of mind-opening books, hard times, and family tensions.

His self-education was not indiscriminate. The library inadvertently provided guidelines, which Lee described years later in his memoirs:

"Every book that was considered unfit for children to read was marked with a black rubber stamp. So I'd go through the stacks and look for these black stamps. Always the very best books. They weren't locked-up books, just books that would not normally be issued to children—D. H. Lawrence, a number of European novels. Reading those books was like doors opening. Don't forget that the fundamentalist South was a closed, fixed society. The world was made in six days; everything was foreordained and fixed in the universe.

"The magazines I'd been brought up on were the *Saturday Evening Post* and *American Magazine*—Alexander Botts and Scattergood Baines and Norman Rockwell. Then to read Upton Sinclair and come upon his irreverence towards education, banks, corporations, pillars of society such as Nicholas Murray Butler and Rockefeller and Mellon and Carnegie—just the idea that you *could* be irreverent about these people and institutions was the beginning of independent thought."

Lee gorged himself on books, as his father had, but on different books. He read in the stacks much of the day and kept right on reading at night. He read fast and remembered what he read. When he wasn't reading, he was listening. At noon, he'd carry his brown paper bag into the library lunchroom and join the table where the talk was most intensely concerned with what was happening in the country.

Long afterward, Lee said about that period, "This was the time of the Great Depression, and there were 'little mags' with powerful short stories, photographs, poems, plays, documentary studies, dealing with the social problems of the country and the world. I'd seen hunger and despair, illness and tragedy. The whole country was in the grip of a terrible sickness, which troubled me as it did everyone else. And I didn't begin to understand it until I started reading the works of Upton Sinclair and the 'little mags.'

"The more I read, the more it seemed to me that something was awfully wrong. That somewhere there was an awful lot of money, and the people who had it didn't have it because they'd worked for it. And everywhere there were a lot of people who needed money who didn't have it, who were willing to work for it and had no chance to do so.

"Somewhere along in there, I became some kind of socialist. Just what kind I've never to this day figured out."

None of the library people could believe how young Lee was.

At sixteen, already topping six feet, with broad shoulders and a barrel chest, he looked like "a big bear of a man" to the other young pages. He rather cowed them with his courtly bearing, his gracious manners, and his confident vocabulary.

He also smoked, drank quarts of beer, never exercised, and ate irregularly and badly by almost any dietary standard. So his largeness ran to flab rather than muscle, and his soft pallor seemed to confirm his frequent complaints about his health.

Physically and socially, Lee so little matched the prototypical sixteen-year-old boy that his age tended to be forgotten. Co-workers, older than Lee, would refer to him as "extraordinarily mature."

Fred Hellerman, with whom he later sang in the Weavers, would say, "Lee was always an old man. And I mean o-o-o-ld."

Times got harder, and Lee read deeper, turning to socialism at about the same time Reuben was rising to prominence on the playing fields of capitalism.

In January 1932, with no sign of a turnaround in the economy, President Hoover and Congress established the Reconstruction Finance Corporation "to provide emergency financing facilities for financial institutions, to aid in financing agriculture, commerce and industry." Reuben organized the RFC's Cleveland Loan Agency, later winning appointment as assistant to the director of the RFC itself. Reuben moved to Washington, D.C. And, in Cleveland, Lee moved to the YMCA.

For a time, he shared a "Y" room with another library page, Joe Sedlak. Lee at eighteen was "so . . . *knowing*" that Sedlak, who was twenty, never doubted that his roommate was considerably older than he.

In a letter written long after their library days, Sedlak remembered Lee's "puckish, sometimes ribald sense of humor. His target, generally, was some politician of the time. He observed, with undisguised scorn, the antics of the national politicians attempting to justify their terms of office to their starving constituents. Lee would project his considerable histrionic ability to mimic, for example, the speech of a political hack at a Fourth of July picnic. There was the thundering voice, the sonorous and grandiloquent phrasing, the false and empty promises of benefits to come, and then, in conclusion, the false humility and the soft-voiced appeal to the Almighty for assistance in that grave moment of crisis. . . ."

The hot-air southern politician remained one of Lee's most appreciated characterizations for years to come. Proclaimed Lee at a Labor Day hootenanny in the late 1940s, "I'm proud to be here amongst working men. I *am* a working man. My daddy was a working man. My mother was a working man. My sisters are working men. And the only way you can ever stop me from being a working man is to elect me and send me to the Congress of the United States.")

Lee and Sedlak worked for about twenty-five cents an hour (after two raises), ate fifty-cent dinners, barely managed to raise the weekly room rent, and tried to look respectable in second-hand clothing. This was in 1932. In 1933, when Roosevelt closed down the banks without warning, they were left with only the small change in their pockets and didn't eat for two days. "We clung to our miserable jobs only because the alternative was the breadline and the flophouse . . . ," said Sedlak.

Often Lee expressed his contempt for a government that could permit decent men to survive only by selling apples in the streets. Others were expressing their contempt, too, from a different point of view.

Lee began to hear some very radical talk. "I thought that we were on the brink of a fascist revolution," he recalled. "There was a very strong right wing. The socialists were attempting to organize, but the system faced such an imminent breakdown that it could have gone in any direction, depending on who came forward. The capitalist system was lucky because Roosevelt came forward and saved it. And helped some people while he was saving it."

Reuben, a Hoover administration appointee, remained in Washington through the Roosevelt transition, continuing to work with the RFC until early in 1934, when he returned to Cleveland as an officer of the Federal Reserve Bank.

A few years later, Reuben would join the First National Bank of Cincinnati, becoming in time its chairman of the board and achieving regional fame as an architect of the master plan that revitalized Cincinnati's downtown sector.

Investment fund officer, banker, Republican—Reuben represented everything that Lee, while in Cleveland, came to see as unfair and unjust. Reuben took the glittering prizes that the system held out to businessmen—wealth, respect, membership on the boards of some of America's largest corporations, honorary degrees,

Lee's oldest brother, Reuben Hays, when he was
chairman of the board of the First National Bank
of Cincinnati. Photo taken around 1958 by Julianne
Warren.

government appointments, country clubs, a winter home in Florida.
All of which placed him with those people who, in Lee's opinion,
had "an awful lot of money, [but] didn't have it because they'd
worked for it." Return on investment never was Lee's idea of "working" for money.

Lee did not go back to his old quarters in Reuben's house. A
family member later suggested that "everything Lee did seemed
wrong" to Reuben's wife, Martha, a "first family" Arkansan. Strait-
laced and a rigid housekeeper, Martha had withheld none of her
complaints either from Lee or from Reuben before the move to
Washington. Lee opted to remain at the Y.

A few months after Reuben's return to Cleveland in his august new position, Lee slipped out of the city without a word to his brother or sister-in-law. Not until 1951 did Lee make contact with Reuben, and never again did they see one another.

The records of the Cleveland Public Library show that Lee left his job on May 24, 1934, "to return to Arkansas."

A letter written to Lee by Reuben on Christmas Eve of 1964— a letter we shall return to in another place—begins, "It has been over 30 years since I believed I knew what was best for the world and you. You, having an equal amount of independence and stubbornness (some things seem to run in the Hays family), said 'To Hell with him! I'll live my life as I damn well please.' "

The way he pleased to live marked him, he later said, as the black sheep. Not at all what his family had expected of their bright kid brother, for all his "old pep and meanness."

3

"In That New Jerusalem"
1934–1935

Organize, organize
Let the will of the Lord be done.

—the REVEREND CLAUDE WILLIAMS

In 1934, the Great Depression staggered into its fifth year; for all the Roosevelt administration's efforts to alleviate the pain, millions remained unemployed and hungry. Nowhere was the devastation more visible and more intractable than in the poor rural states, among which Arkansas ranked as poorest.

Half a century later, events of that time in the South seem unbelievable in the recounting—the whippings, the shootings, the jailings, the lynchings by church-going people when the established order (or disorder) was threatened by attempts to organize labor unions. "It took brave men and brave preachers to work at organizing then," wrote Willard Uphaus, a religious educator.

Out of Arkansas came stories about a fiery radical Presbyterian preacher named Claude Williams and his battle to keep his pulpit in Paris, a small foothills town near Booneville, in the Ozarks. Williams, known to his followers as Claude or Preacher, had been daringly organizing miners and sharecroppers, black and white. The young and the poor who flocked around him worshiped Claude as "Jesus come alive." His opponents denounced him as a dangerous and heretical Communist.

Lee's heart stirred as he listened to the stories. How close Claude's parish to the last Hays parsonage; how far Claude's style of ministry from that of his own father! Claude practiced what

Lee believed, and in Lee's countryside. For the first time since he left, Lee felt an urgency "to return to Arkansas." He wanted to declare himself, on his home grounds.

Claude Williams kept open house for a lot of young people who had no other place to go. Lee would later say, "I got to be his chief helper for quite a while." Indeed, from 1934 to 1940, Claude was the dominant figure in Lee's life—a surrogate father—a man of the cloth but with a radical difference.

"What Claude has tried to do," Lee wrote in his *People's Songs Bulletin* column, "is to take the Bible seriously. Born in a land where the Bible is read from kiver to kiver, and where preachers preach a literal interpretation of the Bible, Claude has said, 'Look here, do you really believe the Bible? Then for Heaven's sake, let's do what the Bible tells us to do.' For of course if we all did that, we'd have no Jim Crow, no hate; we'd have democracy in our plantations and factories and schools and homes and churches; we'd have, Claude says, the Kingdom of God on earth. Who wouldn't want that?"

Simple and clear, put that way. But in time the red preacher ("Are you fer him or agin him?") became a litmus test in the bitter battles of leftist politics.

Lee, an intellectually bursting-out young man at twenty, turned up at the front door of the Presbyterian manse—a four-room frame cottage—in the blistering summer of 1934, after hitchhiking from Cleveland. Claude welcomed anyone who wanted to help in politicizing the underprivileged and propelling them into social action. Lee wanted to help. More than ever, after meeting the magnetic preacher.

Never quite at home in his own heavy and unathletic body, Lee envied the preacher's tall and easy grace and his physical courage. Claude had inherited those qualities, along with his piercing black eyes, from his half Cherokee father. But he'd made his own adventurous life. Born in the hill country of western Tennessee, Claude breathed the fundamentalist religion and antiblack prejudice of family and neighbors. He was quick and naturally eloquent. He seemed destined for the church. Instead, he ran away from home, rode the rails, picked up jobs on farms, on riverboats, on railroads. He joined the army in 1916 and became the best drill sergeant in his regiment. With his comrades, he gave most of his spare hours to gambling and sex. He mightily enjoyed both. When his time in the army was up, he reenlisted.

Still, a voice inside Claude kept surprising him, calling him to the service of God. In 1921, he entered the Cumberland Presbyterian school at Bethel, Tennessee, to prepare for the ministry. There Claude met and married a fellow student, Joyce King, who proved to be as strong, as willing to risk, as Claude himself. Some thought more so.

From his first years in the pulpit, congregations marveled at Claude's fire, his towering presence. "If he ain't the preachin'est man," they'd say. The Reverend Williams surely was headed for glory in the church. But the same inner voice that had called Claude to the service of God to save souls changed its message, importuning him to help save men and women from injustice— economic, social, racial—in this world.

Claude had come to Paris, Arkansas, in 1930 to take over a congregation of about a hundred members. Those who attended met in an old schoolhouse, consecrated to serve as a church. The young people of Paris didn't come at all; they hung out in the courthouse square or at the only recreational place in town, the local pool hall.

Claude figured he could remedy that. He bought a pool table and installed it in an unused wing of his church. The wing rapidly expanded into a recreation center with boxing gloves, punching bags, exercisers, cards, checkers, reading material. The young people flocked to the church, forming clubs and discussion groups. Claude believed in bringing the church into the lives of the people.

As the Great Depression added to the area's chronic economic difficulties, Claude concentrated his fierce energy on the struggles of the miners and the sharecroppers as well as on the young blacks and whites who he felt were taking the brunt. He helped workers to organize, addressed their meetings, brought food and clothing to strikers. Things that hardly struck the established order as proper activities for a minister. Most threatening of all was the free and easy way that the Williamses welcomed blacks into the manse as friends.

"The Preacher," Claude Williams,
in 1936. (Wide World Photos)

"Claude was the only radical with a pulpit in that part of Arkansas," Myles Horton, another southern radical, said. "And he knew how to quote the Scripture to back the Left."

His alarmed opponents, determined to deprive him of that pulpit, framed their attack in theological terms: Williams should be dismissed on the grounds that he had questioned the doctrines of predestination, the Virgin birth, and the deity of Jesus Christ. They tossed in a couple of temporal charges: that he had been derelict in his duty and that he had approved of communism. A judicial body of the denomination had these charges under consideration.

Lee fell in with the young people who all but lived in the manse—an articulate bunch, up on philosophy, economics, unionism, racism, history, and theology. They helped Claude and Joyce each day, then talked through the night about the dark events in Paris, in Arkansas, in the South, in the United States, in the world, and what they, this small but committed band, might do to help turn things around.

A number of the group studied at the nearby College of the Ozarks. They included Zilphia Johnson, the oldest (of five) and favorite daughter of one of Paris's richest men. Zilphia's father, Guy, agreed with those who called Claude "the red preacher" and his young people "a bunch of young revolutionary socialists." That Guy Johnson's daughter should hang out with this Bolshevik crew was intolerable. He issued an ultimatum: Zilphia must give up Claude's place or forever lose her home. To Lee, who had lost his own home through the vagaries of fate, Zilphia's defiance of her father's demand raised her to the heroic plateau on which he had already sited Claude.

Later, Lee would say, "Claude and Zilphia did more to help change and shape my life than any people I can recall." Both were gifted. Claude had the gift of tongues; Zilphia, a musical talent that won her prizes as best classical pianist and best musical soloist in Arkansas. Both knew from childhood on that they were specially favored. With fearless self-confidence, both flouted authority and the established order. They disdained wealth. They enthralled others. Like Lee, both had their roots in the rural South, but unlike Lee (whose Scotch-Irish-German ancestry seemed ordinary indeed to him), Claude and Zilphia proudly claimed streaks of American Indian in their blood. On every count, the twenty-year-old Lee felt admiration and love for Claude and Zilphia. He would walk on the thorny trails they had broken.

Another stranger turned up in Paris in the summer of 1934— Dr. Willard Uphaus, fresh out of Yale Divinity School, newly appointed executive secretary of the Religion and Labor Foundation. Sent by the leftish foundation to investigate the charges against Claude, Uphaus liked the preacher on sight. He would become Claude's most effective supporter in the North.

Lee and Claude fascinated Uphaus, whose background was conservative, Republican, fundamentalist.

"Lee had an intuitive rapport with the Other—people such as miners, sharecroppers," Uphaus recalled. "This requires something beyond the rational, as far as I'm concerned. Something religious, though not in an organized way. Lee was not an organizer in that sense. I can't remember Lee calling a meeting ever, or taking the initiative. Rather, he was an associate, a helper to Claude, an understudy to Claude. . . . Intellectually, Lee was beyond his physical age. Mature. He devoured books. Those scores and scores of books! But I don't know how formalized his concepts were. I think his radicalism was largely a grass roots, native thing. . . . I don't know if he was too much of a Marxist scholar at that time, or ever. It was just a down-to-earth experience."

What Lee experienced in the destitute, violent, segregated South fanned a hatred of injustice that had caught fire in his Cleveland years. As a southerner whose eyes opened to injustice, he responded most deeply to the utter vulnerability of blacks—to daily humiliations, to fear, to beatings, to lynchings—and to the faith and dignity they nonetheless managed to hold on to. He felt a particular anger that his God-fearing family had demonstrated no more interest in the plight of blacks than did their neighbors and parishioners. Wasn't lack of caring a form of complicity? Lee's heart moved further from his family, as he chose to stand with the dispossessed.

Inspired by the example of Claude, who believed the poor of the South could be reached only through religion, Lee entered the College of the Ozarks in 1934 as a student for the ministry. He, too, would work for social justice from the pulpit.

Certainly his family background, his youthful erudition, his imposing bulk, and his resonant bass voice would have commended him to the admissions officer of any southern religious college. On the matter of finances, well, Lee *did* list as "nearest kin" R. B. Hays, Cleveland Federal Reserve Bank. So he couldn't have pleaded hardship and asked for scholarship funds. Perhaps the college sent Lee's bills to Reuben. Perhaps Lee asked them to do so out of anger for Reuben's refusal to pay his way through Hendrix-Henderson. Perhaps (though no record exists) Reuben paid the College of the Ozarks. Neither brother ever mentioned the college in memoirs, letters, or interviews.

The college, founded in 1834 by the Presbyterian church, prides itself on having been the first in Arkansas to admit women, in 1868. Its catalog proclaims, "The over-riding theme on this campus is that it is a place where God is loved and Christ is worshipped, and all of its programs attempt to reflect this atmosphere."

Only a short hitchhike away from Paris, the campus felt the impact of Claude Williams's interpretation of the gospels. Some students idolized Claude. The director of the college considered him a cause for concern.

"The Director was always calling in Claude's friends among the students to try and set them right about the red preacher," wrote Claude's biographer Cedric Belfrage. "His opinion was: 'Certainly there is a lot of Christianity in Williams' ideas—but he is so tactless about it. Why does he have to be so tactless?' "

In every way, the new arrangement suited Lee. He remained close to Claude geographically. He had found the right track, Claude's track, for a worthy life's work. Like his campus friends, he was learning and questioning and seeking ways to help the disinherited. He even joined a college quartet that thrilled listeners by emulating the sound of the popular Southern Jewel Singers.

Lee attended classes (irregularly) in English composition, in argument, in introduction to the Bible, in survey of religion, in physical science, and in psychology.

More often, he sat around the Williamses' parlor, talking the night away with Claude and Joyce and their young people. Nobody stayed longer than Lee.

The Paris establishment had its way; the judicial body deposed Williams. But in the process of losing his pulpit, Claude gained stature as a hero of the Left. He'd be quite a draw at political gatherings, this rare bird—this fearless southern red preacher.

Immediately, he stepped into a new job, as southern secretary of the Religion and Labor Foundation. Uphaus arranged that. Claude would travel, speak, and organize for the foundation, whose stated purpose was to seek ways to help the millions of unemployed. Claude's home base would be a place for inspiration and instruction in elements of economics and trade union principles and methods. He would call the place the New Era School.

Claude moved his family some forty miles west, to Fort Smith, near the Oklahoma border, a city where he'd often been involved in union-organizing activities. In a house rented with the help of a friendly minister (the owner had no idea who Claude was), the red preacher planned to open his New Era School.

Lee and his friends, known in the area as friends of Claude, would drive by night to Fort Smith and slip into the Williams house to work alongside Joyce and Claude. They sent announcements about the new school to everyone, north and south, who might contribute funds.

The New Era School didn't open in Fort Smith. Claude's friends soon forgot the school in their concern for Claude himself. Would he get out of the city with his life?

Claude had unexpectedly and reluctantly taken on the leadership of a proposed strike. He risked the success of his school before it opened. But how could he resist the pleas of relief workers, who voted to strike when the governor of Arkansas knocked their pay down from a miserable thirty cents an hour to twenty cents?

While Fort Smith was in the grip of prestrike tension and the governor threatened to call out the militia, Claude visited religious leaders, asking for their support in bringing about a peaceful solution rescinding the punishing relief-work pay cut. Finding none who would help, Claude proposed a hunger march, hoping the sight of starving thousands would touch the hearts of citizens.

Instead, the sight struck only terror among the observers. What could a hunger march by relief workers be but revolutionary? Moreover, to find the red preacher of Paris in its vanguard was nothing short of incendiary. A few days later, a second hunger march was to take place. As Claude led the relief workers in a prayer meeting preceding the march, the police charged into the crowd and onto the platform, grabbed him, and rushed him to jail.

Around town, they said Claude wouldn't live through the night. Masked men had threatened relief workers with lynching if they didn't drop the plan to strike. Claude, public enemy number one in Fort Smith, could not fall asleep for wondering when the vigilantes would arrive at the jailhouse. Lee and his friends came from the college and spent the nights on guard.

After three days, Claude was given a trial, convicted of barratry (defined in *Webster's* as "the purchase or sale of office or preferment in church or state"), and sentenced to ninety days and a $100 fine. Back to jail the bailiffs took him, as his friends quickly went to work to raise bail.

Claude's biographer recorded that nearly three, desperate weeks passed before his bond was accepted—weeks of nights made sleep-less by fear of a lynch mob, the filth and smells of the cells, and the screams of madmen and -women, thrown into jail to rid the streets of them, as they were beaten into silence.

And then, probably because the story had created a stir in the press, his jailers released Claude on bail. That night a student drove him out of town and smuggled him into the college, into the suite of a professor around whom gathered the Claude-worship-ing students, Lee among them. They'd been waiting for three hours.

"When the preacher came in, very late," wrote Belfrage, "the students clustered around. Some homebrew had been made ready to welcome him. He drank and told about his experiences. His nerves were in a terrible state. His whole body shook as he told of the beatings in the jail. The students wept unashamedly."

Claude was brave, but not foolish. He left Fort Smith, moving his family to Little Rock, halfway across the state. Lee reconsidered taking up the life of a radical southern preacher, being neither foolish nor especially brave. He dropped out of college and did what so many young men of the time were doing. He hit the road.

Little Rock was no more hospitable than Fort Smith to Claude's radical teachings. Nonetheless, he opened a workers' school in one room of the house he rented on a border street between the white and black districts. Willard Uphaus sent money raised from his mailing lists—small contributions, but they enabled the Wil-liams family to eat.

And how did Lee eat in that time?

The question recurs like the chorus of a folk song as one follows Lee's trail through the 1930s. Between 1934, when he left Cleve-land, and the fall of 1937, when he joined the staff of a labor college, Lee had no regular job.

Asked the question in 1955 by an interrogator for the House Un-American Activities Committee, Lee responded, "I have worked in factories as a laborer, and I have worked in a public library as a page, and I have worked on numerous farms as a farm-hand, and I have worked in the undesirable part of a good many greasy-spoon restaurants, and I have worked at warehouse employ-

In the mid-1930s, Lee sometimes turned up at the home of his brother Bill, shown here with Bill, Jr., who called Lee "Grandpa."

ment, and whatever came along, and wherever I was at the time that was sufficient to earn a living and still allow me to pursue my profession."

His sister-in-law, Sue Brown Hays, remembered that Lee "worked around for food" and was "quite a tramp for a while."

An indelible Hays family memory is of a broke and hungry Lee arriving without notice at Sue and Bill's new home in Natchez and, after a week of reconstituting his energy, announcing that he would organize a black Boy Scout troup—about as defiant and hopeless an effort as one could mount in Mississippi. Lee would get the family tarred and feathered, Sue fretted. Bill, in the characteristic Hays family way, found the situation amusing. Why couldn't Sue see it that way? Sue did not—surely Lee's true intention, she thought, was to ruin their lives in Natchez. Lee hit the road again, by request.

Lee never mentioned the episode—not in memoirs or letters or interviews. Perhaps it was as much personal as political; in later years Lee often found ways of discomfiting friends in order to test the strength of their feelings for him. But in this case Lee left with another example of the political gulf between him and his family. He must have seen, too, how foolhardy the concept had been. To use his energies effectively, he would need more shaping, more direction.

And indeed, Lee would soon be learning about the uses of art for social action. He would learn from Zilphia.

"Raggedy"
1935–1937

Raggedy, raggedy are we
Just as raggedy as raggedy can be
We don't get nothing for our labors
So raggedy, raggedy are we

Landless, landless are we
Just as landless as landless can be
We don't get nothing for our labors
So landless, landless are we

Shoeless . . .

Cowless . . .

Hogless . . .

But
Union, union are we
Just as union as union can be
We're gonna get something for our labor
For union, union are we.

—By JOHN HANDCOX,
with added words by LEE HAYS

*W*hen Lee left the College of the Ozarks, in June of 1935, he was twenty-one and homeless again. But he had, in his first year away from Reuben's lectures about what he should do with his life, found a new family—a brotherhood, really—with places where he could get a bed for a night or a week or a year, all over the country.

Within that larger brotherhood stood the brave circle of those who had fought the good fight with Claude Williams. The experi-

ence forged a bond that remained intact long after its members
went off in different political, geographical, and professional directions.

In 1935, no one had yet gone off in any but geographical directions.

Lee looked forward to seeing Zilphia again. He set out for her
new home, the Highlander Folk School, on Monteagle Mountain,
in Tennessee's Cumberland Mountains.

Zilphia had been shipped to Highlander by Claude, to remove
her from harm's way when her father threatened mayhem unless
she came back to the big house on the hill. Claude considered
Highlander only a temporary haven for Zilphia. Instead, she and
Highlander's manly young founder, Myles Horton, had fallen instantly in love. In March 1935, they married.

The marriage compounded Guy Johnson's grievous rage. Good
God, Highlander was as bad, as notorious as Claude! Now his
own daughter—his favorite daughter, his beautiful musical daughter, his headstrong daughter—had become the wife of its founder.

Highlander inflamed a wide swath of Tennesseeans in much
the same way that Claude infuriated Arkansans. Both were perceived as dangerous to traditional values, to the social and economic
structure of southern life. Most dangerous because of their indige-
nousness. Like Claude, Myles was a young southerner with deep
religious roots. But their personalities had little in common. Claude
was unabashedly hellfire and damnation; Myles was gentle and
soft-spoken. Both talked to people they understood, in language
and images and biblical references their people understood. The
editorial writers might (and often did) call them Communists,
but Claude and Myles could never be accused of being "furriners."

Highlander, Myles said years later, has been variously described
since its founding in 1932 as "a community school, we were poverty, you know, a depression school, we were an industrial union
school, a CIO school, we were a farmer labor school, we were a
civil rights school, we were Appalachian. . . . But . . . Highlander
has just been one school all the way through, we were just doing
the same thing with different groups of people. We try to empower
people. We're using these different periods of interest in the South
as a means of educating people to take more control of their own
lives. And although the subject matter differs, the purpose is the

same . . . the purpose is to help people become so empowered that they can begin to have something to do with their lives. . . ."

Zilphia directed Highlander's music, dance, and drama program. As basic to Highlander's curriculum as classes on organizing a union or running a strike, Zilphia's program borrowed heavily from the techniques of the New Theater League in New York City. That's where she'd learned them, she told Lee. He responded as to a revelation: "Concepts of what might be done with music, drama and dance opened up windows on a whole new world."

Zilphia guided workshop attendees in building plays with music out of their own struggles. The best and most relevant were staged at union meetings and labor conferences, their creators experiencing the nervous excitement of a Broadway opening. Zilphia gauged audience response; plays that stirred audiences were mimeographed and made available to labor groups around the country.

Each Highlander session ran from four to six weeks, with ten or twelve "students"—in Lee's time, members of struggling labor unions, trying to develop organizational skills.

No union of that period struggled more valiantly, or against greater odds, than the fledgling Southern Tenant Farmers Union (STFU), formed in a small town on the eastern side of Arkansas during the summer in which Lee cast his lot with Claude Williams in Paris, on the western side of the state. Eighteen men—eleven of them white and seven black—had met in a rickety schoolhouse on a cotton plantation near Tyronza, Arkansas, on the steamy

Zilphia Horton (*right*) square dancing with her husband, Myles Horton (*center*), at the Highlander Folk School, where Lee learned about "art as a weapon." (Photograph courtesy of Highlander Center Archives)

night of July 13, 1934, to form the bold little union, a concept first suggested by the Socialist Norman Thomas during his investigations of the farm tenancy and sharecropper systems.

It was bold because, in the words of a *New York Times* writer, "it challenged social and economic power in the South and attempted to do what unions still often do not do: organize the poor." Bolder because it was launched as an integrated union, when few unions anywhere, and no southern institutions, were integrated. Nothing less than desperation could have brought poor whites together with blacks in that place and time.

"The sharecropping system," said Lee later, "helped perpetuate race hatred because if a white farmer protested or rebelled in any way against conditions the landlord laid down, the landlord could always go out and get a black farmer to take his place. And when times came bad, if the black farmer so much as spoke his mind, there would always be some poor white farmer hard up enough to take the black man's place. So when the sharecroppers began to organize unions, one of the first obstacles they had to face was years of race hatred, and we began to sing, 'Black and white together, we shall not be moved,' to the tune of an old gospel hymn, 'Just like a tree standing by the water, we shall not be moved.' That became an organizing chant of the sharecroppers. Black and white sharecroppers *did* stand together in one instance after another."

Ironically, the movement gained what momentum it had from the *breakup* of the sharecropper system.

The federal government under Franklin D. Roosevelt tried to strengthen prices in the ravaged cotton economy of the South by giving planters money to keep fields idle. Many of the large plantation owners not only failed to give tenant farmers their share of government funds but also, no longer needing their labor, evicted them from their decaying shacks, leaving them landless, homeless, frightened, and in bottomless despair.

While a small minority saw the STFU as their sole hope, the majority of impoverished, uneducated whites remained as fearful as ever of blacks and of unions.

These were the people Claude and Lee hoped to enlighten.

These were the people who made up lynch mobs.

* * *

Claude Williams had jumped into organizing for the STFU. He'd turn up at black churches, or schoolhouses, or cabins, to lead the talking and the singing, always ready to switch to hymns if anti-unionists burst in. After he opened his New Era School, STFU members came around to study trade unionism and radical economics.

Lee, as Claude's "chief helper for quite a while," often accompanied him on organizing trips during his year as a ministry student at the College of the Ozarks. Sometimes Lee stepped into the pulpit of black churches to, well, practice preach, and lead the people in gospel-turned-union songs. Some STFU members thought the union was a new kind of church.

Much of what Lee wrote and sang through the 1930s came out of the STFU experience. The play that Highlander remembers him for and a documentary film that resurfaced in the 1980s were about the attempts of sharecroppers to build a union.

As a close friend of Zilphia's, Lee could come often to Highlander—and he did. But the rules of the school forbade anyone other than staff from remaining on the premises at the end of a session. Lee's first stretch at Highlander had been a watching and learning period only. Although he'd hoped to stick around and create a play, he had to move on before he could come back.

As for *where,* well, if he meant to write plays, he perhaps should do what Zilphia had done—study the work of the New Theater League.

Finding a bed in New York was a matter of making some kind of connection. Claude and Willard Uphaus came through with an introduction to the minister of the Judson Memorial Church, on Washington Square, in Greenwich Village.

Judson is a Baptist church, although hardly a conventional one. In a weekly newsletter of that time, the editors defined the purpose of Judson as follows:

"Judson Church is committed to the task of helping to build a Christian social order. It conceives of such an order as a society based on the universal brotherhood of man with God the Father of all.

"This church believes that the greatest evils of our day grow out of the violation of brotherhood that prevails in our economic life. . . ."

The church pioneered social activism among churches, and its minister, Laurence T. Hosie, served with Uphaus on the executive committee of the Religion and Labor Foundation.

On Judson's grounds stood a building called Neighborhood House, converted by the church into a student residence. Lee, accepted because of his sponsors, settled into one of the small, monastical, two-dollar-a-week dormitory rooms. He didn't quite settle. More often than not, Lee was away, on the road, at Highlander, or at Claude's New Era School.

As soon as he arrived at Judson, Lee became a participant in meetings of the church's Social Action Fellowship—a small group of young people who gathered in a circle in the choir room above the church's sanctuary. Their motivating concept, the Reverend Hosie remembered years later, was "to put religion into practice, to relate religion to the social scene." They invited speakers on diverse social causes.

"The first time Lee came," said Hosie, "he taught the group a song . . .

> Weary, weary are we
> Just as weary as weary can be
> We don't get nothing for our labor
> So weary, weary are we.

"Lee kept talking about sharecroppers and their problems. No one up north knew about any of this. And he gave things a musical twist that made a cause more palatable to young people; they were more responsive because of his songs."

Hosie and the Judson young people responded. They encouraged Lee to do something that would bring the problems of sharecroppers to the wide attention of people in the North. Get pictures. Maybe film. Publicize! Visualize! Make everybody see what's going on down there!

Among those most responsive were two young social-activist brothers, Alan and Seymour Hacker. Alan lived in Neighborhood House; Seymour, a student at City College, visited constantly.

To the Hackers and to most of the fellowship members, Lee seemed "an exotic." Seymour, who became an art-book publisher of international reputation, recalled that Lee "looked like a hick, but was obviously very, very bright. He had astonishing maturity and solidity." "I was brash and abrasive," Seymour added, "but I couldn't make an impression on him—he scared me."

Alan was older, quieter, a serious and talented photojournalist in the era of photojournalism, when, as Lee said later, "the great American photographers went out and recorded the face of America, and for the first time America got a good look at itself."

Alan, deeply dedicated to giving America a good look at itself, eagerly agreed to work with Lee to engrave the injustices of the sharecropper system onto the political agenda of northern activists who hadn't known and so hadn't cared.

If they could raise some money, they would make a film that would touch and move hearts that had been otherwise engaged.

Anyone known for generosity and compassion faced a seeming infinity of causes needing support in that frightening time at home and abroad. To raise money for a film on sharecroppers required proper organization, which meant a committee, for openers.

Thus, the "Sharecropper Film Committee," at 55 Washington Square South (Judson's address), New York City. Its letterhead listed the Reverend Hosie as treasurer and Lee and Alan Hacker as the sole members of the technical staff. Sponsors included Willard Uphaus, Claude Williams, Judson's Social Action Fellowship, and the Religion and Labor Foundation. Myles Horton remembered contributing, and convincing others to do so. The Reverend Hosie said he raised some of the money from Sherwood Eddy, a renowned author and pacifist, who had helped a Quaker group buy land for a new and daring social experiment—an interracial cotton-farming cooperative in the Mississippi Delta. Lee and Alan would do much of their filming at Delta Farms.

Fund-raising letters put the budget at $1,000, for the 16-mm sound film. "This of course is no Hollywood production," they said. "It is simply the best that can be done under the circumstances."

It was not only no Hollywood production but barely qualified as a shoestring operation. With the most meager of startup funds, Lee and Alan set off in the summer of 1936, "having got a car, and borrowed or bought a tent," Hosie remembered.

Still, the two young men did not go off without doing some

On stationery of "The Sharecropper Film Committee," Lee wrote to his brother Bill in Little Rock on November 5, 1936, sealing the envelope with a stamp showing a white man flogging a black man. In his letter, Lee expressed concern about their institutionalized mother but added that because of his "activities on the lunatic fringe" he had been unable to do anything to help.

homework. Lee gives a glimpse of their preparation in a letter written years later to Pare Lorentz, whose documentary films, produced under government auspices in the 1930s, were widely admired and emulated:

"In 1936 I studied briefly with Paul Strand and Leo Hurwitz [radical filmmakers then prominent in the left-wing Film League] who coached me in my efforts to make a small documentary film about sharecroppers; they quoted you extensively and so frequently that I have never forgotten their instructions . . . about the 'spinal' treatment of ideas and materials. . . ."

The "spinal" treatment in filmmaking (but also, Lee learned, in the writing of songs, short stories, and essays) meant thinking out the spine of the piece—the main thing it is to say—and ruthlessly discarding material that does not bear directly on it.

Lee and Alan agreed on the spine of their project: the desperate plight of the sharecroppers, and their stirring efforts to build the Southern Tenant Farmers Union. (Fifty percent of the film's earnings were promised to the STFU). Clear on their main point, writer and cameraman drove south with the hope of doing the job within budget.

Intentions and actuality didn't quite coincide for the novice filmmakers. Their mailed reports, headed "To Contributors and Friends of the Sharecropper Film Committee, Greetings," told of adventures and misadventures and of the need for more donations.

In an interview years later, Lee referred to the project as "kind

Lee, then twenty-two, on location in Mississippi for *The Dispossessed*, a 16-mm documentary on the efforts of black and white sharecroppers to unionize.

of a disastrous effort," adding, "I think it was in Mississippi that I got beaten up by the riders of the big plantation owners, who raided our camp and stole our shooting script, so we had to shoot from memory. . . ."

The event sounded less dramatic in a report from Hillhouse, Mississippi, dated September 17, 1936, and signed by Hays and Hacker: "Here is news of a really tragic sort: Our notebooks, containing scenario, continuity, records, etc., have been stolen. It happens that we know it by heart and can rewrite it with some effort, although it will take time. . . . Add tragic note: We are out of film, due to great distance from New York. . . . This sort of thing is getting monotonous. . . ."

From Hays and Hacker, in Colt, Arkansas, October 20, 1936: "A few small gifts have been sent directly to us, and these we appreciate. We have no more money in the treasury, although we have here about enough to finish the work and get us home. We do not yet know how much will be required to finish the film. Sound, titling, editing, and the purchase of a few necessary stock shots unobtainable here. . . ."

Myles Horton remembered "having to explain to others who'd kicked in some dough that these two young men didn't just go off and have fun with the money."

Lee later said about the project, "We brought back a jumble of film which was eventually put together into a documentary with some sharecropper songs."

In fact, the footage they brought back rarely veered from the spine. Hacker's powerful photojournalistic images could have done with less narration than the novice filmmakers supplied.

"This is the story of the sharecropper," Lee's script begins. "A story of hunger and discomfort, a story of poor people in a rich land. A story of their struggle against oppression and of their hope for the future.

"When the Civil War freed the slave, it left him without land or tools. The plantation owner, helpless without workers, or the money to hire them, put the ex slave on his land, furnished him with tools and a shack, and promised him half the crop as his share, thus the sharecropper. Those whites who lost their lands gradually were forced into the same status.

"Today the South's three million sharecroppers, black and white, are still without security, possessing as nearly nothing as any people in the world.

"They are America's disinherited."

("Possessing nearly nothing"—that's how Lee lived then, and always. "Never own more than you can carry on your back," he advised young people in later years.)

America's Disinherited previewed at Judson on May 14, 1937, to an audience of contributors and friends, including, as Seymour Hacker recalled, "a number of elegant ladies from the uptown organizations that helped finance it." "[The film's] impact was brief, all too brief," he said. "I remember it as being a very ephemeral event. The sharecropper thing was awfully peripheral, in the face of huge stirrings of the labor movement, the CIO and its battle with the AFL . . . the violent strikes that were happening then, and the European situation, Spain, the Nazis."

Less global but equally daunting was a technical problem facing the young filmmakers. Few of their target-audience groups had access to 16-mm projectors. Still, Tom Brandon, another prominent member of the radical Film League, agreed to act as distributor for the film. Correspondence through 1937 affirms a number of screenings at schools and churches.

Few of Lee's later friends ever knew about the film. His reluctance to speak about it perhaps had to do with its "all too brief" impact, or perhaps with the fact that his friend and cinematographer, Alan Hacker, died soon after the film was completed, of an illness contracted on their adventure.

Lee assumed that the film had vanished from the face of the earth. Today, *America's Disinherited* is in the film archives of the Museum of Modern Art.

Between the wrap-up of the film and its preview, Lee hitchhiked back to Highlander, eager to lead a group of resident students in creating a play he'd been plotting since his earlier visit. *Gumbo* (a word used by sharecroppers to describe the heavy, black mud of the Delta country) became one of the most requested plays in the Highlander repertoire.

The drama tells the story of a black sharecropper murdered by white planters whose attitude is simply "There's goin' to be an end to this union stuff around here, or I'll build me a dam across the Arkansas River with the bones of you union niggers!" Its poignancy is heightened by songs—the same songs Lee used for the sound track of his film, "We Shall Not Be Moved" and "No More Mourning."

Powerfully written, *Gumbo* lost some of its dramatic effect in southern meeting halls, where black characters had to be portrayed by whites in blackface. Nonetheless, the play was performed widely at union and community gatherings, unfailingly moving its audiences.

Watching audiences respond in turn unfailingly moved the play's creators. In this involving way, Highlander's resident students—tenant farmers, miners, oil workers, most of whom who had lived their lives without stage shows or concerts or even electricity—got the message that art could be put to the service of empowering people.

Lee, only twenty-two years old during the making of *America's Disinherited* and *Gumbo*, didn't think of himself as an artist. Having given up on the possibility of becoming a minister, he tended to think in terms of union organizing and of teaching. The people he most wanted to help, in both roles, were the sharecroppers.

And so, on April 2, 1937, having just turned twenty-three, Lee sat down at a Highlander typewriter and addressed a five-page, single-spaced proposal to Hosie and Uphaus. Four points summed up Lee's plan to work among the sharecroppers, black and white, in east Arkansas:

"1. To buy land and build a place to live, for myself and for one or two families concerned; to develop all the resources for farming that can be developed on submarginal land. . . .

"2. To study the educational needs of the people as the basis for developing, with expert help, a program of workers' education designed to become an integral part of the affairs of the people;

"3. In a larger sense, to aid the Union struggle for socialized agriculture; and to join in immediate struggles for better conditions;

"4. To develop my own mental and physical resources, now sadly lacking."

He would, he said, begin by traveling some of the ground that Highlander had already covered. Funds were needed, of course, to buy a piece of submarginal land ("$100 or less") and a few pots and pans.

The plan never materialized. Instead, a few months later, Lee had a job as a teacher in a very unusual college in Arkansas, thanks to his mentor and surrogate father, Claude Williams.

5

"I've Got a Home in That Rock"
1937–1940

Oh what is that I see yonder comin', comin', comin'
What is that I see yonder comin', comin', comin'
What is that I see yonder comin', comin', comin'
Get on board, get on board.

It's that union train a'comin', comin', comin'
It's that union train a'comin', comin', comin'
It's that union train a'comin', comin', comin'
Get on board, get on board.

—From "*Union Train*," adapted from
"*The Old Ship of Zion*,"
by LEE HAYS

*L*ong before Myles Horton founded Highlander Folk School in the Cumberland Mountains of Tennessee to "try to empower people," a small labor college opened its rough-hewn doors in the Ouachita Mountains of Arkansas. Its announced aim was to train leaders for a new and different society in which the workers would have power.

Commonwealth College grew out of the socialist, trade union, and cooperative movements. Established originally in 1923 as part of the Newllano Cooperative Colony in Louisiana, it had since 1925 been situated on a bluff overlooking a valley, ringed by piney woods and mountains, near the Arkansas town of Mena, four miles from the Oklahoma border.

Although Commonwealth's dreams of a new society with workers in power seemed to coincide with Highlander's dream of empowering people, its student body and program were considerably different. So, in the end, were its direction and its fate.

Students sought in Commonwealth a genuine alternative to a traditional college education. They enrolled after graduating from high school, and they expected to remain for four years. On paper, Commonwealth's course list, outside of its labor movement classes, looked like that of many small traditional colleges.

Teachers and students came from as far as Germany, Cuba, China, and Japan. Few Arkansans attended, and of those few, none were black. The founding fathers, buying land in Mena, had settled their college into a county where blacks dared not show their faces after sunset.

At the time of the founding, no one had considered the possibility of blacks attending Commonwealth. Later, the fact that this radical college stood on "lily-white" territory created much anguish among students and faculty.

As early as 1926, Commonwealth had come under attack by an Arkansas American Legion leader for advocating "bolshevism, sovietism, communism and free love." The Department of Justice, J. Edgar Hoover wrote in response to an inquiry, had not issued any statements on Commonwealth. Nor did the important newspapers in Arkansas rise to the bait. For a while, the heat was off.

But more and more the school and its people were drawn into the struggles of sharecroppers, hill farmers, timber workers, and miners, as drought and depression made hard lives harder. Militant left-wing groups—Communist, Socialist, Trotskyite—began organizing rival unions among textile workers, miners, tenant farmers. Commonwealth students supported them all, marching in picket lines, supplying material aid to strikers. In geometric proportion, attacks on the college increased. Investigations of the college became a way of life.

Inevitably, Claude and Commonwealth had connected during the preacher's pulpit days. Their common interests brought them together on picket lines, at conferences, in courtrooms. As 1937 began, the college named Claude its director.

Claude had appeared on the front pages of newspapers across the country in June of 1936, when he and a well-born Memphis woman, driving through Crittenden County, Arkansas, in search of information about a missing black STFU member, were beaten almost to death by six white men. Claude couldn't seem to stay away from danger. His growing notoriety made him a draw on lecture platforms organized by Willard Uphaus to raise money for his New Era School. And the preacher never failed to thrill audiences with his spellbinding style and his wizardry at finding biblical passages in support of every radical idea. For Commonwealth College, snaring Claude seemed a coup. Claude immediately invited Lee to join the teaching staff.

From the Commonwealth College *Fortnightly* of September 1, 1937:

"Lee Hays, native of Little Rock, will join Commonwealth's faculty with the beginning of the fall quarter, October 4, to teach Workers' Dramatics and to supervise Commonwealth's drama groups.

". . . He has been assistant to the drama director at Highlander Folk School and was a member of the Sharecropper Film Committee which produced 'America's Disinherited.' Lee brings with him to Commonwealth valuable experience and ability."

The campus of Commonwealth College, in Mena, Arkansas, in the 1930s, the house-like buildings serving as classrooms, offices, and dormitories.

Well, he *had* assisted Zilphia, if not officially. And beefing up one's résumé is a good old American tradition. Certainly, Lee had more experience and ability than most twenty-three-year-olds.

Claude brought as his executive secretary a young Commonwealth graduate named Donald Kobler, who had been the preacher's chief associate at New Era. In a letter years later, Kobler remarked on the strength of Lee's bond to the Williamses and on the lack of other connections: "When Lee appeared at Commonwealth, it was obvious that he regarded Claude as a surrogate father. He was also deeply attached to Joyce. . . . Although we worked closely together during the ensuing year, Lee did not talk with me about family or friends. To my knowledge, no one ever came to visit him at Commonwealth."

Probably not, but Lee had a way of creating a family for himself from whatever people he happened to be sharing a place or a goal with. There would be many families along the way.

Meanwhile, Lee had a curriculum to organize. Perhaps from his exposure to New York's leftist film and theater groups, Lee promised a great deal in an article he wrote for *Fortnightly*. He would offer a full program of workers' dramatics, with emphasis on "the drama as a weapon for union organization." He planned "a survey of professional plays of social content and of special interest to labor." Students would study the "professional theater and the motion picture, as institutions influencing and molding opinion."

In addition to professional plays, his class would study "the many labor plays . . . produced by workers' groups and published by labor schools and unions" and would produce some of them. Students would learn labor songs, mass chants, and "other theatricals."

"Most important," Lee wrote, "students will write and produce their own plays out of their common experiences and ideas. They will learn how to use dramatics in attacking their own social, economic and organizational problems. These plays will be produced on the college stage and before workers' audiences in the Southwest."

An ambitious program—and one that in fact marked the only new direction taken by Commonwealth in the Williams years, wrote Raymond and Charlotte Koch in their history of the college.

Lee, they noted, "organized The Commonwealth Players as an experimental performing group. He wrote and directed the first production, 'One Bread, One Body.' It toured and was a hit. More original scripts were written and produced. These dramatic expeditions . . . were (among) the high points of educational achievement during this period."

"We wrote 'zipper' plays," Lee related in a *People's Songs Bulletin* column a decade later, "so constructed that the local union members could play roles in the plays—committee men, plantation thugs, and so on.

"All plays opened with a prayer, by a local preacher who often as not stepped out of character to pray for the play, its authors, producers and actors. Claude would play the part of the visiting union organizer, and at certain points in the play he would deliver lectures on local union problems.

"Perhaps we borrowed considerably from 'Waiting for Lefty,' for the burden of his lectures was usually, 'Don't wait for the organizer to come and tell you what to do. Fight your own fights. Make your union strong the way you want it to be, the way you can make it strong by your own efforts.' "

From Claude, as from Zilphia, Lee absorbed the importance of music in stirring emotions and action.

"All Claude's meetings are singing meetings," wrote Lee. "He has dug up folk singers and songwriters and set them to work fashioning songs for particular meetings or causes. . . .

"It was in the plays that we first sang 'No More Mourning' and 'Roll the Union On' and 'What Is That I See Yonder Coming.' And always we sang songs like 'Let the Will of the Lord Be Done' and 'When the Struggle's Over We Shall All Be Free, in the New Society.' Sometimes at meetings way out in the backwoods or in the heart of the dismal cotton country, Claude would sing an old song like 'We Shall Not Be Moved'—prepared to break into the old hymn words if gun thugs should appear."

Lee was the most talented of Claude's people, it seemed to Waldemar Hille, the young dean of music at Elmhurst College, who came from Chicago to spend the Christmas holidays at Commonwealth College in 1937. "Lee was able to lead and make things hum," Hille said later. "Claude and Lee collected songs and turned them into labor songs, but while Claude was very much a part of this, Lee was the one who polished them and created the final accepted version. Lee had a 'polishing' sense. Claude accepted that."

"In the evening," Kobler remembered, "when we were all involved in some common task—perhaps some mindless job like getting out a mailing—Lee usually led us in singing. His improvisations were often amusing, sometimes inspired, and I realize now that songs he later made famous were tried out on us on those impromptu, often boisterous occasions. The Commons would ring with the excitement of a revival meeting as Lee led us, his 'audience,' through variations of a folk song or hymn—songs such as 'When the Saints Go Marching In' and 'We Shall Not Be Moved'— making up new lyrics as we sang along."

Hille was enchanted by Lee's store of folk songs, so many of them "aimed at people's social condition."

Lee took Hille to visit a neighbor—Emma Dusenberry, old, blind, and perhaps the single greatest repository of folk music ever found rocking on a front porch. The two young men listened to her sing, and Hille "made notations on a number of them, such as 'The Candidate's a Dodger.' " "Lee," Hille said, "got a kick out of my ability to do this." Hille would set down many songs for Lee in the years to come.

Lee led another kind of outing that Hille joined on his Christmas holiday. They and several Commonwealth students piled the campus truck high with stage equipment and set out for Tulsa, where they put on "progressive" entertainment, art as a weapon, for striking oil workers. Hille never forgot "the dragon, which represented 'the spirit of evil and capitalism,' and which actually spat fire. The program was presented in a rented hall; it had a favorable reception."

The group stayed for two nights at the home of the strike's organizer; its members learned later that police raided the house and arrested the organizer the day after they left.

Those were the chances you took at Commonwealth.

Life as a social activist in Arkansas was precarious indeed. In a *People's Songs Bulletin* column published in 1948, Lee made vivid the fears that went with the territory.

"The car in which we were riding through the cold Arkansas

night was kind of rump sprung from being overworked by its owner, a union organizer. I suppose if you'd been chased sixty miles down the blacktop by riding bosses you'd be rump sprung, too. When you saw the car by day it looked like an old hound dog with his rear end way out of line; and when you rode in it you had the feeling of being in a sailboat, tacking. . . .

"I was scared. We were riding through a part of the country where the car was known, and where the owner was known and hated. He was hated so much that once the riding bosses had caught him and flogged him with the belly band of a mule harness. I had never been beaten up, and I was scared and nervous. We knew of men who had been active in union work who had vanished, and it was said that only the red waters of the St. Francis River knew where they had gone. . . .

"I've heard it said that there are organizers who aren't afraid of anything; but I've always considered they worked for other unions, for I never met them.

"Now, nothing happened this night, except that we had a flat tire, and that we sang. Still, we were scared. The organizer drove warily, hunched over the wheel. The young Negro boy beside him watched the road just as carefully, and his feet pressed the floorboards every time the organizer stepped on the brakes. The Negro man and the white woman who sat in the rear with me were tense, and I could feel their bodies tightening up every time we passed a car or went through a town.

"The organizer started singing.

"Now here we were, all union folks, and in our meetings we sang the old labor songs, and the new songs of labor that were being written by union people. We were proud of our songs that sang of the dignity of labor and of a bright future. But in this cold night we sang hymns . . . sang them as we drove along, harmonies swelling and breaking . . . all the voices searching, working for harmonies unheard and unknown, perfect blends of tones and feelings and fears.

"I wondered about this, why we found such comfort in the old hymns, we whose eyes were fixed on a new day and a new way of life. For a while it was possible not to be scared, even.

"But the answer was there, and it came to me that the words of the song didn't matter. They were there and we sang them, but what mattered was that we were singing. It was a drawing together of inner strengths, and what mattered was that each offered his voice to the others, and his own strength. Yes, the hymns were written for people who had come together after long absences in the wilderness, and the writers of the hymns made them songs for people to sing together. . . . I said, 'I wish we had as many labor songs as hymns, and that folks sang them with the same feeling.'

"The organizer said, 'We will, someday. And who do you think is going to make the new songs?"

" 'Why,' I said, 'I guess WE will.' "

Lee's reputation as a stirring presence in labor battles made its way up north. In 1938, he hitchhiked to Chicago to sing for the city's striking newspapermen. Wally Hille backed him on the piano.

"Lee participated in meetings and sang union songs, labor songs, radical songs," Hille recalled. "He had all this wonderful material that he and Claude had created with a few word changes out of gospel songs, making them into inspirational labor-organizing songs. Such as 'Organize, Organize, Let the Will of the Lord Be Done.' "

For rousing the spirits of strikers, you couldn't beat "Roll the Union On." That "zipper" song, a product of Claude's New Era School, brought howls of laughter each time Lee zipped in the names of the union's enemies.

And if the boss is in the way
We're gonna roll it over him
Gonna roll it over him
Gonna roll it over him
If the boss is in the way
We're gonna roll it over him
Gonna roll the union on.

We're gonna roll (Gonna roll)
We're gonna roll (Gonna roll)
Gonna roll the union on
We're gonna roll (Gonna roll)
We're gonna roll (Gonna roll)
We're gonna roll the union on!

A zipper song is a simple folk tune built on repeated lines and, in Lee's words, "so constructed that you have to zip in only a word or two to make an entirely new verse. 'Roll the Union On' is the best example, with its structure allowing you to roll the union over anything you want to roll over, but there are many more. . . .

"Now these are obviously songs that don't call for much brainwork. They are songs you can sing three seconds after you've heard the first line. And, because they are very rhythmic and full of bounce, they're inviting—as a matter of fact, that's just what they are, because they derive from the invitational hymns of the old camp meetings.

" 'Join the Union' is 'Come to Jesus.' 'Roll the Union On' is 'Roll the Chariot On.' So today the same music invites people to join churches and unions."

While Lee's social-action dramas about organizing unions and overcoming the spirit of capitalism played to appreciative workers, Commonwealth itself, under Claude, faltered. More and more, the school came to be perceived as dominated by members of the Communist party, and broader-based labor support began falling away. Some felt Claude abetted the change. Others, the school's historians suggest, thought Claude simply "had the dubious luck to be available at that particular time . . . in Oregon farm language, 'no blame attaches to the buggy horse we harness to the plow.' "

At the time, the specter of communism began to dominate labor union politics. Claude and his politics became a critical issue within the young and vulnerable Southern Tenant Farmers Union.

"When Claude was kicked out of the STFU in 1938," Myles Horton said later, "he was for the first time called a Communist by people of the Left. Before that, everyone who was left of Genghis Khan was called a Communist, so it didn't matter. But at this point it began to matter."

J. R. Butler, president of the STFU, resigned from Commonwealth's board, charging that the college had violated its nonfactional policies.

Claude responded that Commonwealth was "an independent labor school" and had "no affiliation or connection whatsoever with any political party." He added, "Neither am I a member of the Communist Party." The dispute, he insisted, originated in his championship of "progressive trade unionism, in opposition of the bureaucratic policies of the Memphis office."

Whether or not you believed the preacher depended on where you stood politically.

Nobody relented; the college further narrowed its political orientation; the right-wing press began to print "exposés" of the Bolshevik college in Arkansas where people ran around nude and practiced free love.

Perhaps the sense of downward drift affected Lee. From a visitor to the campus, one hears about a trait mentioned with increasing frequency by those who knew Lee later.

Magda Fink came to Commonwealth in 1938 with her young child to recuperate, inexpensively, from a divorce. (She went on to become head of a progressive prep school in Connecticut.) She later described Lee as "sick all the time . . . always in a bathrobe, always badly disheveled," adding, "The only thing I remember his doing was at Christmas services for the neighbors, where I played the piano, Lee led hymn singing, and Claude preached in his hellfire-and-brimstone way."

That was a different perspective on a young man previously seen hitchhiking up and down and around, following the red preacher into mean and dangerous places, staging agit-prop plays on southern platforms, filming black and white sharecroppers together in the Mississippi Delta, trying to organize a black Boy Scout troup in Natchez.

From this point on, a running subtheme is Lee's health, and the degree to which his ailments were real or imagined.

Another 1938 Commonwealth visitor remembered Lee's ear for speech, the attribute of a true writer. Hope Hale Davis came to Commonwealth to research material on sharecroppers for a serial commissioned by *True Story*. The magazine's editors wanted more realistic and socially aware material in those troubled times, as background for the romance. In Davis's serial, the narrator is a sharecropper's daughter with whom the plantation owner's son falls madly in love. An important role in their story is played by a fearless left-wing preacher patterned on Claude Williams.

Davis spent much of her time at Commonwealth with Lee, whom

she described as "big, disheveled, sloppy, brilliant, and helpful." He worked with her on the cadences of plantation country dialect. "He did that brilliantly," she said, "and that lent verisimilitude to my work."

She never saw him again, and never forgot him.

In later years, Lee looked back on Commonwealth as one of his "golden places." He loved Claude and Joyce, he enjoyed being the person who "made things hum," and he sensed that he had picked up the kind of experience that would lead to something bigger.

Perhaps "golden places" glow brighter from afar. Lee didn't hang around for the end of Commonwealth, though it wasn't long in coming.

By the end of 1940, the school was out of business. Months earlier, Lee, with sixty-five dollars collected from the college's student body and faculty, had headed north, carrying Commonwealth's labor songs to the unions up there.

6

"Roll the Union On"
1940–1941

If you want higher wages let me tell you what to do,
You got to talk to the workers in the shop with you;
You got to build you a union, got to make it strong,
But if you all stick together, boys, it won't be long.

You get shorter hours,
Better working conditions,
Vacations with pay,
Take the kids to the seashore.

It ain't quite this simple, so I better explain
Just why you got to ride on the union train;
'Cause if you wait for the boss to raise your pay,
We'll all be waiting till judgment day;

We'll all be buried,
Gone to Heaven,
Saint Peter'll be the straw boss then, boys.

—From *"Talking Union,"*
words by the ALMANAC SINGERS

*A*fter six years of radical life in the South, the move north had to bring some relief. Despite his size, Lee didn't scoff at physical danger the way Claude Williams did. He was tired of having it always lurking about. Moreover, what could be accomplished by staying in Arkansas?

The STFU, on which much of his passion had centered, all but disappeared during the labor battles between pro- and anti-Communist factions. Claude's influence withered with the demise of Commonwealth.

Meanwhile, an international event had thrown the Far Left into an isolated shambles. On August 23, 1939, Stalin signed a nonaggression pact with Hitler, freeing the Nazis to pick off other countries without concern about their eastern front.

"I do remember," Lee told an interviewer in 1979, "that the signing of the Hitler-Stalin pact was a very hard pill to swallow. . . . To this day I don't quite follow the line of reasoning behind that one, except to give Stalin more time."

That the pact gave Stalin more time was the story then put out; millions around the world didn't buy it, and at that point lost faith in the Soviet Union as the exemplar of the great socialist experiment. (Many others had lost faith earlier, during the Moscow purge trials.)

But as a disciple of Claude's, Lee in 1940 held firm with those who continued to believe that America and Britain were maneuvering not to defeat Nazi Germany, or rather not just yet, but first to turn Hitler to their desired end of destroying the Soviet Union.

(If such reasoning seems paranoid today, consider the August 18, 1985, *New York Times Book Review* article on *Atomic Diplomacy: Hiroshima and Potsdam*, a scholarly book first published in 1965 and reissued in 1985. There Gaddis Smith, the Yale history professor, stated the book's premise: the atomic bombs that destroyed Hiroshima and Nagasaki were meant by President Truman "to send a threatening message from the United States to the Soviet Union." This premise, he concluded, seems less startling in 1985 than in 1965, for "the preponderance of new evidence that has appeared since 1965 tends to sustain the original argument. It has been demonstrated that the decision to bomb Japan was closely connected to Truman's confrontational approach to the Soviet Union.")

The prewar unpopularity of the Soviet Union escalated when, in the winter of 1939, the massive Russian bear attacked Finland, which, instead of rolling over, fought surprisingly and effectively into 1940, stirring hearts everywhere for the brave little underdog of a country.

In short, 1940 was a bad time to say a good word for "peace." Worse, the only other voices opposing the war emanated from the extreme right, particularly America Firsters, a group suspected of harboring the hope that Hitler would eventually triumph *über alles.*

Whatever uneasiness the Hitler-Stalin pact churned up, Lee hoped to submerge by throwing his unvast energies into the service of the dynamic young Congress of Industrial Organizations—the challenger to the fat and lazy and bureaucratic old American Federation of Labor.

A singing labor movement, that was the goal. If you got the unions singing, peace and brotherhood had to follow. It seemed so clear and simple. Well, not simple. "It wasn't as easy as writing good songs and then going out and singing them," said Lee in 1948. "What we had to do was to tap that root of the people's own culture—to mine out a particular vein."

A vein, perhaps, such as he'd mined at Commonwealth. Hymns and gospel songs, with religion zipped out and pro-union lyrics zipped in.

You could find them all in ten mimeographed pages headed "Commonwealth Labor Songs—A Collection of Old and New Songs for the Use of Labor Unions." Lee had gathered and edited the collection, which Commonwealth sold for five cents per copy, plus three cents for postage, reduced prices arranged for quantity orders.

The people at Commonwealth praised the collection and agreed that the songs could help the bold young CIO unions in their awesome battles with industry. It wouldn't happen without a push. Who better to push than Lee, a veteran song-leading crowd rouser at twenty-six?

Lee's destination was New York City, but he hadn't gotten beyond Philadelphia. He'd stopped each night on his way north at "friendly houses." Claude and others at Commonwealth had drawn up lists of people they knew along Lee's hitchhiking route, at whose homes Lee could turn up unannounced and be sure of a bed and a welcome. That's how he got to the doorstep of a three-story house on Regent Street in Philadelphia on a winter's night early in 1940. And there, unexpectedly, Lee found a new surrogate family to replace the one he'd left behind. From that night through the greater part of the 1940s, home to Lee meant the intellectual, political, and children-everywhere ferment of Walter and Lillian Lowenfels's noisy, friendly house.

Angela, a Lowenfels daughter, said later, "Ours was the kind of household where there was always chaos and confusion, and people who wandered in and stayed."

Lee wandered in and stayed.

Here the politics was familiar and the head of household (Walter, like Claude) something of a legendary figure. But life and legend at the Lowenfelses' were strikingly and beguilingly different from those at Claude's.

You might come upon Walter Lowenfels's name in books about Paris in the 1920s and 1930s. An avant-garde poet of impressive reputation, he'd hung out with the great American literary figures of that place and time—Anaïs Nin, Henry Miller, Hemingway, Fitzgerald.

In 1935, he returned to America, profoundly concerned about recent international developments, convinced that only Marxism could or would turn back the Nazi tide. Still sporting his Paris beret over his balding head, he'd signed on as Philadelphia editor of the *Daily Worker*, a surprising step for a Lost Generation poet. But then, little about the 1930s was predictable.

Claude's lifelong companion, poverty, had not yet touched Walter, scion of a well-to-do family. Not that Walter and Lillian could get by without jobs. But their lifestyle went beyond their salaries, into the realm of unearned income. The tall and craggy Walter had a strong sense of his own creative importance. Lillian, short, constantly battling obesity, hardworking, and devoted to Walter's talent, ran a large and bountiful house, warmly welcoming friends old and new. Their four little girls—Michael; the twins, Judy and Manna; and the youngest, Angela—learned to cope with their far from typical home.

Everything about the Lowenfels household captivated Lee.

"There was lots of music making," recalled Angela. "Father loved classical music. He and Lee banged on the piano, and wrote songs. Father banged with panache. Lee and Mother played anagrams. Lee did lots of the cooking, and he and Mother made things for the house. He built a great kitchen table which we ate at, on high stools, and which Father took everywhere after. Judy has it now, I think. Having Lee around was like having another father."

"My dear boy," Lillian called Lee, and he adored her. Among Walter's lasting imprints on Lee was a passion for Walt Whitman, of whom Lowenfels wrote a biography.

Lee would later urge young songwriters to remember Whitman's charge that poets should "sing worthily the songs these States have already indicated: Their origin, Washington, '76; the picturesqueness of old times, the war of 1812 and the sea-fights; the incredible rapidity of movement and breadth of area—to fuse and compact the South and North . . . to express the native forms, situations, scenes, from Montauk to California . . . the working out on such gigantic scales, and with such a swift and mighty play of changing light and shade, of the great problems of man and freedom. . . ."

In that spirit Lee, with Walter's collaboration, later wrote one of his most memorable, and most political, songs, "Wasn't That a Time!"

Living with the Lowenfelses kept the creative juices flowing. Lee resumed writing poetry and began writing humorous essays. He submitted pieces to national publications, with some success.

The prestigious *Poetry* magazine published his poem "Deadbuggy" in its November 1940 issue.

> Death is a rubbertired fact
> F O B America.
> A 6% investment
> in a 7' plot
> paid off in gold of angels tooting trumpets on that day.
> Hold your teeth grampa here we go
> razmadaz
> bring on your rubbertired pulpits
> your seventeen silvergeared moaners
> your firstclass A One super special deluxe
> deadbuggy
> with a New York Times in every flowerpot
> and the Gospel of Saint Matthew standing out before.
> Enjoy yourself! You only die
> once.

Years later Lee said, "Sometimes, reading this poem, I think I know what it means." He also said it didn't mean anything but had "some pretty good images." Images that just happened to describe the way his father died.

His father's ghost wouldn't lie still in Lee's repressions. Lee tried to exorcise it by turning the Reverend Hays into something of a comic character. In rural rhythms and biblical references, Lee spun stories about his father's mishaps with devices purchased to enhance his dignity in the pulpit: a hair tonic that restored natural color, individual screw-in false teeth from St. Louis. The *New Republic* published "My Father with Purple Hair" in its May 27, 1940, issue; and "The Forty-Ninth Chicken" (a parish family ate forty-eight chickens before finding the one who'd gobbled the Reverend Hays's false teeth off their window sill the night he slept over) in the August 26, 1940, issue.

Here was a natural storyteller out of Arkansas, a tall-tale spinner in the Mark Twain tradition. Readers responded; the magazine forwarded fan mail to Philadelphia.

Among the letters of admiration was one from another young writer who'd published in the *New Republic*, Millard Lampell. (Lampell would go on to write for radio, television, the theater, and Hollywood.) Lee replied with kind words about Lampell's pieces. After another exchange of letters, they arranged to meet in New York City, where Lampell lived, and where Lee knew he had at last to go to push the labor songs project. He wished he could stay forever in the comfortable and nurturing household of the Lowenfelses.

Another young musician was thinking about putting out a book of labor songs at that time. His name was Pete Seeger. He had returned to New York after knocking around the country with an Oklahoma folk singer named Woody Guthrie. Pete, at twenty-one, burned with a passion to right the injustices of the world. The descendant of an aristocratic New England family, Harvard-educated, immersed for a year in Alan Lomax's historical collection of folk music at the Library of Congress, Pete had been persuaded by Woody that he'd "learn more from hitting the road than from hitting the books." And off they'd gone, Pete and Woody, in appearance an odd couple—Pete tall and skinny and acne scarred and desperately shy, Woody short and scruffy and feisty. They'd traveled for months, swapping songs with each other and with "the people"—workers, farmers, mountain folk, every kind of folk—and singing in redneck saloons to earn some quarters for food and gasoline. Woody was Pete's "finishing school."

But now, in New York City, Pete found himself "really at loose ends." "I didn't know quite what I was going to do with myself," he recalled. "I still wanted this book of labor songs out, I still wanted to learn more songs, I didn't know quite how to make a living singing, but I was getting occasional offers to sing for a fund-raising party, five dollars here, five dollars there, which was good pay in those days, it seemed to me, for singing a few songs."

He heard that a man who'd taught at Commonwealth had come to town with a bunch of labor songs he hoped to publish. "It seemed kind of sensible," he said later, "that we should pool our resources and put out one book which would be a better one."

Lee and Millard Lampell had "hit it off pretty good and become had roommates," Lee wrote later, adding, "Within a week or two we met a guy named Pete Hawes, and he brought Pete Seeger around."

"Lee and I found we got along well," said Pete. "He liked the sound of my banjo accompanying him, and I really admired his way with an audience. I was relatively shy and inexperienced in many, many ways. So we took bookings together."

From that time on, the central figure in Lee's musical life, and the force field that drew his love and anger in equal parts, was Pete Seeger.

Their very first booking, a luncheon at the Jade Mountain restaurant, raised funds for the remnants of Loyalist Spain. The organizers paid them $2.50. Pete gave the money to Lee, saying, "You take it. I got five bucks for singing ten days ago, and still have most of it left. You need it more than I do."

Suddenly, they were singing for all the "worthy causes" (as they termed them) in town. They sounded terrific together, these two tall young men—the skinny one, the Yankee, in his farmer's overalls, and the heavy one, who seemed to be some kind of southern minister, in his rumpled black suit—singing all these radical songs that they'd dug up, or written, or rewritten.

They forgot the labor songbook project (Pete would return to it in the 1960s) in the rush of writing and singing songs that bounced off the headlines. In New York City, you could find groups and leagues in every profession that worried about America's and Britain's true war aims. Pete and Lee were becoming their minstrels; soon Lee's roommate, Millard, a dazzlingly quick and clever verse writer, started coming along to join in on the choruses.

Millard dashed off what Pete later called "a real sassy song—'I hate war, and so does Eleanor/But we won't be safe till everybody's dead'—against the efforts of President Roosevelt to get America drawn into the war between England and Germany." "It seemed to us," Pete remembered, "that Churchill wasn't interested in fighting Hitler so much as he would have preferred to sic Hitler on Russia. And the fact that England and France and the U.S.A. had not supported the Spanish Republican government was one more piece of evidence that these countries weren't really against fascism."

So the first songs they wrote were songs for peace. "They were sentimental and pacifist . . . written from the point of view of a bunch of young fellows who didn't relish spilling their blood on some 'furrin' battlefield to make profits for Standard Oil," said Lee. "But they were full of guts and just as poignant as hell, and very effective."

They needed a name for themselves, and they found it in a letter from Woody, who had bobbed up once, sung with them for a week or so, and blown town again.

As bookings increased, they felt confident enough to take a loft, on Fourth Avenue and Twelfth Street.

"A friend designed a beautiful table for us along the wall," Pete said. "We had weekly rent parties. Lee would bake the bread, we bought a keg of beer, we'd sing up a storm, and pay the rent and a little bit more. In April 1941, we recorded some of the peace songs. The company was scared—they wouldn't put their name on the label—just called them 'Songs for John Doe' by the Almanac Singers."

Pete, Lee, and Millard sang on the album. Backing them on guitar was their friend Josh White, who like Lee was the son of a southern preacher, only black. He and Lee seemed to have many other things in common: their religious roots, their feelings about the South, their links to the sharecroppers, the poverty they'd experienced, their wanderings around the country, their politics, and music. They loved swapping stories and songs out of their heritage, often over a bottle of what Woody called Old Overcoat. Lee looked up to White, who had already gained some fame as a guitarist and singer of authentic folk songs and blues. Their friendship became a casualty of the McCarthy era, when White, blacklisted, purged himself by testifying in his own behalf before a congressional committee in Washington, D.C.

The little album of peace songs got around. Pete remembered that the *Daily Worker* gave it "a fine writeup, and from coast to coast people said, At last, songs that tell people's feelings about the war drive."

That, at least, is what the people they heard from said.

One of the songs in particular produced the most startling effect on audiences he'd ever seen, Lee later wrote: "It stunned 'em. Its story of the strange death of a young man who died for no reason, and its last line which gave the reason—'A bayonet sticking in his side'—hit people right between the eyes, like a nine pound striking hammer."

A month later, the Almanacs put out an album of union songs. The album, entitled *Talking Union*, has remained in print ever since. Pete, like many others, thinks "it's still one of the best albums of union songs there is."

Among labor union audiences, the title song was an instant and solid hit. Lee, Pete, and Millard traveled the subway circuit, singing their song in meetings and on picket lines. Their record went out to unions across the country. After hearing it, the Committee to Defend Harry Bridges (the Australian-born, left-wing head of the CIO Longshoremen's Union, threatened with deportation by the FBI), asked the Almanacs to write a song for their cause.

"One weekend," Pete recalled, "up at Camp Unity, we sat down and worked, and by gosh, at the end of the day we had a song:

> Oh the FBI is worried, and the bosses they are scared,
> They can't deport six million men, they know.
> And we're not gonna let them send Harry over the seas,
> We'll fight for Harry Bridges and build the CIO.

This was a single record, and the Longshoremen's Union paid for it and sent it around the country"—to other CIO unions, the six million men of the song.

All in all, Lee and Pete had reason to believe that their records and performances might do more to spur a singing labor movement than a book of labor songs ever could.

On June 22, 1941, Hitler's armies marched without warning into the Soviet Union, certain of quick victory because of the Russian armies' dismal performance during the invasion of Finland.

"Our whole politics," Lee said later, "took a terrible shift from 'the Yanks ain't coming' to 'the Yanks ARE coming.' All of a sudden it became one war, instead of two, and there was some chance of beating fascism on its own ground, which everybody was for. But it sure knocked hell out of our repertoire."

Their peace songs, of course, went right out the window, with no regrets. Eventually, the rousing union songs went on hold, because anything promoting labor unrest interfered with the war effort. Not that a booking ever had to be canceled for lack of material; the Almanacs could always whip up new songs to fit the goals of the moment. But when events brought the group into confluence with the mainstream war effort, torrents of new songs flowed forth.

Hitler's invasion coincided with the Almanacs' preparations for a kind of CIO grand tour of the country.

"We bought a $125, eight-year-old Buick, a big old seven-passenger limousine," Pete recounted. "It only got about ten miles a gallon and seven miles on a quart of oil. But it purred along.

"About a week before we were to leave, who knocks on the door but Woody. He'd hitchhiked and ridden freights, split up with his wife again, and we said, 'Woody, we're about to leave for the West Coast, wanna come with us?' Woody scratched his head and said, 'Well, I just got here, but I guess if you're going west I'll go with you.'"

Before they left, Woody helped them record two more albums, *Sod Buster Ballads,* songs of America's pioneer days, and *Deep Sea Chanteys,* both for General Records. Then they set out. Woody sent back word of their adventures in a newsletter:

"We rolled the gasoline hose down into our tank and left it there to suck and blow till we hit our first union hall stopoff. We made up songs. 'From the Allegheny to the Ohio she's all gonna melt up CIO, Pittsburgh! Lord God! Pittsburgh!'"

Woody started the Pittsburgh song off, and they all tossed in words, a common technique among the Almanacs, according to Pete: "One person would get an idea for a song and try it out, and the others would add verses. If it worked, it worked."

The Pittsburgh song worked. Some of its verses ("Pittsburgh is a smoky old town/Solid iron from McKeesport down/In Pittsburgh, Lord God, Pittsburgh") are still sung in the city's schools. Pete's favorite is the verse they *don't* sing in the schools:

> What did Jones & Laughlin steal, Pittsburgh,
> What did Jones & Laughlin steal, Pittsburgh.
> All I do is cough and choke
> From the iron filings and the sulfur smoke,
> Pittsburgh. . . .

The Almanacs drove and sang and whooped and hollered.

"We went into union halls," Woody's report continued, "and sang before, during and after the speakers had spoke, and took up a collection to buy gas, oil, and to grease the breezes. We sang: Union Maid. Talking Union. I Don't Want Your Millions Mister. Get Thee Behind Me Satan. Union Train a'Comin'. And made up dozens and dozens as we rolled along or as we stayed overnight at a friendly house. . . ."

Millard had to restrain Woody occasionally, Pete remembered, "when Woody started drinking too much and goosed the wife of the head of the union."

"We rolled on out to Denver," wrote Woody, "then onto Frisco and sang for five thousand longshoremen at the Harry Bridges Local. We sang for the Ladies Auxiliary. We sang for the farm and factory workers around lower California, and then back to Frisco."

There was more, lots more, for Pete and Woody, but Lee and Millard cut out after San Francisco—Millard because he missed his girlfriend; Lee because the pace had utterly exhausted him.

Pete later recalled the anger he felt: "I didn't realize. . . . I thought, surely he can keep up. But he went back to New York, saying he'd get things ready for us—'You'll be back in a month or two.' "

And so only two Almanacs—Woody and Pete—went north

expect much money for doing exactly what they wanted to do?

As for the groups who'd booked them, they often registered surprise and disappointment at who showed up and how they sang. (Woody called the Almanacs the only group he knew that rehearsed onstage.) Groups knew the Almanacs from their antiwar and union song records; they assumed that Pete and Lee *were* the Almanacs. Pete singing "Talking Union" and Lee singing "Roll the Union On"—that was *it*. But Pete would have had to replicate himself to appear at all the gatherings whose organizers asked for him, and Lee wouldn't turn up, because . . . well, more about that in a minute.

Meanwhile, the Almanacs' low booking fees couldn't cover their house rent. Before 1941 ended, they'd given up the house and moved two blocks away, into a large, sixty-dollar-a-month apartment, where they kept on writing.

"We made up songs against Hitlerism and fascism homemade and imported," Woody wrote. "We sang songs about our Allies and made up songs to pay honor and tribute to the story of the trade union workers around the world. . . ."

They sang "Round and Round Hitler's Grave" and thrilled the nation with their patriotic song "The Reuben James." The Office of War Information (OWI) hired them to sing on overseas broadcasts beamed to frontline fighters.

But by the time of the OWI broadcasts, Lee was out of the Almanacs, having been asked to resign by Pete, who would in retrospect feel he'd made "one of the biggest mistakes of [his] life."

In the annals of protest songs, folk groups, and labor music, Lee's ouster from the Almanacs is an event. Questions arise and explanations or theories are floated.

Pete, since Lee's death, has chivalrously assumed sole responsibility for this and future breaks with Lee. He has spoken of differences in work habits.

And indeed, it would be difficult to imagine two more incompatible metabolisms than Pete's and Lee's. Pete could fall asleep on a hard floor in seconds and spring up ready for action with the first light, thirteen ideas to the dozen, a cyclotron of energy, exhausting the mere mortals who lived and worked with him.

Lee's furnace burned on a low flame. He had never glowed with good health, and his habits ensured he never would. (Later, he liked to quote the comedian who said, "If I'd known I was going to live this long, I'd have taken better care of myself.") More and more often, he'd take to his bed before a booking, professing to be too ill to sing that night. He slept fitfully at night and took hours to pull himself together in the morning. He puffed up theories about how "the creative power comes from loafing and inviting the soul."

The other Almanacs were no happier about Lee's immobility than was Pete. Nor did they appreciate Lee's constant critiquing of the songs they so energetically, if not always consummately, crafted. Lee questioned everything. What is the central thing we're trying to do with this song? What is its spine? Where is the rhythm? Where are the images? And so on and so on. Good questions, but when you had to finish a song for tonight, and he sat, or lay, there sticking pins into your work . . . "It seemed to me that the best thing would be that Lee resign from the Almanacs," said Pete, "and I was the guy who had to ask him." Pete did the job, but not without a consensus.

Lee, in a letter to Pete four decades later, wrote that he'd been asked by Jim Capaldi, interviewing for *Sing Out!*, whether political disagreements had anything to do with the ouster.

"I told him, as I'd told Joe Klein [biographer of Woody Guthrie], that I was kicked out of the group . . . because I was not doing my job, and that as far as I have ever known, politics had nothing to do with it. . . .

"During most of the Almanac period I had low-grade fever and during the latter part of my tenure I spent a lot of time in bed (quite hungry, most of the time) and was not able to go on bookings and do my share of the group work, following which, in an official meeting, I was 'terminated.' I recall absolutely no discussion of politics at that meeting. It was a rude shock, to say the least. . . ."

Pete remembered talking to a friend of Lee's in Greenwich Village soon afterward. "Are you sure you did the right thing, asking Lee to leave?" she inquired. And Pete said, "Really, it didn't seem we were getting anywhere, just continually embroiled in arguments." She sighed, "Well, it's a great hurt to him."

(In 1948, Lee wrote, "The Almanacs were my own brothers and sisters, and I have never had any better ones, or loved any more.")

The ouster was the first of three major ruptures between Pete and Lee, two giants whose talents and beliefs kept bringing them together, and whose personal traits and idiosyncrasies kept driving them apart.

Lee moved out of the group house. The Almanacs, after a brief blaze of national glory, sputtered out of existence, as the members, "quite a shifting personnel," went off to war. The Almanacs' history did indeed prove to have many versions and many interpretations. But its essence was Lee and Pete and Woody and Millard, and of those the indispensables were Lee and Pete.

7

"Tomorrow Is a Highway"
1941–1946

I saw the people walking, walking two by two,
And what men can dream, men can surely do.
If two can walk together along the way
A million can walk together some bright day.

—From *"Walk Along Together,"*
words and music by LEE HAYS,
derived from a spiritual theme

The war period, Lee would say afterward, passed by "as a blur"; it didn't stick in his memory.

Pete had joined the army. Woody and his buddy Cisco Houston were on the merchant ships. Everybody had scattered. Lee, with vestiges of tuberculosis, couldn't pass a physical and sought some way of being useful in the city.

Even before the others enlisted, Lee, terminated by the Almanacs, felt he had lost another family. The excitement, the productivity, the group living, the albums, the impact, and, well, the *importance* of being an Almanac, were difficult to come down from. The aftermath was an unshakable depression that led to long bouts of drinking. Not that Lee and booze were strangers; even in good times, Lee occasionally used beer or whisky as a crutch; in bad patches, his drinking turned everything into a blur.

He found a job with War Prisoners Aid, a Geneva-based organization that provided what its title said, worldwide. Working for the New York office meant aiding war prisoners captured by the United States and brought to camps in this country, German and Italian soldiers. Down was down, to Lee.

As head of packaging and shipping operations, Lee brought in Wally Hille, the music professor he had met at Commonwealth College, to package recorded music for the prisoners. "Beethoven, et cetera, in concerts of about an hour and a half each," Hille remembered.

There were long stretches at the Lowenfelses', and at farmhouses of friends, during which he tried to get into shape. With his health in mind, he took a summer job at the left-wing Camp Unity, in Dutchess County, New York, as a night watchman.

According to a woman who worked as bookkeeper in the camp that summer, Lee's chores included picking up papers scattered about the campgrounds. "He read whatever he picked up," she recalled. "He knew everything. We wouldn't have been surprised if he'd become the president of the United States." She assumed he worked at the camp primarily because "it was a good place to be, healthful, and one got fed, even if one hardly got paid. He sang, but not as an entertainer. Everybody liked to be around him."

Lee whiled away a year as a nonpaying guest of Jean Karsavina, a Polish émigré writer. Karsavina had studied at Smith College, and worked with the League of American Writers to help German writers (including Thomas and Heinrich Mann) slip out of Germany and relocate. In 1939, she'd leased a pre–Revolutionary War clapboard house at 27 Jane Street, in Greenwich Village, a house said to be haunted by the ghost of Alexander Hamilton. Few single and beautiful young women rented houses on their own. Her independence, and the orderliness of her surroundings, appealed strongly to disorderly friends such as the Almanacs. Once they'd pushed open a window in the middle of the night—rather than frighten her by ringing the doorbell, Pete explained—and asked if she'd put them up for a night or two, between rentals. They'd stayed a week or two. She didn't mind.

Now, with Lee in need of a home, Karsavina volunteered. "I thought it would be a good idea to have a man in the house for protection," she remembered. "The Lowenfelses had shipped him back to New York. I gave him a small bedroom and said, 'Here, this is yours. Do whatever you want in here.' And the place was always a mess. But Lee was an excellent cook. He took over the cooking.

"I learned a great deal from him about the American language.

His writing, his speech, his rhythms, his humor, were Mark Twain Americana, and when I told him so he would reply, 'Well, he got it where I got it.' "

Lee wrote, but in an undisciplined way. He couldn't seem to pull things together.

"There wasn't anybody around, nobody to form a group with," Lee said later.

Karsavina saw in Lee "emotional turmoil" created by his father's death. He told her about the accident, his father's brains splattered on the country road, the image that wouldn't go away.

Lee's emotional turmoil, some old associates believed, had another source: a sort of sexual ambiguity. Beyond some experimental teenage encounters, Lee was never known to have a romantic involvement with a woman or, for that matter, with anyone. "Did Lee ever marry?" ask people who knew him long and well. Subtext: "What about the sticky sex question?"

The evidence suggests suppression. A captivating woman like Karsavina could share her home with Lee and never worry about sexual advances. The young men who flocked around Lee over the years (Lee, the old philosopher; Lee, the surrogate father) belonged to whatever community he shared with them. And Lee sought community and family above all else. Finding them, he had to be careful not to endanger them by deviant behavior. And so friends and neighbors tended to think of Lee, when they thought about such matters at all, as asexual, as inactive as an old volcano. Whatever activity there might have been took place outside, and not within the musical, political, familial, or communal worlds, beyond whose territories he rarely ventured.

And such restraint is a sure path to emotional turmoil.

Wrestling with his demons brought on crabbiness, irascibility, argumentativeness. Still, his humor prevailed. Asked about a cross-country flight he made soon after a two-plane midair collision had been in the news, Lee responded, "I didn't put my full weight down the whole trip." Things often "put him in mind" of other things, like the story about the preacher who said, "I've married a lot of people and I've buried a lot of people. Not all the couples I've married have stayed married, but I haven't had a single comeback on one of my funerals."

Lee made people laugh. Among left-wingers wallowing in earnestness, Lee stood apart because of his wit and humor and musical talent. If his bad habits got him kicked out of a group, well, he'd rise to the top again. Usually to the accompaniment of Pete's banjo.

Pete, with the army in Saipan, dreamed about moving mountains with music when he returned to the States. "I had a feeling there were people on the West Coast," he later said, "in the Midwest, in the South, and North, who ought to be in touch with each other. We were all thinking of union songs, and peace songs, and one-world songs, and songs against racism. Using songs to help change the world, not just help it survive, as I tend to think now. That's probably the main ideological shift to overcome me with age.

"Lee would write me and say, 'We could start an organization, put out a monthly newsletter, and we'd have broad support from coast to coast.' "

Despite Lee's unhappy ending with the Almanacs, Pete knew he would be a major player in the next push for "a singing labor movement." Lee simply was too valuable a resource to exclude— as a singer (Pete had never teamed up with a better bass, and never would), as a crafter of songs for a cause, as a Will Rogers-of-the-Left raconteur. For all his undisciplined, unruly, and aggravating ways, Lee had stature and talent to burn. Too often he burned it instead of using it. But maybe the Almanac lesson had sunk in.

On the night of December 30, 1945, twenty-five songwriters and singers gathered at Pete's in-laws' house on MacDougal Street, in Greenwich Village, "pitching in their efforts," Woody Guthrie wrote, "to make out of all their little works one big union called People's Songs."

The group elected Pete president and Lee ("Arkansaw Hard Luck Lee," Woody called him) executive secretary of their new organization. Woody, from his perch on the executive committee, took a somewhat apocalyptic view of the need for People's Songs: "Unless we do hear the work songs, war songs, and love songs, dance songs, of all the people everywhere we are most apt to lose the peace and this world along with it."

Woody Guthrie (*right*) and Cisco Houston (*second from right*), in port from merchant marine duty in 1944, record a cantata, *The Chisholm Trail*, for the BBC with Lee and Burl Ives.

In February 1946, the first *People's Songs Bulletin* came out, mimeographed. "Lee and I," Pete related, "were the two main full-time people behind it, in many ways Lee more than me. I was traveling more, singing, and Lee manned the office more."

The long blur ended. Lee had a group and a purpose again, and a publication that would print as much as he'd write.

"Organized to create, promote and distribute songs of labor and the American people" was the credo of People's Songs. In practical ways, the organization offered its services in realizing the dream.

People's Songs would happily help a union put together a songbook for its members. Or compose a special union song. Or produce a record of a union's own songs.

Songwriters, amateur and professional, were encouraged to submit songs for publication in the *Bulletin*—songs "about Gerald L. K. Smith, the Freeport murders, the high cost of living, picket lines, labor unity, housing for veterans . . . songs about atomic power, about labor's role in the peace, and our concern for suffering minority peoples everywhere."

A greater than expected response to their first *Bulletin* encouraged the fledgling organization to abandon the mimeograph machine in favor of photo-offset. People's Songs was on its way.

In later years, making appearances in South America, Pete would be asked if the U.S.A. had a new-song movement. He would reply, "We don't use that term, but in a way we'd had one since Woody and Lee met in NYC, or when Lee and I started People's Songs. There'd been songwriters (Joe Hill, et cetera) and singing in various organizations, but we tried to start a national movement. . . ."

The time, in the victorious aftermath of a war fought for the right reasons, seemed gloriously auspicious. Nazism and fascism had been defeated by "the common man." Now "the common man" wanted something more than the economic hard times of prewar years. In America, unions that had bridled their members' demands during the war for patriotic reasons gave them free rein in a wave of tumultuous strikes. In England, the Labour party defeated Winston Churchill's Conservatives and began to implement its socialist platform. Among workers in both countries, the war had left a residue of admiration and goodwill for the Soviets; the word *socialism* had a less threatening ring. Why shouldn't alliances continue?

The era of goodwill, however, would soon dissipate in an already-building countertrend that would culminate in the dismal McCarthy years, when fear and loathing would equate such phrases as "one world" and "brotherhood" with Stalinism and when every kind of liberalism would be thrown into long and dark disarray.

Lee loved his job at People's Songs. Sitting at a rolltop desk, heavily and with great authority, in a small and cluttered office at 130 West Forty-second Street, he tossed out lines to old friends and new, enlisting them in the process of exchanging songs and encouraging songwriting.

He wrote to Zilphia Horton at Highlander, asking her to do "a two hundred word comment on the monologue 'Lynching! Lynching!' from the album 'Scent of Magnolias' " for publication in the *People's Songs Bulletin.*

He wrote to tell Myles Horton, "What we [People's Songs] are trying to do for PAC [the CIO's Political Action Committee] campaigns is to write general songs which can be adapted for local situations. . . ."

He sent off postcards to young singers he thought might be the right stuff for People's Songs, suggesting they drop around and visit. (Fred Hellerman, attending Brooklyn College under the GI Bill, doing "the all-purpose fuck-off thing, being an English major," and singing topical protest songs at school parties, came to People's Songs after receiving one of Lee's postcards.)

He corralled his old friend Wally Hille to serve as the organization's music editor. Hille took over the second room of the two-room office and installed an old upright piano. His "music room" had to double as an art room, a bit of space reserved for work on *Bulletin* layouts.

Old friends helped with chores of copying music, with the artwork, with mailing lists. By the second edition, the *Bulletin* had a full-time editor, Bernie Asbell, a young singer-writer, and People's Songs had an office manager, Bernie's wife, Millie. They shared the front office with Lee daily and with Pete when his bookings didn't take him out of town.

Bernie and Millie, in their early twenties, were thrilled to find themselves adopted as Lee's "young people." "He was an ex-Almanac," said Asbell, "and that was important. And he was a genuine, 'out-there' American, one of those 'real people' that New York City kids loved and looked up to. His stories about Commonwealth and Highlander, about the STFU and sharecroppers . . . he *knew* them.

"He was an elder. [Lee had just turned thirty-two.] He was the ages. He authenticated what the others believed, and were doing."

Asbell, who went on to become a successful author (his books include *When F.D.R. Died*), looks back with a historian's eye: "When I think of that period, I think of Pete and Lee, Lee and Pete. Lee's deep bass singing 'Roll the Union On.' He and Pete are the two guys who made folk songs serve political purposes. More than Woody. Woody was an individual creator, but Lee was the one with the sense of history, who tied it all together. He was the one who brought the sharecroppers in, and the union songs based on hymns. His images inspired us. 'Raggedy, raggedy are we.' It couldn't have happened without Lee.

"He was the one who convinced us that the Left was the great continuum of the American tradition, or at least that it was part of the mainstream of the American tradition. Lee thought in terms of events, history; he saw large, and that rubbed off on the rest of us. He was the philosopher of the folk music movement. He stretched the canvas. And he was funny—and God, we needed that. There wasn't much humor around."

Lee, making out a check to the musician Sonny Terry, enters the comment "For Good Singing."

Lee, having crabbed and bitched in the car all the way from New York to Philadelphia, greets an audience with some words about having listened en route to a local radio station (he hadn't) whose announcer pronounced the city's name "Phiddle-a-deddle-phi-a." (Laughter) A few numbers on, he announces a "meddle-dee." (Louder laughter) "I did say meddle-dee, diddled I?" (Sustained laughter)

Lee, taking the mike at a union meeting with a small turnout and low morale, relates an appropriate fable. "It's a story of a boy rabbit and a girl rabbit who went out walking on a Sunday morning, skipping along and enjoying the countryside, listening to the birds chirping and the butterflies zipping around. But after a while a couple of foxes spotted them and took off after them, and they started to run. The foxes got closer and closer, and they were feeling the foxes' breath on their little rabbit heels when they came to a hollow log. In they scampered. The hole was too small for the foxes to follow them in. They could hear the foxes huffing and puffing outside. After a while the girl rabbit said, 'Honey, what do we do now?' The boy rabbit said, 'There ain't but one thing *to* do, sugar. Just stay here 'til we outnumber them.' "

With the *Bulletin* under control, Pete came up with a new idea. They'd round up all the folk singers in town for one big performance,

Climax of the first hootenanny, at Irving Plaza in 1947. Lee had argued against the concept and refused to participate. He came around after the smash success of the original hoot.

so that people could get to know the kind of music People's Songs was promoting. One of Pete's crazy impractical ideas. Where will we do this? We'll rent a hall. We don't have any money! We'll sell tickets. How can we find enough people who'll pay to listen to a night of nothing but folk and political songs? We'll advertise. But we don't know how to do any of these things! We'll learn.

That was Pete, always pushing for the next step. And there was Lee, expressively impatient with Pete for his unworkable ideas (that usually worked). A tension was building between them: a tremendous respect for each other's talents, but once again, as in Almanac days, a downhill slide in Pete's tolerance for foot-dragging criticism.

The event—named, after long and intense debate, a hootenanny rather than a wingding—was a sellout and a smash. Among the

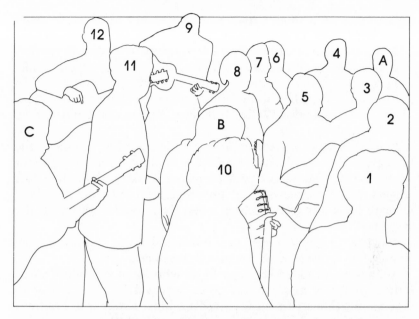

1. Pete Seeger   2. Blind Sonny Terry   3. Woody Guthrie   4. Bernie Asbell   5. Brownie McGhee   6. Betty Sanders   7. Charlotte Anthony   8. Bess Lomax   9. Oscar Brand   10. Bob Claiborne   11. Alan Lomax   12. Tom Glazer (A, B, and C unidentified; photographer unknown)

singers: Pete, Woody, Brownie McGhee, Sonny Terry, Alan Lomax, Bess Lomax, Betty Sanders, Bob Claiborne. But not Lee. Not at the first hoot. Afterward, Lee shrugged and got aboard, singing regularly at hoots and often emceeing.

For hoots were here to stay. Their success changed People's Songs from a kind of casual, almost bohemian operation to a business requiring frequent and serious business decisions. These rarely related to the *Bulletin*, which never topped two thousand in circulation. But soon the organization, representing the folk singers, found itself operating in the arcane managerial world of bookings, schedulings, concerts, and fees.

Nobody had expected this, and many arguments (also called "policy discussions") followed. Was it profligate to give hoot audiences a dozen performers? Did hoot appearances undercut a musician's value as a money-maker on his or her own? How many times could you, or should you, sing for free for People's Songs?

(Lee, complaining about young performers who wanted twenty-five dollars a booking, mused about the old days when people sang for two dollars a night, or for coins thrown into a hat on the saloon floor. They were willing to be destitute to sing those songs. Yes, responded Wally Hille, but it costs much more to be destitute today.)

People's Songs sprouted an arm, People's Artists, to handle the bookings, after a gigantic snarl of a "policy discussion" about whether Pete should get paid more per booking than the other singers. If he did, wasn't that undemocratic? If he didn't, who'd want to book any of the others when they could get Pete for the same fee?

As growing success spawned more and more "policy discussions," Lee threatened to resign at least once a day.

Arguments crackled between those who cared about folk songs only as political material and those who valued them as songs. One memorable argument involved a scholar-singer who had built a reputation on exhuming and performing Civil War songs, among them Confederate soldiers' plaints of longing for their wives and grief for lost comrades. Should People's Artists book him? The ideologues argued that singing Confederate songs was racist per se. Lee, threatening to resign, insisted that Confederate songs, too, belonged to history and had to be allowed. As one of the participants later said, "Lee didn't believe a song wasn't a song unless it had a message written all over it."

On the other hand, Lee very much believed in the power of songs with messages, provided the songs worked as songs.

Possibly the best, certainly one of the most popular, of People's Songs in 1946 was "The Rankin Tree," Lee's rural tall-tale cut-down of Congressman John Rankin, of Mississippi, a politician who embodied all that was most reactionary in postwar America. Hootenanny audiences led by Lee laughed and cheered and repeated each line after Lee:

> Well I had a farm (*Well I had a farm*)
> And on that farm (*repeat each line*)
> There was a tree

And the name of the tree
It was the Rankin Tree
It grew so big
That it hid the sun
For miles around
Poisoned everything in the ground
It poisoned my potatoes
It poisoned my squash
It mildewed all
Of my Monday wash
It killed my horse
Killed my pig
In fact that tree
Got too damn big
So I got my little axe
And put it on the stone
And I turned the stone
Around and around
And whetted the blade
Till the edges shone
Then I went to the tree
And one, two, three
I chopped it down
And I laid it on the ground
And I chopped it up
For kindling wood
I built me a fire
And the flames went higher
And I said to myself
As I sat by the fire
That's the only time
That Rankin Tree
Ever did any good
When I chopped it up

For kindling wood
This is the end
Of my melody
About that terrible
Rankin Tree!

Every issue of the *Bulletin* that first year carried a timely new song by Lee.

A coal mine in Pineville, Kentucky, blew up, sealing twenty men in a mine tomb. In following up the story, Walter Lowenfels found figures showing that at least a thousand coalminers died in accidents each year. Lee wrote a song called "Pineville," which began as follows:

> Do you know how the coalminers die
> To bring you coal from the earth?
> They die by the hundreds and they die by the thousands
> And that is what your coal is worth.

"Walk Along Together," another 1946 song, returned to the haunting theme of injustice to blacks.

> See the lynch rope a-swinging, see the torches burn
> The people said, wake up, it's time to learn
> Time to get together, drive the evil men out
> And make a new land in our own South.

Of Lee's songs in the 1940s, the most enduring is "If I Had a Hammer," written with Pete to warn of the dangers to liberty loose in the land. Later Lee remembered how the Hammer Song was written. "In the course of a long executive committee meeting of People's Songs," he said, "Pete and I passed manuscript notes back and forth until I finally nodded at him and agreed we had the thing down."

Those were good times, the busy days at People's Songs sometimes running into song-filled nights at the Lower East Side apartment of Martha and Hudie Ledbetter, the black ex-convict folk singer known as Leadbelly, a man all of them—Pete, Lee, Woody, Cisco Houston, Alan Lomax, and every folk singer and folk song maven—worshiped and learned from.

Lee wished Leadbelly could break the habit of calling them "Mr. Pete" and "Mr. Alan" and "Mr. Lee," but Leadbelly couldn't, or wouldn't. On the other hand, Lee chuckled over the irony (which he pointed out to Pete) that Leadbelly dressed in a dignified shirt-and-tie fashion while Pete, the New England aristocrat, turned up everywhere in farmer's overalls. Pete didn't see the humor at all.

Sometimes Leadbelly would stake Lee to a bottle of bourbon when Lee's always minimal money ran out. Lee swore he sang louder and better with booze lining his vocal chords. Woody and Cisco kept right up with Lee. The nights began to last until the mornings. Pete, never deflected from his work by old-boy carousing, cast a cold eye on the proceedings. Hadn't Lee learned that Pete's patience could give out?

But when Lee stood up and led a hootenanny, Pete had to love him. What could be more effective than this big southern preacher type calling out, in his marvelous deep bass voice, stingingly funny lines about antediluvian southern congressmen? When you lived in New York City, you couldn't be sure how far protest went in the country. Lee and Woody most especially could make you believe that "the folk" could be pretty durned radical.

Lee and Woody were a pair, close and competitive as brothers, always finding something preposterous to argue passionately about. Bernie Asbell remembered a trip they and he and Sonny Terry took to Washington, D.C., that year. "Three things stand out," he said. "One, we were barred from a restaurant right across from the Capitol because of Sonny. Jim Crow, in a real greasy-spoon joint. Two, we weren't allowed to enter the Capitol building, because a guard saw the sign on Woody's guitar, 'This machine kills fascists,' and he wouldn't let us in. Three, a venomous, intense argument, of the kind only brothers who love each other carry on, between Lee and Woody on whether or not to leave a tip in the restaurant where we did eat.

"Woody contended we shouldn't, because tips encouraged employers to underpay their help, and thus we would be supporting a rotten system. Lee argued that was ridiculous—there are some things not worth taking a stand on—and the only person who'd suffer was the poor waitress. They went on bickering the whole afternoon."

One day, a friend of Pete's from their army days in Saipan walked into People's Songs, an attractive young man named Felix Landau. He was living on 52–20 (fifty-two weeks of twenty dollars, standard World War II veteran termination pay) and volunteered to help out with publicity. Energetic and resourceful, Landau did the work so well that Pete began to envision him as head of the whole operation. It made sense to Pete and, without much urging, to others on the board.

With People's Songs and People's Artists expanding into big business, Lee as executive in charge had become more and more anachronistic. Nothing in his experience or temperament prepared him for dozens of decisions a day on rentals, on equipment, on printing jobs, on advertising, on pricing, on negotiations, and on other such matters. Even his attitudes—harking back to old days—seemed antithetical to a future glittering with promise, if they would but take risks. Pete charged with great leaps into the future, oblivious of peril. Lee could always come up with a dozen reasons why a new idea would never work.

Late in 1946, at a national board meeting, Pete asked Lee to resign as executive secretary of People's Songs. Everybody on the board complimented Lee on all the good things he'd done, and Lee said drily, "It sounds like you're making remarks at my funeral."

"In retrospect," Pete said in 1982, "I think it was a mistake. Lee's perceptions were probably truer than mine. I was willing to barge ahead, thinking that energy and love would conquer all, and he had doubts. Musical doubts, philosophical doubts—perhaps a physical disagreement—and I didn't realize it. He couldn't keep up with my extraordinary energy. . . . I pushed myself hard, and people near me in trying to keep up with me have got pushed hard too. . . ."

Lee, in shock because he'd had no idea he was about to be sacked, got on a train to Philadelphia, "to stay with Walter Lowenfels," said Pete, "and lick his wounds."

This second Seeger-Hays rupture somehow went underground. Presumably, a cover story was put out, perhaps that Lee had gone off to Philadelphia to work on a novel. No reference to the incident turns up in Lee's papers, letters, taped remembrances. Yet Pete never forgot. For Lee, the ouster could only have reinforced the humiliation of his Almanacs experience; it was just one more trauma in his complex relationship with Pete.

Around People's Songs, Lee's flight to Philadelphia caused few comments. So he'd chucked the office routine—what writer wouldn't? Within weeks, Lee had created a new role for himself—that of columnist for the *Bulletin*—and in time he returned as a fixture of the popular hootenannies.

"The Un-American Blues"
1946–1948

. . . you just ain't nobody at all
If nobody calls you a Red,
If you go by what the papers say
There's one under every bed.

Now wait a minute. Who's a Red?

Well . . . let me see. There's . . .
Henry Wallace, Mrs. Roosevelt, Shirley Temple,
(add your own well-known local names)
Movie Writers, Radio Actors, Broadway Playwrights, Ballad Singers,
And that ain't all. . . . There's also

Union Members, Organizers, Preachers, Teachers, Workers,
ALL OF THEM. They're a bunch of so-forths.
A lot of Reds!

You ain't got no style,
You ain't got no fame,
If the Un-American Committee hasn't scandalized your name,
  because
You ain't nobody at all
If nobody calls you a Red!

> —From *"Ballad for Un-American
> Blues,"* words and music by LEE
> HAYS and WALTER LOWENFELS

*O*f all the questions Lee asked in later years, the most searching
and nagging was what he called, variously, The Question, the Central Question, or the Big Question. The Question wasn't carved
in stone; it seemed never quite to hold still, reflecting changing

moods and times. But whatever the phrasing of the moment, The Question stemmed from People's Songs days.

"We tried to start a national movement," said Pete, long afterward. A singing labor movement, they called it at the time.

The Question: Had they in any way succeeded? Had their "purity" of anticommercialism been an obstacle? Had they, in fact, made a difference?

Just as The Question reflected changing moods and events, so did the answers. Certainly, their confidence was badly shaken by the events of the late 1940s.

Pete had his own way of measuring impact.

"We knew we were beginning to be successful when redbaiting articles appeared against us in leading New York papers," he later wrote, about events in the summer of 1946. "They didn't bother us, nor, at this time, PAC [the CIO's Political Action Committee]."

Soon, however, CIO unions would purge their left wings in a general stampede by organizations to prove their anticommunism, and People's Songs would become more and more isolated from the labor movement it had hoped to serve.

But even in the promising beginning of People's Songs, the vision of unions asking for help in putting together songbooks and composing and recording songs for their members never became reality.

Unions waging strikes and battling internally hadn't time to worry about songbooks and phonograph records. On a picket line, strikers might take heart roaring out choruses while Lee led them through "Roll the Union On," or listening to Pete sing "Talking Union." But who expected steelworkers and longshoremen and electrical workers and auto workers regularly to sing out of union songbooks? "A *listening* labor movement" might more accurately describe the early People's Songs period, and even that description stretched it.

Still, labor unions, along with colleges, accounted for most of People's Artists' bookings. On campuses, guitar pickers were learning from songbooks published or publicized by People's Songs as folk music began to take root among the young. Within unions, perhaps an education director would figure that bringing someone in to sing could help an organizing drive or bolster morale on a picket line. Perhaps the education director learned to love that kind of music as a guitar picker in college. Nobody could claim that the labor unions turned from Tin Pan Alley to folk labor songs.

Nonetheless, the songs are there when needed; you can hear them today in a union hall or on a picket line—"Talking Union," "Which Side Are You On," "Roll the Union On," "Union Train a'Comin'," "Union Maid."

All came either from the struggles in the South in the 1930s or from the talents of the Almanacs in the 1940s.

Lee, in Philadelphia licking his wounds, talked over his hurt with Lillian and Walter Lowenfels, who propped up his ego and urged him to use the *People's Songs Bulletin* not only for songs but also for essays.

And so, the first issue of the *Bulletin* in 1947 introduced "A New Monthly Feature Column by Tall & Substantial People's Songster Lee Hays."

"I propose," wrote Lee, "to run a column in the *Bulletin:* personal observations on singing, with a high percentage of anecdotes and stories about the way I have seen singing used in past struggles. . . . I would like to put in stories about the way we ran our singing sessions in Commonwealth; the way we used singing at our sharecropper meetings; the way singing was used in the miners' fights; the way music was used at country funerals; and so on. . . ."

Labor music history just might edify those young city folk (sometimes referred to, privately by Lee, as "interlopers") trying to write "people's songs" in New York City or LA or Chicago in the 1940s. City folk didn't know, when they started reading Lee, who or what Claude and Zilphia and Commonwealth and Highlander were. But they kept on reading, because he told good stories. He made connections. They learned that people's songwriting wasn't merely a postwar, big-city phenomenon. Its roots were deep and broad.

Claude "is one of the papas of People's Songs," wrote Lee. "Whenever you hear 'Roll the Union On' or 'What is that I see yonder coming—coming—coming' you are hearing what can only be called Claude's songs. A good many of the Almanac union songs and certainly the spirit of all of them derive largely from Claude's work. . . ."

Zilphia started him song leading, at a miners union meeting in Tennessee. "When Zilphia got up and said, 'Brother Lee Hays will

now lead us in singing,' I damn near went through the floor,"
Lee wrote. "There was no backing out; I had to take the plunge;
I had to get up and sing; and I've been doing it ever since."

On the craft of songwriting, Lee's columns promoted the old-
fashioned virtues.

A song is "firstly and mostly poetry." And rhythm makes a
poem memorable: "English blank verse, the Greek hexameter, the
epic verse of the Iliad, the funeral dirges of the Gullahs,* or a
pretty little jingle that 'strokes us with the wings of a butterfly'
and no more—each takes its character from the rhythm that Homer,
or whoever, selected."

Nor should the songwriter write without rhyme, which "gives
to a narrative ballad or poem or song a feeling of strength. It is a
definite statement. Its cheap and expedient use will turn a fine
poem into a jingle (outrageous, wages). The occasional absence
of a rhyme can have the reverse action of giving strength to a
poem too. But in general the songs we remember and sing are
those with strong rhymes.

"And we have not yet come to the problems of thought and
imagery and symbolism—the content of our poems, which is after
all their only excuse for being. But if we think that we can write
good people's songs that are not poems and that are not subject
to the mechanics of poetry, we're fooling ourselves. Only a genius
or a damn fool would try it."

In fact, People's Songs' writers produced many more jingles than
fine poems. Clever, topical—and ephemeral. The Hays-Lowenfels
song that heads this chapter, "The Un-American Blues," did not
survive its brief usefulness. Another Hays-Lowenfels song from
the same period—"Wasn't That a Time!"—strong in rhythm and
symbolism, remains vibrantly alive.

Lee wrote out of Philadelphia for about a year; then he was
back in New York, living in a Chelsea loft, the second floor of a
two-story building, with a pudgy watch repairman named Harold
Bernz and a slender young working-class lad from Philadelphia
named Fran Dellorco.

Bernz gave hours of volunteer time each week to People's Songs,

---

* A group of blacks who live on sea islands in the South and have their
own dialect.

laying out the *Bulletin*, doing odd jobs, and being so altogether sweet and generous that everybody adored him. Dellorco rather puzzled the regulars. Lee brought him into People's Songs, extolling his as yet unevidenced talents, and putting him to work creating filmstrips for hoots.

"This was before tape recorders," recalled Fred Hellerman, by then a People's Songs regular, "when wire recorders were in, and Fran used them for sound to accompany the filmstrips. He'd had no experience at all at this. I keep remembering him constantly snarled up in acres of wires."

Lee, introducing the filmstrips at hoots to illustrate songs or news events he meant to make funny comments on, never knew if the technology was going to work. More often than not, it didn't—which the audiences found funnier. Ah well, said Lee, the things *were* homemade.

"Something there is about a hoot that calls for the best I can give it," wrote Lee to Pete in 1948. "I love the audiences, and find them wholesome and inspiring—most of all, sure. I am sure of their response. I know this audience. But beyond [hoots] I don't feel eager to go anywhere and sing."

Perhaps he and Fran could develop filmstrips into some kind of artistic venture that would earn them a few dollars. Lee would do the voice-overs. He'd recently had a very enjoyable and satisfying experience doing the voice of a union organizer in *Seed for Tomorrow*, a docudrama directed by Julian Roffman for the National Farmers Union. (Lee was always the one to do the serious work during the recording sessions, "and then during breaks regale the actors and recording crew with songs and anecdotes," Roffman related later, adding, "I can still hear him speaking and singing and I will for all my time.")

If he and Fran could make some small success out of filmstrips that Lee would write and record, he'd have more time to work on short stories and articles. That's what he ought to be doing. He would, of course, continue to sing at hoots. And perhaps take an occasional booking to help pay for beer. But performing, Lee proclaimed to friends, would be peripheral to his writing.

Lee often suggested that singing, even later with the Weavers, impinged on his valuable time.

*   *   *

Bernz, with his small but regular salary, paid the rent, bought the food, and, on his way to work each morning, stopped at a corner store to buy a pack of cigarettes, which he tossed up to Lee, who then didn't have to leave the loft for the rest of the day. And he didn't.

As executive secretary of People's Songs during those idealistic if argumentative early months, Lee managed to show up at the office every day. Through all the threats to resign, he clearly enjoyed his lofty perch. But when the job ended, Lee took up his old posture, sitting behind a typewriter in his room, smoking, and drinking beer. He'd budge for few things—hoots, an occasional booking, and invitations to the country in the summertime.

Everybody knew the loft and dropped in to swap stories, share a beer, try out a song. You never knew how you'd find Lee.

Fred Hellerman remembered going up to the loft one night when Lee was "piss-ass drunk" and hearing Lee moan, "Oh, Fred, I'm dying. Don't let them give me a Baptist funeral."

Since the day Lee's postcard had brought Fred to People's Songs, they'd been friends, the "o-o-o-old man" and the bright Brooklyn College student with the lean talmudic face, the quick mind, the sound musicianship.

Years later, Fred would say, "Of those young people who flocked around him like bees around the flower, he demanded much, but gave so much of himself in return that they always felt they were getting the best of the bargain, as indeed they were. I know because I was once one of them."

After he'd met and talked with Fred, back in 1946, Lee had suggested they might work up some material and take bookings together. (Lee couldn't perform solo, because he didn't play an instrument.) The joint performances hadn't happened, but the two had established a solid relationship.

"Lee had a way of making young people feel very comfortable with themselves," said Fred, "of making them feel they were worthwhile people, that they had something to contribute. You walked away from Lee feeling a lot better. Lee convinced me I had something to say."

Neither of them, of course, could know that within a couple of years they'd be saying what they had to say high on the charts, in songs and arrangements at the top of the hit parade.

One of the minor perplexities of Lee's career is why so many of his songs were written in collaboration—and why so many different collaborators?

Bernie Asbell played guitar for Lee the first time he sang "Wasn't That a Time!" in public. "Do you really think it's good enough?" Lee kept asking. Asbell believed that Lee had to have someone else hold his hand, metaphorically, and go forward together: "Lee always needed a coauthor, needed not to be totally responsible for a song, in case it didn't turn out wonderful. He needed to share credits because sharing made him a little less vulnerable. But he was the poet and idea man."

In needing to share credit, Lee pushed friends and associates into writing songs.

Pete, talking about the early Almanac days, said, "Lee was a very creative force. He had one idea after another for songs. I had never been a songwriter, but I found myself writing songs under his impetus."

Pete admired Lee's talents, loved sharing a stage with Lee, felt enhanced by what Lee offered.

Lee, feeling lost without Pete's banjo behind him, resented the dependency and alternated between praising Pete and bitching about him. He brooded, too, about the way Pete kicked him out of groups.

Pete's whirlwind existence left him no time to brood about anything. He laughed, but he must have wondered, long after People's Songs days, when Lee spoke to him of the Eleventh Commandment, "which according to Lee," said Pete, "is 'never give up a grudge.' "

Summertime in New York City could wipe out a 300-pound beer-drinking writer living in an un-air-conditioned top-floor loft. Lee would budge in a minute if the countryside beckoned. Camps, farms, country houses, wherever things grew Lee felt he belonged. He didn't have a dime, so he couldn't have his own place. He often enjoyed someone else's.

He was a "a hay-pitching guest" at Asgaard farm, the artist Rockwell Kent's Adirondacks home, "the loveliest spot on earth." During the days, hay-pitching guests worked, but nights resonated with music "good enough to make an album."

"Music at Kent's," Lee wrote in his column, "would have to

At Rockwell Kent's farm near Ausable Chasm, New York, *left to right*, Kent, Lee, and Mandel Terman, a friend from "the movement."

include Paul Robeson singing by the fireplace at the picnic grounds, Mrs. Kent playing the piano and singing in her ineffably lovely soprano, Marc Blitzstein doing one or another of his new songs, a group of musicians from a neighboring symphony orchestra, a well-known harpsichordist playing Bach on the long grand, Kent playing the flute or singing duets with me, usually old salvation hymns . . . and of course, all of us, guests and hosts, singing people's songs. . . .

"The night I left the Kents gave a picnic in my honor, and the farm people came with their families, and Blitzstein came over from the farm where he was composing his new opera, and the campfire glowed for hours as we sang. In the course of the evening I stumbled over the carrier tray, spilling four dollars worth of hot dogs and spaghetti on the carpet of pine needles, but rescuing the beer. I must have been overcome with sentiment and regret at having to go away from those wonderful singing people.

"One of the great men there presented me with a bottle of Scotch, and the Kents and the farm people gave me a bottle of genuine Kentucky corn whisky with a label reading: 'This whisky is guaranteed to be less than one month old.'

"Well sir, you never heard such singing. . . ."

Quite a different atmosphere from that of the night of hymn singing in the labor organizer's car down south in the 1930s.

Boozing it up was integral to life with those good old boys Woody and Cisco, or to a night of barhopping with a hard-boiled pro like Dashiell Hammett, or to a walk on the wild side with the Chicago writer Nelson Algren. Citing anecdotal evidence, Lee could almost have made a case for booze being essential to life as a writer. Or to flouting authority, a habit developed during the aggravating days of Prohibition.

Perhaps, for Lee, this was another form of rebellion against his upbringing—drinking being one of the evils his father inveighed against in sermons and in small tracts he published and sold, "Price Five Cents Per Copy," the same price as Lee's collection of labor songs published at Commonwealth College.

Pomposity in any form—that of earnest musicologists no less than that of orotund southern congressmen—raised Lee's hackles. He counterattacked with humor and common sense, as in his column "The Incidence of the Word 'Roll' in American Folk Music."

He told how "a gal named Gertrude came South during the

good old WPA days, to collect material for a research paper on symbols in American folk music, like tree, or bird, or rock, as they appear in songs.

"Now you'd think a rock would be a rock. One's a-plenty, if somebody's hitting you on the head with it. But Gertrude found 48 different meanings of that little word. Some of them, I recall, were heaven, faith, lack of charity (as in 'heart hard as a', etc.), strength, steadfastness, stubbornness. . . .

"In order to fall in stride with the girl, I decided to develop one or two little research projects of my own. I'd already collected and catalogued every union songbook I could lay hands on, but Gertrude pointed out that this was a mere librarian's job. I saw right off I'd have to get into something deeper than that.

"I came up with a title for a paper (above). It had struck me that every time I sat down to work on a song, I found myself wanting to put that word 'roll' into it. It was a very convenient word—meant anything you wanted it to. It then came to me that the word appears in many and many a spiritual—indeed, in almost any kind of song you wanted except Methodist songs.

"I had it, and straightway began to compile my paper on the incidence of the word in American folk music. Incidence is a good word, too, for researchers. Well sir, in no time I was rolling along (see?) in high gear. Before I even stopped to take breath, I had over 100 listings and at least a dozen main usages. 'Roll Jordan Roll' and 'When the Roll Is Called Up Yonder' of course; and 'Sweet Moments Roll On,' 'If You Don't Roll the Devil He'll Roll You,' 'The World Is A-Rolling,' 'Roll the Chariot On,' 'Rolling Through an Unfriendly World,' 'Timber's Rolling,' and so on.

"I found that the word meant travel, push, move, die and go to heaven, subdue an enemy, a record of good works, money, what you do with dice, drumming, etc. . . .

"Of course what I really learned out of all that nonsense was that the word is the best singing sound of all good words that fit well in the voice. It's the beauty of the 'o' sound itself, the 'r' gives it a good foothold in the throat, and the double 'l' tapers it off nice and sweet. A good singer can sing anything, I've heard, but for real topnotch unrefined hightoned singing, give me a song full of 'o's,' preferably surrounded by 'r's' and 'l's.'

"I should have rolled up my project before I rolled as far as the blues, for I found certain usages of the word that definitely did not interest Gertrude. I wasn't being bawdy at all. I was just rolling up my listings and usages in purely objective fashion, and it wasn't my fault that Gertrude decided to roll on to another state to roll out some more rocks and trees and birds.

"Scholarship has been a little dull ever since."

Some readers remember the column as the first time the words *rock* and *roll* came, if only glancingly, together.

In 1947, the United States attorney general issued the first list of organizations that the Department of Justice and its investigative arm, J. Edgar Hoover's FBI, considered "un-American." Supplementary lists followed, flowed. The worst of times for the Left were coming on fast.

From the thousands of theories by thousands of authors about the backdrop for the triumph of anticommunism in the post–World War II period, we quote just one, by Larry Ceplair and Steven Englund in their book *The Inquisition in Hollywood*, published in 1979: "Intensive class conflict, following a decade of gains for labor unions and four years of enforced wartime labor-management 'harmony,' formed the economic backdrop. The rallying of an impressive number of labor organizations to the left-center coalition during the war had deeply antagonized powerful economic interests in America: an anxious cartel of bankers, industrialists, and media barons represented by the United States Chamber of Commerce and the National Association of Manufacturers. The war, by massively increasing sales, productivity, profits, and the government's need for managerial expertise in the newly created war bureaucracies, had reintroduced corporate influence into Washington to an extent greater than at any time since the inauguration of Franklin D. Roosevelt in March 1933. To the business and financial elite, anti-communism had far less to do with putting the GOP back into power than it did with combating recurrent worker restiveness and weakening organized labor. Thus anti-communism functioned in this period in the same fashion as nationalism had in other periods: naked class, economic, and political objectives were dressed in more appealing, demagogic garb. In the guise of a loyal opposition and protectors of the public interest, the elites launched their attacks on liberals and labor—the un-Americans."

At the same time, Stalin's Soviet Union, with its aggressive moves and oppressive puppet governments, thoroughly undermined the goodwill it had built up through its heroic victories over Hitler's armies.

The Far Left nonetheless clung to the belief that Stalin's actions resulted from the belligerent anti-Soviet posture of the Western governments. The culprit was the Cold War. And the villain who gleefully maintained the Cold War as the foundation of U.S. foreign policy was President Harry S Truman.

Such views led to the creation of a new party, the Progressive party, and the candidacy of Henry A. Wallace for president of the United States, a campaign waged with Pete Seeger at Wallace's side, energetically leading audiences in song.

People's Songs plunged into the Wallace campaign as the entertainment arm, sending members to sing at street meetings, rallies, whatever. ("Most members," Pete recorded in his *Bulletin* files, "although not all, certainly—some were against him.")

They wrote and published and sang "Songs for Wallace." Songs like "I've Got a Ballot," with words by Yip Harburg to the tune of "I've Got Sixpence." The chorus:

> The Republicans they grieve me,
> The Democrats only deceive me,
> I've a brand new party, believe me,
> As we go rolling up the vote.
>
> Roll it up FOR WALLACE!
> Roll it up FOR TAYLOR!
> There is magic in that ballot when you vo-o-o-te.
>
> Happy is the day
> When the people get their way,
> As we go rolling up the vote.

Another Harburg lyric, "Friendly Henry Wallace," opened with a line more hopeful than realistic:

> Everyone wants Wallace
> Friendly Henry Wallace
> Everyone wants Wallace in the White House

If you want the right man
Now's the time to fight, man!
Fight to put the right man in the White House.

Exuberance and hyperactivity filled the offices of People's Songs. The organization didn't have enough personnel, enough singers, enough entertainers to handle all the requests, Fred Hellerman remembered. "But theater people, who weren't part of People's Songs, volunteered, and there were attempts to put together whole units, where there'd be acting, sketches, skits, singing and so forth. It wasn't terribly well organized; it wasn't terribly good; it was all sort of slip-shod, but in a way it was a very exciting time."

In the initial enthusiasm, and from the parochial vantage point of New York City, they convinced themselves that Wallace could actually win or, at the very least, pull in ten million votes.

Lee's doubts surfaced early, in an April 1948 *Bulletin* column meant as a goad and inspiration, "A Sermon to Songwriters."

"700 unionists marched down Constitution Avenue in Washington. In the middle of the long line two girls and I walked singing, and half a dozen forlorn voices fore and aft tried to take up our melodies and sing with us. Even without a sound truck to guide them, those 700 people could have sung to raise the lid off that town—if they'd wanted to. If they had been trained to sing, and knew how to sing together, and if they had had the songs to sing. That procession had about as much pep as a third-rate funeral, and it was hot, and the marchers were harassed by the taunts of sidewalk Fascists, and gov't workers leaned out of windows to jeer and boo. A singing parade would have drowned the hecklers, and inspirited the marchers, and told the world who was marching, and why.

"Where there is no unity, the people perish. Songs help to create unity, which is understanding; and songs are born of unity, too. The music of horns blowing has torn down walls in battle. Gideon's army had trumpets to blow, as well as pots to smash and swords to fight with. Where is the music for today, for 1948, for peace, for Wallace and our own First Party?

"One dreams of a great people's song, of our marching song which will come again, but hasn't yet; of the great song which is still unsung. It will be a hymn, for it will be born in faith, and love, and united purpose. It will be a battle hymn, for we are at war against the powers of evil. It may even be a topical song, for the topics of the day are no smaller than peace, and democracy, and a future of hope. When it comes, no committee of songwriters will pass judgment upon it, for it will be a people's song, and the people will know it for their own.

"And that song will be sung in many days of defeat; and it will be sung on the day we celebrate our victory. . . ."

This describes precisely the unifying, inspiriting force of the song "We Shall Overcome" in the civil rights movement a decade and a half later.

Apart from an occasional march or meeting, Lee didn't budge much more during the Wallace campaign than before. The word *consultant* appealed to him; he'd happily discuss potential campaign songs with friends who came around to the loft.

Even a Wallace campaign couldn't keep Lee away from the countryside in the summer. A new place this time, a country house rented by the Lowenfelses outside of Reading, Pennsylvania, but the same warm welcome. The girls, as always, happy to see their "other father." Twelve-year-old Angela felt particular relief to have Lee back. She'd stewed in guilt over something she'd said before he moved from Philadelphia to New York in 1947. Had her words caused him to leave?

A fragment of an undated letter from Lee to Walter reveals the source of the child's concern: "I remember Angela saying, 'Lee, I have been wanting to ask you this for a long time, and I'm embarrassed, but are you married?' She asked this as I was hustling around getting ready to go to NY—in the excitement of folks wishing me well, and making plans to meet, the question that came up was not concerned with the hour or the times, but came up from the deep well of interest which is in the minds of babes and sucklings and such fools as the rest of us are. . . ."

"That was the most intriguing question in our lives," said Angela years later. "Had Lee ever married?"

The question never would go away.

Election day buried Henry Wallace and the Progressive party. They'd pulled under a million votes, fewer than the Far Right movement of the segregationist Strom Thurmond.

Wallace campaigners sifted through the rubble for rationalizations. Perhaps people who meant to vote for Wallace realized he couldn't win and, in a last-minute cop-out, voted for Truman because Dewey as president was unimaginable. (But nine million of them?)

Fred Hellerman looked back at the 1948 campaign as "the end of the enthusiasm and the rah-rah of the Johnny-come-marching-home period. People's Songs was born when the country was in great turmoil in the transition from wartime to peacetime. There were all kinds of problems to be dealt with—housing, jobs, education, continuing price controls, all kinds of issues, and a lot of enthusiasm among those who grappled with them. And all the hopes of the brave new postwar world came crashing down at the end of the Wallace campaign."

Under a mountain of debt piled up during the campaign lay People's Songs, its life signs flickering.

Pete's notes of that time record his hopes and disappointments: "Right after the election we threw ourselves into putting on the best series of hootenannies we had yet produced. Lee was back in town and wrote scripts for them . . . we all felt super-confident and put everything we had into a big push that would make us solvent. It seemed generations since we'd started this little organization, we had a reputation and a following, and we felt that if only the NY hoots, which had always supported the deficit of the national organization, could only grow larger still, we would have no troubles. Alas, we were wrong . . . they didn't quite make it."

What could they add to make hoots better? Someone suggested dancers. They staged the first post-Wallace hoot on Thanksgiving weekend. In the one-world spirit of People's Songs, it featured dances representing America, Russia, Jews, and blacks. Lee, Pete, Fred, and Ronnie Gilbert—a radiant young New Yorker who'd sung with a topical-songs group in Washington during the war years—worked up music to accompany the dancers. "Flop-eared Mule" for an American hoedown, a Slavic dancing song, an Israeli hora, and "Hey li-lee li-lee-o" for the West Indies. They called the number "Around the World." The audience went wild, and

Lee, Pete, Fred, and Ronnie wondered if maybe they were onto something.

Issues of the *Bulletin* came out later and later. One of the last, in December of 1948, reported the appointment of Harvey Matt as head of the new People's Songs Music Center, to sell albums and books. (He'd turn up later as an FBI informer.)

A fund-raising hoot in Carnegie Hall on March 7 was the last chance to keep People's Songs from going under. It failed.

In a final note attached to his copies of the *Bulletin*, Pete wrote, "Swiftly we moved to close up. In lieu of back salary several important items were given to staff members (Wally, owed over $2000, got the library). Within a week there was no more organization or publication, nationally, that is, known as People's Songs."

"Hold the Line"

1949

We live in the best of all possible worlds and we must put a favorable construction upon all events and happenings. If the cat has kittens in the oven, call 'em biscuits.

—LEE HAYS

*P*rofessionally, 1949 began and ended on unexpected high notes for Lee. The months in between, however, included some of the most impoverished of his never affluent life, with hunger that took him back to the 1930s.

Politically, 1949 marked for Lee the beginning of a sickening realization that from the vasty deeps of the North's historically liberal, tolerant essence, ugly spirits could be called up, as dangerous and terrifying to a dissident as anything he'd known in the South.

The violence of Peekskill happened in 1949.

The bankruptcy of People's Songs came at a time when Lee's career as a short-story writer seemed to be taking off.

On the December 1948 cover of *Ellery Queen's Mystery Magazine*, one scans an impressive list of the month's authors: John Dickson Carr, Cornell Woolrich, Edith Wharton, Ellery Queen, Georges Simenon, and—Lee Hays. In good company.

Lee cracked the publication with an adaptation, in rural southern dialect, of Chaucer's "Pardoneres Tale." His story, entitled "Three Against Deeth," takes from its source the theme that gold is bad.

"Yes, it's a classic theme," wrote the *EQMM* editor in an introduction, "but Mr. Hays comments wryly that no one ever offered him a pot of gold in exchange for his soul, although many a time a beefsteak would have been sufficient temptation. . . .

"You'll hear more from Lee Hays in the pages of *EQMM*. We think he has a rare talent in his own right. He has spent most of his 34 years delving into the mysteries of American folk lore, and soon we will bring you an earthy sample of how Mr. Hays combines folk music with foul murder—a haunting and unforgettable medley."

The promised second story, "On the Banks of the Ohio," in the March 1949 edition of *EQMM*, is Lee's imaginative version of the event that inspired the song:

> I drew a sword acrost her breast,
> Gently in my arms she pressed,
> Cried, "Willy, oh Willy, don't murder me!
> For I'm unprepared for eternity!"

Words and music, arranged by Wally Hille, were printed along with the short story. The caption noted, "To the best of our knowledge this is the first time in detective history that a murder story has been offered complete with music. Why not some night, between singing 'The Blue Tail Fly' and 'Foggy Foggy Dew,' put this page on the music rack of your piano and see how it goes?" (Folk music, before the Weavers, tended to mean the songs of Burl Ives to non-folk folks.)

About the story, the editor wrote, "Here, my good friends, is a reading experience in wild rhythms, in mounting melodrama, in the feverish, tragic, soul-stirring accents of backwoods America— as authentically American as the mountaineers' feud, the illicit still, and the need for an anti-lynch law."

And about Lee: "This man, Lee Hays, is a big fellow—make no mistake about that. Potentially, he has the stuff of great talent. You will be hearing from him, more and more, and in the voice of truth."

The *EQMM* people took Lee up as, in his words, "a country boy genius of sorts, kind of lionizing [him]."

One of the lionizing people, Robert Mills, *EQMM*'s managing editor, remained a fan, speaking years later of Lee's "marvelous talent for writing—he had a wonderful touch for, in a few words, making offbeat people into very real people."

Lee's productivity was quite another matter. *EQMM* readers did *not* hear from him more and more, did not hear from him again for five years.

On Wednesday afternoons, Lee would go to Pete's place, or rather to Pete's in-laws' place, on MacDougal Street to sing with him and Fred and Ronnie, working up material. They'd been doing that since the Thanksgiving weekend hoot. They'd sounded so doggone good together that Pete and Lee started talking about their becoming the new Almanacs, only with rehearsals.

And wasn't this a time for new Almanacs, with the House Un-American Activities Committee on a rampage, Hollywood writers fighting in the courts to keep out of jail (they'd soon lose their appeals), indictments under the repressive Smith Act picking up steam?

What could they do, these four young leftist singers?

So bad was the climate that Pete genuinely considered the possibility of taking a factory job to support his family. *Pete*, the only one of the four getting any bookings at all.

Fred lived with his parents, middle-class business people, in Queens. Ronnie, the child of factory workers, had gone to work in the CBS typing pool, to "colonize" for the office workers union. Lee's loft days had ended with the demise of People's Songs; Harold Bernz moved uptown; Fran returned to Philadelphia. Now Lee was bunking with a married couple only slightly less poor than he.

Once they sang at a fund-raiser for the Photo League, a collective of left-wing photographers. So much did their spirited singing add to the event that the league offered to let them use the organization's clubhouse, in the basement of the Hotel Albert, on Sunday afternoons.

The quartet called their Hotel Albert performances "open house." People would come and drop whatever they wanted into the hat. At the end of the afternoon, the twenty or twenty-five dollars collected would be divided up among the four singers. Lee lived on his share.

Once they sang on Oscar Brand's WNYC radio show as "The Nameless Quartet." The need for a name hadn't arisen.

Pete's nature simply couldn't sustain negativism. Hearing the sound of the four of them, he began to dream again.

"In a way, we thought we could pull together the experiences of the Wobblies and Joe Hill," he said years later, "the experiences of the black churches and white churches, the experiences of folk musicians—who would have wondered what we were talking about if they'd ever heard that term, *folk musicians*. We were thinking of singing cowboys, singing sailors and miners and housewives and farmers, fiddlers and banjo pickers and rattlers of bone and beaters of tom-toms and congo drums and mouth bows and many kinds of instruments. The idea of pulling all these together and making greater music than had ever been heard before. And this great music, this great synthesis, pulling together wonderful ideas from many different cultures, would be part and parcel of a great movement which would put an end forever to racism, would put an end forever to poverty in the midst of plenty, would put an end forever to war, sexism, agism, all sorts of stupidities.

"Looking back on it, it was either awfully premature or awfully simplistic, a utopian way of looking at things. But we were fired up with inspiration. Lee even wrote a song, 'Tomorrow is a highway broad and fair/We are the many who'll travel there.' "

Ronnie Gilbert said it more simply, "We felt if we sang loud enough and strong enough and hopefully enough, somehow it would make a difference."

As the ill-paid weeks and months rolled on, Fred watched Lee's evident lack of nourishment with concern. Lee's friends shared their food, but they had little enough for two.

In the summer of 1949, Fred and Ronnie took jobs at a Catskills resort run by the left-wing Yiddish newspaper *Daily Freiheit*, Fred as a singer, Ronnie as a secretary in the office. Out of Fred's fifteen or twenty dollars a week, he sent Lee five. Said Fred, "Lee had nothing. He was literally starving."

Pete and his wife, Toshi, were spending the summer up in Beacon, New York, clearing a piece of hilly, wooded land they'd bought for $1,700 borrowed from family and friends.

Lee continued to write, but the easy promise of *EQMM* proved ephemeral. *EQMM* had strict requirements—murder or mystery being an essential. He felt dry in that line at the moment. Sending pieces cold to other magazines was an expensive shot in the dark. Who had money for postage to try this publication and that, along with self-addressed stamped envelopes if you hoped to have the pieces returned when rejected?

He completed a long pornographic novel, of the Fanny Hill–Frank Harris genre. Fred read it with delight and considered it a sure bet for publication. Then Pete's mother-in-law asked to read it. Lee brought the manuscript to the MacDougal Street house, from which it never reemerged—lost somewhere in the heaps of papers and books strewn through every room. Fred remembered his astonishment at Lee's laconic reaction to its loss: "Just 'eh.' After all that work. I never could understand that."

Fred and Ronnie, working at the *Freiheit*'s summer camp, entered the Lakeland Picnic Grounds in Peekskill from the north and departed the same way. Not until later did they hear what had happened along the main exit route.

None of the quartet had been on the grounds two weeks earlier, for an outdoor Paul Robeson concert. Pete, scheduled to sing, tried to get there but found the roads blocked. State troopers told him the concert had been called off.

Even as Pete turned his car around, to drive back to Beacon, three hundred war veterans were beating the bejesus out of concert organizers and audience who'd arrived earlier. Clubs and fists and rocks and screams of "Kill the nigger!" (meaning Robeson, who wasn't there, because he'd been warned); blood everywhere. The novelist Howard Fast, the concert's master of ceremonies, in the center of the battle, began loudly to sing "We Shall Not Be Moved." The concertgoers picked up the song—"Just like a tree that's standing by the water/We shall not be moved." They linked hands, holding until the police finally arrived, hours later, after a second onslaught by the veterans. In the darkening night, the attackers threw every songbook and pamphlet they found onto a bonfire, and in case anybody missed the message, they left behind a fiery cross.

Thus ended part one.

Robeson, seething, insisted on trying again. A second concert was scheduled for September 4. Its organizers sought an injunction against any further veterans' demonstrations. The judge turned down the request on the Friday afternoon before the concert. The town of Peekskill, meanwhile, was awash with bumper stickers ("Wake Up America, Peekskill Did!") and talk about what the townsmen would do if the Commies dared show up.

Showing up that day took guts. The only hope was in numbers.

Pete, of course, agreed to perform; perhaps Lee and Ronnie and Fred would do a couple of their Nameless Quartet numbers with him. And so Ronnie and Fred arrived from the north. Lee called on Fran Dellorco, who came up from Philadelphia and drove him and Woody to Peekskill in an old borrowed Buick.

What happened at the end of the concert has been told by many writers, but it's Lee's version that belongs in this book. He wrote it soon after the event, still shaking with rage and fear and passion. He sent the article to the *Sunday Worker*—he didn't know where else to send it. Yet he doubted its editors would print it. Lee knew that by comparing events at Peekskill to events in a novel by Albert Maltz, he was touching a tender nerve.

Maltz had brought on a messy Communist party dispute in 1946 about the role of the committed writer. In a *New Masses* article, he criticized the concept of "art as a weapon," terming that approach "a straitjacket for the writer." He'd been roundly chastised and soon recanted. The affair left a bad aftertaste. Maltz was hardly the writer to quote in submitting a piece to the *Worker*. Which may have been why Lee did it. He loathed rigidity. To his surprise, the editors took the piece.

Under a four-column headline, "Simon McKeever at Peekskill," Lee's article opened with a quote from Emerson: "We know the austere condition of liberty, that it must be re-conquered over and over again; yea, day by day, that it is a state of war; that it is always slipping from those who boast it to those who fight for it."

Lee then moved to a scene from the Maltz novel, in which men armed with guns and clubs break into a local IWW (Industrial Workers of the World, or Wobblies) hall where a hundred people are dancing and, "by obvious prearrangement, and under the direction of an efficient police sergeant," wreck the hall.

After the attack, Lee continued, Simon McKeever carried fright within him. In the words of Maltz, "It was not a physical fear but something worse: a fear that his life as he had lived it and believed in it, was a fraud; a fear that men walked the earth like blind moles to a blind and aimless end. . . ."

Peekskill felt like that. At the concert's end, the safety of numbers evaporated. Each departing car was its own isolated, self-contained trap.

"The gauntlet outside the concert grounds seemed dark," wrote Lee, "as if the air had changed, and there was no sun. Running through it was like being propelled through a long gray tunnel with no promised light of exit showing ahead.

"A tunnel lined on both sides with the enemy. And docks, boards, bottles, rocks. Police slowed down vehicles so the hoodlums could get better aim.

" 'Jesus! How long can this go on!' It was a journey of incredible length and while the hoodlums were strung out for miles it was strange to know that we, the many, were being so horribly punished by the few. Hoodlums all along the tortuous passage, and police and troopers; and when we came to where there were no more police, there were no more hoodlums.

"It didn't take so many hoodlums to do so much damage. They had as many as they needed. Their gauntlet was ably organized, efficient, with the law herding and driving us like cattle to a single file of slaughter. . . .

" 'All those people behind us! The thousands still on the concert grounds—they don't even know what's going to happen when they drive out!'

"On the grounds they waited in busses and cars, and all those who had walked could not ride out. Negro men and women, and their children—main objects of the fascist attack. All getting ready to run the gauntlet but, like us, not knowing how bad it could be. . . .

"Woody said, 'I've seen a lot, but this is the worst.'

"America Wake Up—Peekskill Did! If these were fellow human beings, these goodlooking boys and girls with their printed signs, their screams, and the older men, and the uniformed troopers making no attempt to stop the violence, then the world was a jungle and would never be changed. . . .

". . . the young voice of the driver, trembling, but with confidence: 'Take it easy. We'll soon be out of it.'

"And his skillful driving, the hands on the wheel, no protection for himself though the rest of us had free arms for shields, plunging ahead only a few feet from the bus ahead, never swerving . . . until 'We're all right. Here's the end of it!'

"He was a hero, like the drivers of all the other cars who had to run the gauntlet, like the thousands of 'our guys' who had held the line all day and who would wait for many hours before they could get away, like those of 'our guys' who had never driven busses before but who drove them through the gauntlet when regular drivers decamped.

"Parents shielded their children with their bodies. We heard of these and other brave acts and many of us wept with pride that so many thousands of people were not on the rock-throwing side of the gauntlet, but with us, and that we had stuck together and come through. . . .

"A long procession of smashed busses and cars, and people along the way astonished.

" 'What happened?' from a car alongside.

" 'Peekskill!'

" 'Oh.'

"The people in the busses singing. Woody leading, 'I'm worried now but I won't be worried long!' Our battle song, 'We shall not be moved!' Between songs Woody making fine edgy comments: 'Anybody got a rock? There's a window back here that needs to be opened!'

"And then:

" 'I'll sing out danger! I'll sing out warning! I'll sing out love . . .'

"Now, that was it, the final understanding, the only faith which could banish the jungle, put an end to a man's doubts, set the world to turning again, restore motion to life. It was a faith which had been built by Howard Fast and the bravery of 'our guys' who held the line in order that Chopin and Moussourgsky and 'Old Man River' could be heard under a free sky.

"Then we knew that we had won a victory. We had again reconquered liberty. But we knew also that we would have to fight for it again as long as this state of war against culture and the people should continue.

"Then it was possible to know what Simon McKeever at last came to know, during his journey, that he had seen men and women striving together and knew he was not alone. He knew 'that in spite of everything he still heard the music, and he still believed that there was a good path to be trod'. . . .

"Sometime before Peekskill I heard the young fellow who drove our car through the gauntlet say, perplexed, 'I know there's a lot of things wrong with the world, but I don't know what one man can do to change it.'

"Now he knows. For the world can never be the same after Peekskill; it has been changed by our victory; and he and all the veterans of the battle of Peekskill changed it. . . ."

That was the posture: Peekskill was a victory. Lee and the soon-to-be Weavers wrote "Hold the Line":

Let me tell you the story of a line that was held
And many men and women whose courage we know well . . .

With Howard Fast and Paul Robeson, they recorded the song. But if you'd given Lee a few shots of booze, he probably would have admitted that Peekskill had felt a lot more like the sky falling in.

Passions cool. In later years, Lee lived in the country, not far from the concert grounds.

Peekskill "is a very ticklish subject around these parts," Lee told an interviewer in 1979. He spoke of his article, and the book Howard Fast wrote on Peekskill, and about "Hold the Line."

"I don't know whether I'd stand by it [the song] today or not. Howard's book calls these people out-and-out fascists. Since then I've met some of them and I wouldn't call them fascists by any strict definition. They were misguided people filled with ha-tred. . . .

"I'm not sure whether I'd go in for anything like that today. I'm not sure whether I think that was a good thing to have done or not. I think it was done in all innocence. It probably had to be done as a demonstration of strength against that outpouring of hate."

A few months after Peekskill, in December of 1949, the Weavers opened at the Village Vanguard for a two-week Christmas-season engagement that extended to six months and catapulted them to the top of the music world.

"Shalom, Chaverim"

1949–1950

WEAVER THEME SONG

RON: My name is Ronny, I used to go
With a feller I called my beau;
We tied that wedlock marriage knot;
It wasn't too long ago.
I'm trying hard to meet and beat
The troubles of married life;
I guess I'll weave and spin my songs
As long as I'm alive.
FRED: You c'n call me Freddy The Weaver Man;
I sorta like song spinnin';
Been in th' weavin' way mosta my life;
I spin lotsa tunes for the wimmen.
I'll weave ya tears or weave up a smile;
With my gittbox I'll keep weaverin';
Long's I'm headin' this hit parade,
My weavin's lots better th'n thievin'.
PETE: My name is Pete, my ma & my pa
Wove a jillion tunes before me;
They wove tunes in the classic vein;
I reckon that's why they bore me.
I was born up north of New England,
Then I walked my way down south;
Spinnin' tunes witha million hillfolks
Weavin' on my banjo head.
LEE: Lee Hays is my name, down Arkansaw's way;
I've outwove the best of these weavers;
Fr'm the best of tellers I stole my tales;
Baptized with the True Believers.
I've weaveled my trail fr'm coast t' coast;
Spun webs from sea to sea;
Just look where people go weavin' their ways
And 'mongst 'em you'll find me.

> —From *"Weaver Theme Song,"*
> words and music by WOODY
> GUTHRIE.

*A*ny two or more people, with Lee as one of them, was a talky group. The members of the Nameless Quartet went on endlessly about what to call themselves. They wanted something strong, something to do with labor, with basic industrial occupations—hammering or mining, perhaps.

Fred, in his final year at Brooklyn College, came upon a play by the German dramatist Gerhart Hauptmann, *The Weavers*, about a strike in nineteenth-century Germany by premachinery textile workers.

Nice. That took care of the militancy angle. And the *craft* of weaving, as opposed to assembly-line stuff: they liked that. Weaving threads of music together to create new patterns, new ideas, new hope.

Lee joked, "We are the warp and woof of history; Pete's the warp and I'm the woof."

That left Ronnie and Fred as the supporting cast. Not unreasonably, it seemed then, though Ronnie soon enough would burn with feminist rage at what the others assumed on her behalf. Pete and Lee, Lee and Pete. The big guys, the ones who'd made it all happen. Imagine being twenty-two years old (as both Ronnie and Fred were) and singing in a quartet with Pete Seeger and Lee Hays! Not for fame or money. For the glory of trying to make a difference, alongside the best singers in the world of trying to make a difference.

Certainly, making *money* in any real sense of the word had no place in their thoughts. Nothing could have seemed more preposterous. Pete barely supported his family on booking fees. And any group that booked him couldn't afford to pay more for four singers than they paid him alone.

Fame? Well, of course, in Almanac terms; not in hit parade terms—who could think that way after Peekskill? They'd never thought that way *before* Peekskill. (Excepting Ronnie, who in her teens often fantasized being the "girl singer" in a big band, a cultural hangover she never confided to the male Weavers.)

After Peekskill, the question was whether they could survive at all. Fear polluted the air. Their kind of audience was going for cover, battening down the hatches. People were plain old scared after Peekskill.

And who were the Weavers, anyway? Pete would try, when he

did get calls for bookings, to bring the Weavers in, if only for the exposure. "Don't know 'em," was the usual reaction. "We want *you*, not the Weavers." Maybe the callers remembered booking the Almanacs and having three unknowns arrive to perform.

They *were* the warp and woof of their branch of history. That's why Pete did it again—formed the nucleus of a small, intensely together group with Lee. Despite all the aggravating experience with Lee's difficult, disruptive ways; despite the tensions between them; despite their incompatible metabolisms and the memory of two traumatically unhappy endings.

Talent is talent—it kept coming back to that. And listen, if you're optimistic enough to think you can improve the whole goddamn world, why can't you hope to improve the working habits of one old friend?

Every Weavers fan knows the legend. They went into the Village Vanguard as unknowns and came out as stars.

But the scenario wasn't quite that of *42nd Street*. The Weavers were incontrovertibly leftists, at a time when any entertainer with a list toward the left was being swatted down by the growing legions of red-hunters.

Nothing on paper or in their recollections indicates that the Weavers felt any concern about walking into the limelight with their Vanguard engagement. Their thoughts were on earning a few bucks and eating. They'd been on the verge of breaking up for lack of bookings when Pete or Toshi suggested that they audition for Max Gordon, the Vanguard's independent-minded proprietor. Pete had played the Vanguard successfully several years earlier, and Max liked him.

Gordon listened to the quartet and said fine, for two weeks, as long as the Weavers would accept the same fee, $200 a week, that Pete alone had been paid. In addition, they could make themselves hamburger sandwiches in the Vanguard kitchen. The beefsteak rather than the pot of gold.

Perhaps the Weavers figured that at the end of the two weeks they'd collect their grand total of $100 each and go back to waiting for the worthy causes to call again.

Meanwhile, they stoked up on hamburgers and argued a lot.

They argued about singing in nightclubs, much as Lee and Woody had argued about tipping waitresses.

By appearing at the Vanguard, were they singing for the class enemy (nightclub audiences, ugh), and thus doing something reprehensible? Or were they doing something laudable, singing to more people, to a wider range of people than the already committed?

But the embarrassment to these people's singers of how they were expected to dress!—to Pete, Lee, and Fred, that is. Ronnie, the only Weaver raised in the working class, knew that real workers loved dressing up, and had little tolerance for their discomfort.

"The hell we went through those first few weeks at the Vanguard," Fred recalled, "just on the matter of what we should wear. We went to some junk place like Robert Hall, with Toshi in charge, and bought three green corduroy jackets. We had a hard time with the idea of being commercial in that sense, all of us wearing matching jackets. Lee kept complaining, 'It isn't comfortable, it doesn't fit.' Everything was wrong. What wasn't comfortable, what didn't fit, was us wearing uniforms, for God's sake!"

And yet, they were singing at the Vanguard because Pete had earlier played the tiny Greenwich Village club, so the place couldn't have held many surprises. Nor was the Vanguard your typical long-stemmed-American-beauties-parading-half-nekkid nightclub. Leadbelly, Josh White, Burl Ives, and Susan Reed performed there. The Vanguard *majored* in folk music and black music, blues and jazz. Authentic musicians loved playing the club.

Moreover, taking Pete at his written word, we see that an enhanced commercial image was in fact his intent.

In his book *The Incompleat Folksinger*, Pete tells a story that starts with a call to People's Artists from the American Labor party in Brooklyn. The ALP wanted to book a well-known performer for a fund-raiser. If that performer couldn't make it, the booker asked, would Pete Seeger do? "Oh, we know Pete," the ALP caller responded, "he's sung on our soundtrucks and parties for years. But we need someone who can bring in a mass audience. We need to raise money."

That, writes Pete, started him "doing some hard rethinking" about his own work: "Here I'd been knocking myself out all these years, congratulating myself on not 'going commercial,' and the result was that I was not as much use to the Brooklyn ALP as was my friend, a highly conscientious and hardworking artist, but one who also set out in a more conventional fashion to build a Career. He could bring in a big audience for them. I couldn't.

"Later that year I started working hard with the Weavers, and we took the drastic step of getting a job in a nightclub. . . ."

Why drastic, if he had pioneered the trail? Pete, Lee would say later, contained a multitude of contradictions. Whatever his original motivation, Pete was the one who started the Weavers. And Pete was the one—the only one—whose discomfort level rose in direct proportion to the rising tide of their astonishing commercial success.

Lee sometimes said Pete started the group in an attempt to reproduce the magnitude of Leadbelly's sound. It took four of them to equal what one black singer created with just his own voice and his twelve-string guitar. Leadbelly was dying when the Weavers began singing together, of amyotrophic lateral sclerosis, Lou Gehrig's disease. He died a month before they opened at the Vanguard. They signed off their first performance in the club with Leadbelly's theme song, "Goodnight, Irene." It felt so right that they signed off every performance with the song.

Lee had a special memory of Leadbelly each time he sang it: "Long before the Weavers became commercially popular," he said, "a number of us folk singers, including Leadbelly, were singing at a hootenanny, and when we came to 'Goodnight, Irene,' I sang the verse, 'Stop ramblin,' stop gamblin'/Stop stayin' out late at night/Go home to your wife and your family/Stay there by your fireside bright.'

"Leadbelly liked the way I sang that verse so much that he gave it to me. After the show was over he said, 'That's your verse.' And forever after I always sang that verse."

Their first two weeks didn't exactly break any house records. Still, Max Gordon had become a fan, and he extended the engagement. He also upped the weekly fee to $250 and cut out the kitchen privileges, a less unprofitable arrangement.

The Weavers were glad to stay on.

At first, Lee thought, it seemed "somehow wrong for our kind of music to be put into a nightclub. But when I got the hang of it, I started to enjoy it."

He got the hang of it quickly, being an old hand at winning an audience with his pointed stories and dry introductions.

Lee, sending up those earnest folklorists who claimed to have collected all their songs traveling through the Kentucky mountains: "This next song we learned while on an extensive folklore-collecting tour through the pages of an old hymnbook."

Or: "We're now going to sing an old folk song that we wrote last week."

Lee, feeling perhaps a nightclub audience might relate to this: "I remember hearing about a successful revivalist who came to town and preached so good that he set adultery back fifty years."

Lee, *sure* that a nightclub audience would relate to *this:* "We had a cow at home used to get drunk . . . find her way over to these mash barrels a neighbor had, and she'd get so drunk she couldn't come home by herself. We'd have to get about two dozen neighbors to carry her home on a barn door. If you ever saw a cow with a hangover, it's a pitiful sight. Poor thing had a sad end. One day she commenced to give milk bourbon punches, and we milked her to death."

Lee enjoyed drinking stories. He also enjoyed drinking at discount rates, which performers could do at the Vanguard. As Max Gordon extended the engagement again and yet again, Lee reverted to a bad old habit—failing to show up for performances. Laryngitis, he said, exacerbated, the others knew, by brandy.

His laryngitis lasted for weeks, during which Max Gordon continued to pay Lee's "small but inadequate salary."

The other three felt disheartened, appalled, angered, betrayed. How could Lee *do* this just as audiences started to build? Just as word began to spread around town that the Weavers were the show to see? They'd had a terrific publicity boost after Carl Sandburg visited the Vanguard—the press had picked up his poetic remark "When I hear America singing, the Weavers are there."

"We may have to take the bull by the horn," Pete told Fred. "If we have to, we have to. I've done it twice before." Yes, but on reflection the Almanacs never did sound like the Almanacs without Lee. How would the Weavers sound without his ministerial bass, his authenticity, his stories?

No one could replace him; the others knew that. But neither could they tolerate his irresponsibility.

Week after week Pete, Fred, and Ronnie performed as a trio, looking, Lee began to hear, for a new fourth. "I learned a great lesson then," said Lee in his memoirs, "which was that alcohol and music don't mix. I came back just in time to save my job."

Lee remembered the lesson well. Not that he turned tractable. Contentious, argumentative, disruptive, Lee had to be Lee. In the years ahead, he would often torpedo rehearsals, but at least he showed up for performances. Another violent split with Pete lay in the future, the most traumatic of all. That, too, would be Pete's decision, the difference being that Pete would go, and Lee would stay.

They started out a bit klutzy—Lee, Fred, and Ronnie—making their way onto the tiny Vanguard stage in the first weeks of their engagement, bumping and tripping and generally looking ill at ease. (Nothing strange about the Vanguard stage to Pete.)

But their singing! To their new audiences, the Weavers' music was a revelation. Here were these four rather oddly assorted people, with an unlikely combination of voices, singing this weird collection of songs—African chants and Israeli horas and hymns and Christmas carols—and when they finished you felt as if you'd been through some kind of religious experience.

Once you'd heard them, everything out of Tin Pan Alley sounded false, cheap, jerry-built.

Their music soared. It blew you right out of your seat, with its passion and integrity, its strength and clarity and simplicity. They rarely sang a song the same way twice, but somehow every chord and harmony they hit was *right*—never a word or note that rang false.

Whatever gave them the strength to fly in the face of conventional politics may also have provided the steel in their unalterably high musical standards.

But it was their music that their audiences responded to, not their politics.

The four Weavers gloried in a sense of discovery and excitement, of plowing new ground.

"When new songs came in," Lee said later, "no matter who

brought them, everybody was supportive and willing to work hard. That's when I learned the phrase *woodshedding*, a phrase of Pete's which simply meant getting together and hammering away on an arrangement.

"More than once, we had a song on paper, in a book, which just would not come to life until all of a sudden something would happen, a new chord would be thrown in, a new rhythm or a new line or sound would emerge that brought the song to life off the page."

The audiences kept on growing. Gordon Jenkins, the big-band leader, came once and returned every night for a month. He would become their champion, ignoring warnings and providing the way to bring their music to the nation.

Born in Webster Groves, Missouri, the son of a church organist, Jenkins responded to the rural flavor of Lee's stories almost as much as he did to the Weavers' music.

"In a more innocent time than today," said Lee in his memoirs, "perhaps before the tube, people looked on stories kind of like songs, as things they could hear over and over again. It was not uncommon to sit around at a party or social gathering and say, 'Tell that one about the such-and-such again.'

"So it was when we met Gordon Jenkins for the first time at the Village Vanguard. He gave me a new lease on telling stories because he enjoyed the same ones so often.

"Every night I told the same stories. I could hear his high-pitched giggle, which sometimes would crack me up, night after night on the same stories. After we got to know him better and began to meet and socialize with him, he would ask me to tell that story about the such-and-such.

"One of Gordon's favorites had to do with a bunch of men sitting around in a saloon one Saturday night. It got kind of late and the clock in the town hall began to bong, bong, bong—eight, nine, ten—bong, bong—eleven, twelve—bong! Thirteen! One of the men finished his beer and got up and said, 'Well, fellas, I guess it's time to go home. It's later than I've ever knowed it to be before."

Talent agents, hopeful managers, learning the Weavers had no professional representation (Toshi had done all their managing so far) began hanging around the Vanguard, asking, "Who's handling you kids?" They represented an alien world to the Weavers. Why couldn't Toshi keep on managing them?

Before they'd resolved the management problem, Gordon Jenkins brought them in to audition for Decca Records, his recording company. Decca's chiefs listened; then one of them nodded toward Pete and said, "I know him, he's an old leftie, he's not commercial," which seemed to be the end of that.

Not for Jenkins. As the Weavers left the room, he whispered, "Never mind, I'll bring you in on my next recording date," a promise he kept. Things clearly were getting beyond Toshi's expertise.

(In a 1963 letter to Lee from his home in Malibu, Jenkins wrote, "I still have your first Decca audition tape, which I often play, whilst sipping a touch of vodka, and gazing back into a little cellar saloon [the Vanguard] where music, talent and truth had such a wonderful blending. It was a wonderful privilege to hear you all, and thank God for tape.")

Help on the management front arrived one spring night when Harold Leventhal brought his date to the Vanguard to hear the Weavers.

The only Weaver he had known personally was Pete. "When I went backstage after the show to say hello to him," Leventhal recalled, "he says to me, 'Hey, you're just the guy we're looking for—you want to be our manager?' I promptly said yes."

The connections were politics and music. Leventhal, like Pete a young old leftie, had been a song plugger for Irving Berlin and had recently taken his first steps into music publishing.

Pete introduced him to Lee, Ronnie, and Fred. They liked him at once. His eyes twinkled with humor rather than dollar signs. He was short and a bit round and had a high, raspy voice and a Pickwickian gentleness, and he said very funny things deadpan. Leventhal definitely would do.

Thirty-seven years later, Leventhal still manages Pete, is Fred's music publishing partner, produces concerts for Ronnie, and is executor for Lee's (and Woody Guthrie's) estate.

The Weavers' first record with Gordon Jenkins and his orchestra had "Tzena, Tzena, Tzena" on one side and "Goodnight, Irene" on the flip.

Pete remembered, "In the month of June, we had a hit record with 'Tzena,' and the song on the other side was zooming up on the charts. Just about the time we quit the Vanguard, 'Goodnight, Irene' was on every jukebox in the country, week after week after week. The summer of 1950, no American could escape that song unless you plugged up your ears and went out in the wilderness someplace. Hard to imagine how ubiquitous that song was, and how ironic that Leadbelly, the man who put the song together, died only eight months before."

Another irony: just as their record zoomed up the charts, the first issue of *Red Channels: Communist Influence on Radio and Television* appeared. Pete was among the artists cited.

Looking back, Fred saw "the rise of repressive action against the Left coinciding with the commercial birth of the Weavers."

The Weavers were hardly surprised. They were far more surprised by their commercial success. In fact, they were "in a state of shock about the record," said Fred, adding, "As for the other, well, the thought never occurred to us that we could ever be anything other than what we were. The only question really was *when* we would get our subpoenas. Meantime, we'd just go on doing what we were doing."

With the instant and spectacular success of their record, the usual American celebrity things began to happen. They appeared, self-consciously ill at ease, on America's most popular program, "The Milton Berle Show." (Berle, in rehearsal, said, "Now at this point the girl will bounce up and down the stage going 'Tzena, Tzena, Tzena.' " Ronnie replied that she wouldn't, and she didn't.) Advertising agencies dreamed up formats for Weavers television shows that their clients might sponsor. Van Camp Foods acted fast and first, lining up the Weavers for a summer replacement series on NBC-TV. Then *Red Channels* struck. Van Camp canceled the Weavers.

Lee, increasingly comfortable in the role of successful commercial performer, thought perhaps the right kind of letter might repair the damage. He wrote to a Van Camp executive:

"The Weavers regret that malignant charges against us have forced your agency to cancel our appearance on the Van Camp's Television show.

"We had looked forward with much pleasure to taking part in

this program, and were very happy that our songs had been selected as the kind of material which could help to sell your products to the public. [Lee had to know that Pete could never be happy with the idea that his songs would help sell canned beans.]

"Particularly we were pleased at your personal reaction, and of others associated with you during your New York visit, to our songs, and wish to thank you again for the manner in which you expressed your liking for us and our work.

"It is our belief that folk songs will endure long beyond the malice of self-appointed traducers and inquisitors—with whom this country seems to be swarming today. If a large company is not free to select the material it needs to sell its products to the American public, then we are indeed in a bad way. . . ."

The Weavers remained canceled.

After six incredibly eventful months at the Vanguard, and with Snooky Lanson singing "Goodnight, Irene" as number one on "Your Hit Parade," the Weavers took the summer of 1950 off.

Ronnie finally had time to marry her beau, Marty Weg, a dentist. Pete and Toshi ran a gang of volunteers, including Lee and young Angela Lowenfels and sometimes Fred, clearing more of the land they'd bought upstate in Beacon.

For all their sudden success, the Weavers ate a lot of lentil soup. They'd used their Vanguard salary for daily living expenses; royalties hadn't started coming in. Later that summer, they received checks for $3,000 each, their first royalties. They'd never seen such large sums in their lives.

Pete Kameron spent the summer lining up bookings. Kameron, a boyhood friend of Leventhal's, had been brought in by Harold as comanager because he himself had other business obligations at the time. Any boyhood friend of Harold's, the others said, is . . .

Decca, elated by the enormous demand for the first Weavers record, put the group under contract and plotted a campaign of new releases.

The confusion of it all—the highs and the lows—the mind-boggling success and the incursions by the Right. How soon before their roots would become a media issue?

Pete later figured, "They [the blacklisters] must have wondered, how'd we let those sons of bitches slip through our fingers? I mean, they're not even supposed to get *started*, and look, they're right at the top of the hit parade, and every one of 'em's got a leftie record of some sort."

Everything was a problem, a big decision, under the circumstances. Mainstream success meant press attention, interviews, stories about the Weavers. How should they deal with their biographical material?

Omission and a bit of laundering seemed the safest course. Lee wrote their press kits with an ingenuous air:

"The four people who call themselves the Weavers came from totally different backgrounds, and might never have met except in such a big and cosmopolitan place as New York. There they became acquainted through their common love for a style of music variously labeled as 'folkmusic,' 'hillbilly,' 'corn,' or even 'esoteric'. . . .

"It's one of the characteristics of a big city that people who like the same thing can get together . . . whether it's stamp collecting, rare books, classical music, squaredancing, or, in this case, singing folk songs. Thus at many an all night song session the four Weavers started harmonizing together, till they decided that they would like to go so far as to rehearse some of their arrangements . . . never intending to make a living at it. Fred Hellerman, of the strong voice and driving guitar, was studying for his M.A. at college. Ronnie Gilbert, whose vibrant alto can easily be heard above the three men, was planning to leave a typist's job to be a doctor's wife. Lee Hays, at 37 the eldest of the four, had long since been a writer of novels and short stories. Pete Seeger, the only one to have made half a living singing folksongs, had sung for every imaginable audience in the country, high and low, respectable and not quite so. . . ."

A fine touch, that last bit about Pete, more or less covering any questions that might be raised about his pre-Weaver bookings.

Publications like *Time* magazine, however, didn't go for press handouts, and when they got around to writing up the Weavers, in September of 1950, with both "Tzena" and "Goodnight, Irene" on "Your Hit Parade" for the eleventh time ("Irene" number one), their description of how the singers met was emphatically more political:

"After the war the four met at Greenwich Village get-togethers, soon decided that their voices, plus Pete's banjo and recorder, and Fred's guitar, made just the right blend. Sponsored by Red-tinged People's Songs, they got enthusiastic but unremunerative backing from fellow travelers who have long claimed folk songs as their particular province. . . ."

Imagine having your long-lost brother turn up in *Time* magazine (that was Lee, all right, in the picture), as one of the singers you'd been listening to the whole summer long, never suspecting.

None of the Hays family had heard from Lee since the 1930s. Reuben, not since 1934. Minnie Frank had put Lee and Alan Hacker up for a weekend on their travels to shoot that sharecropper movie. Alan had taken wonderful pictures of her brand-new baby, after totally upsetting the front parlor by moving all the furniture and setting up his special lights.

Sue and Bill had lost track of Lee after 1936, when they were living in Little Rock and he "simply showed up." He'd stayed (Bill saw to this) at the YMCA, and then in a room let by a friend of a friend. Billy, Jr., aged three, had kept calling Lee "Grandfather." After a month or so, Lee left, "without settling any bills." He hadn't worked. "He just read. He read and talked," Sue said later. "He used to say, 'If I had a million dollars, I'd start a revolution.' " Then Lee had absolutely ripped it with Sue and Bill by mailing them a letter from the North, sealed with a stamp depicting a black tied to a post, being flogged by a white man. Was Lee *determined* to get them tarred and feathered?

Now he was a celebrity, or at least some kind of national success. Amazing! Well, of course, they felt pride. As for that red stuff, well, people have their eccentricities. Basically, he was a Hays, the baby of the family, the one with so many God-given talents and as many sloppy ways of wasting them, and now he'd risen to the top. They rejoiced when Lee sent them the record of "Goodnight, Irene" with a note that said simply, "This is what I've been doing."

Minnie Frank, plugging away at her own typewriter, writing poems for the local newspaper, laughed and cried with excitement.

Reuben acknowledged receipt of Lee's record with a letter, cool and bankerly over the bridge of sixteen years, indicating he'd kept informed: "The Weavers seem to be quite a hit and the folk songs which you sing are attracting the attention not only of your audience, but also of magazines." After some words of congratulation, Reuben issued a remote invitation: "Should you be out this way at any time, I hope you will stop in for a visit." He would try to get in touch with Lee next time he came to New York. Cordially.

It was almost as though Lee had had to prove himself before he could make contact with his siblings again.

In September, the Weavers opened their engagement at Max Gordon's uptown club, the Blue Angel. A week later, they were doubling into Broadway's Strand Theater (for a total of $2,250 a week, *Time* reported breathlessly). They played the Hippodrome in Baltimore, a big vaudeville house, where they shared billing with Yvonne De Carlo. They wound up 1950 with a concert in Town Hall, as they would 1951 and 1952.

They continued to argue about clothes. The question escalated from matching corduroy jackets to tuxedos when they prepared for Town Hall.

"Boy, the hell we went through on *that* one," said Fred. "Not just from Lee—I'm not sure what side Lee was on, probably both sides at once. On the one hand, there was Us, what the hell were we doing in tuxedos? On the other hand, I remember Lee bringing in a picture of Paul Robeson doing a concert in Russia in a tuxedo. That settled that."

Between performances, they turned out one hit record after another: "Wimoweh," "On Top of Old Smoky," "So Long, It's Been Good to Know You." They were the recording stars of the year, but the ground under their feet could give way any minute, and they knew it.

Lee couldn't disguise the pleasure that success and its perks brought him. Grandly, he sent records to old friends from Commonwealth College days, along with repayments of amounts they'd advanced him for his journey to New York, and lofty observations on the futility of small isolated movements, as compared with influencing large audiences.

Given a choice between singing for fifty people and singing for five thousand, you're going to sing for five thousand. They felt comfortable with that formulation, Lee and Fred and Ronnie.

In their "top of the charts" days, Weavers
appearances were publicized in a "three guys
and a gal" manner. (O'Neil's Photos)

Lee making the best of formal regalia in the Weavers'
preblacklist period. (Photograph by "Popsie" of New York)

Some of their old associates on the Far Left felt otherwise. They carped that the Weavers were in the process of abandoning their old audiences and activist songs, chasing the bitch goddess Success, falling into a rut with their music to please their upper-class nightclub audiences. Pete heard this kind of fault finding regularly from Irwin Silber, the editor of *Sing Out!*

Furious, Pete scribbled these notes: "Perhaps he is right; perhaps it is a rut. But his methods remind me of a neighbor of mine in the country. I was carrying a typewriter across a field when it fell in a post hole, and got wedged in the soil so I couldn't seem to pull it out. My neighbor came up with a crowbar, and said, here, I'll get it out for you, and commenced prying and poking, until, b'gosh, he did get it out—so mashed and torn by the crowbar that it was quite useless as a typewriter from then on. I was naturally quite angry, and after first feeling that he was a stupid irresponsible fool, that possibly he knew it would break the typewriter, but didn't care. This led me never to trust him again."

Also from the left came heavy, humorless dissections of their music, and what roads it should seek in the future, from Walter Lowenfels—the sort of thing that sent Lee and Fred up the wall.

For a time, they held more meetings than rehearsals, trying to resolve tensions and problems created by a success under fire from both right and left.

Pete didn't see the point of fame if it kept him from singing to his old audiences.

Kameron said if the Weavers sang at left-wing affairs, they'd lose their record contracts and their personal-appearance contracts.

Pete wanted to turn the Weavers into a racially mixed group, so that they could help defeat Jim Crow.

Kameron said things were getting rougher—they'd have a hard enough time getting bookings as they were now constituted; with a mixed group it would be impossible.

In *The Incompleat Folksinger*, Pete writes, "Our then manager would not let me sing for the hootenannies and workers' groups. Decca—hungry for more hits—insisted on teaming us with a big band; predictably, the result was almost the opposite of how we wanted to sound."

Lee, taking issue with Pete's version, said in his taped memoirs,

"It's true [our then manager] believed we should concentrate on our commercial work and not sing for any unrespectable things like hootenannies or what Pete calls workers' groups. But it is also true that we had a meeting at which we decided that at that point in our career and at that point in history, we should try to continue to be as commercial and successful as possible in order to beat the blacklist on its own ground and to avoid any controversial appearances that would work against our reputation as commercial singers.

"That was a joint decision which Pete agreed to. It is also true that having agreed to it he said, 'I'll go along with it, but I will feel like a prisoner.' All during the rest of our time together, he felt and acted like a prisoner.

"Life became very uncomfortable for all of us."

Said Ronnie, "Pete made us pay dearly for what pleasure there was to be had out of it."

By way of contrast, here is Lee's attitude toward what the Weavers had given up, expressed in a letter written at the time to a close left-wing friend, the composer Earl Robinson:

"Poor Pete is in anguish, so unwilling to accept the demands of this new day. I am myself fearful of what is to come but at least I have broken with the restrictive notion that we can go on forever in the same old way and with the same old methods and techniques. Maybe this is a sign of maturity, to be able to give up the shining glories of youth without too much hurt. I am so wrapped up in the problem of what to say to this big new audience of ours that I am not in the least ashamed that the old audience is gone, or that we did so little to keep it alive."

About that same time, Lee outlined chapter ideas for a book proposed by a University of Minnesota Press editor, a book about folk songs and folk singers. Lee's outline, never submitted, started with labor songs, and ended as follows:

"The Weavers. Who do not believe in themselves. Who believe that money is wonderful, but somehow evil. Who have done the greatest work in folk music that has ever been done in America."

| **11** |

"Times Are Getting Hard"
1950

I want to say a few good words about the blacklist, when all you
had to do to become a hero was just keep your mouth shut. Didn't
have to do anything, just not name names. Right on.

—LEE HAYS, 1976

*I*n his book *False Witness*, Harvey Matusow, whom last we
glimpsed as "Harvey Matt" at the end of chapter 8, describes how
the blacklist against the Weavers started:

"We [Matusow and members of a publication called *Counterattack*] discussed the careers of a well-known quartet who, at the
time, had the top-selling phonograph record in the United States.
One of its members was listed in *Red Channels*, but there was
nothing that could be pinned on the group specifically—they could
not be placed in the Communist party. Having known all four of
them, not as Communists, but as friends, I triumphantly said, 'I
know them, and they are Communists.' "

Needless to say, his recantation never caught up with the damage
he had wreaked.

Perhaps the blacklisting of the Weavers would have happened
without Matusow's triumphant report. It was everyone-to-the-left-
of-Genghis Khan time again, with the red-hunters methodically
setting about to deprive of their livelihood all who didn't recant
and name names (even if untruthfully).

One has only to cast back to the debacle of the Wallace campaign
to realize how little of the Left remained in the United States by
1950. But for finishing off the job, the moment couldn't have been
riper. The Cold War's first hot offshoot, the Korean War, burst

| 135 |

into the world on June 25, 1950. Spy trials of atomic scientists in Britain and the Rosenbergs in New York threw Americans into a frenzy of fear that Russia would soon develop and drop an atomic bomb on the United States. If respected scientists and ordinary little lefties were handing secrets to the Russians, where was safety? Who else might be doing what?

In this fertile ground flourished Senator Joe McCarthy, the House Un-American Activities Committee, the strange operation called *Counterattack*, its sister publication *Red Channels*, and people like Harvey Matusow.

Counterattack, formed by three ex-FBI agents with access to "confidential information," ran a "clearing house" that checked out performers' loyalty for advertisers, at a hefty yearly fee. The publication often ran stories about "pinks" and "fellow travelers" working on shows whose sponsors and their advertising agencies had failed to engage *Counterattack*'s services. Most came quickly to heel. Dread and suspicion seeped through the offices of advertisers, agencies, and networks.

Writers who have compared FBI files with material in *Counterattack* and *Red Channels* deduce a strong connection between the bureau and the privately operated loyalty-enforcing business.

One such writer is David Dunaway, who, while working on a biography of Pete Seeger, *How Can I Keep from Singing*, brought a Freedom of Information Act suit and won access to FBI files on Pete.

Counterattack, writes Dunaway, served as "the FBI's unofficial leak."

Red Channels's thirteen citations on Pete replicate material Dunaway found in the FBI files—clippings from the *Daily Worker* about Pete's performances. The citations in *Red Channels*, we have seen, instantly torpedoed the scheduled Weavers' network show for Van Camp Foods.

More, much more, was to come.

As 1951 began, the Weavers set out for six months of bookings that included some of the plushest nightspots in America—Ciro's in Hollywood, the Empire Room of the Palmer House in Chicago, the Nicollet Hotel in Minneapolis, the Shamrock in Houston, the

Thunderbird in Las Vegas, and the Riverside in Reno—class book-ings, as befitted a group whose recordings topped the charts. Pop charts, folk, country and western—the Weavers' music crossed lines the music industry thought uncrossable, their songs scram-bling previously well-defined categories.

Personal appearances sold more records, they knew that, and first-class bookings helped build the group's bio as a solid main-stream hit act, which *maybe* could keep them a step or two ahead of the whirlwind, which just *might* lose its force before it tore them apart.

Pete Kameron, the comanager who ceaselessly promoted a grand-hotels-and-glamorous-joints approach, shepherded the group on the road. Harold Leventhal remained in New York, dealing with the music-publishing and financial aspects of their careers. Lee, sensing that he minded the store well, gradually turned over to Harold the management of his personal finances. The job took more pa-tience than investment wizardry. Little of the money earned on a tour by Lee survived the tour. He discussed the things he spent his money on (or wanted to) almost daily in letters to Harold.

"Sky Coach is unbearable," wrote Lee from Las Vegas. "There are Constellation flights for $99 which would be much better than this one at $88. Everything—delays, small seats, no leg room, lousy food, many landings. . . . *Please find out* which the *best* non-scheduled lines are—take my word Sky Coach is not among them. . . ."

From Chicago, he wrote, "I have not told you how eager I am to have a bass recorder. . . . I know I can play the damn thing, as I have not been able to play anything else. . . . I know $100 is steep. But is it possible to get any kind of discount? Do you know anyone at Schirmer's? Could you, anyhow, inquire about this? . . ."

Frequently, Lee requested shipments of books, and underwear in his size. Everything he asked for required research or shopping trips. Lee did need taking care of.

The glitzy hotel and club dates promoted record sales, so they were important. But they also heightened differences between Pete and Lee.

Puritanical Pete could barely conceal the contempt he felt for such places. Everything, Walter Lowenfels used to say, was grist for the writer's mill, but at Reno and Las Vegas the grist reached the top of Pete's long neck.

The others got a kick out of the slot machines; Ronnie and Fred, "bored silly," Lee wrote to Harold, even took to the tables. After a lifetime of unappeased appetite, Lee's discovery of room service rivaled the excitement of a youngster at the foot of the Big Rock Candy Mountain. Pete, observing Lee's unabashed consumption, did not pause to reflect on childhood deprivation or the like; disapproval radiated from him.

Their metabolisms, Pete's and Lee's, remained as incompatible as in the Almanac days. Pete, a mass of kinetic energy, escaped the hotels each day, roaming the surrounding areas, visiting historic sites and waterfronts, prowling pawnshops in search of musical instruments to master, scouring art stores for materials with which to create plaster Icelandic statuary and other such exotica.

The others would be "sleeping off the work of the night before, sometimes the excesses of the night before," Lee said in his memoirs. In the afternoons, he and Fred and Ronnie "were content to buy cheap paperbacks in the hotel lobby or go to movies or whatever. Pete was desperately trying to exercise his artistic interests and to keep life going full steam ahead, always with great difficulty."

Room service threatened to be Lee's undoing. His "excesses of the night before" arrived in his room on ice, immediately after the last performance, with one simple phone call. During their engagement at Houston's Shamrock Hotel, the actor Arthur Treacher ran into them in the lobby, heard Lee coughing, and asked, "Hard night, old boy?" No, Lee replied, he'd gone to bed early with some kind of infection. "Nonsense," snapped Treacher. "I know bourbon when I hear it."

By this time Pete, too, knew it when he heard it.

Ronnie characterized the four of them, in a letter to Harold, as "Laughing Boy" (dour Fred), "Camille" (her own theatrical self), "The Messiah" (world-saving Pete), and "The Drunkard."

Two notable things happened in Lee's life during the Houston engagement: he flew to New Orleans to see his brother Bill's family for the first time since 1936, and he wrote his first will.

Once the Weavers gained fame, Lee reestablished contact with his family. *Right*, brother Bill's wife, Sue.

Lee had habitually spoken with scorn and disdain about his establishmentarian brothers—the one a banker, the other a corporate manager—so it surprised the Weavers to hear, on Lee's return, how marvelous a visit he'd had.

It struck Fred that Lee enjoyed being able to afford to fly to New Orleans, to return as something of a success—and that that might have had something to do with why he hadn't seen them before.

Extrapolating from the satisfaction of his visit to Bill and Sue, Lee proposed a similar visit to his sister's family in Greensboro, North Carolina, in June, after their Palmer House booking. He tried the idea out on Kameron, then wrote to Harold, "He (PK) thought I could combine this visit to my sister and my family with some disc jockey interviews. . . . In Greensboro I should stay in a hotel. . . . I could be a big shot for a change, and not a supplicant for food and lodging, as I used to be when I was a part of the labor movement. And I could make a maximum impact as I did in New Orleans—presents for the nephew, and all that. . . ."

While they were playing the posh Shamrock Hotel in Houston in 1951, their manager, Harold Leventhal, visited and drew up Lee's first will. Fred Hellerman (*left*), Leventhal, Lee, Ronnie Gilbert, and Pete Seeger.

"I want," added Lee, "to establish myself with my sister and her son."

The black sheep enjoyed the idea of homecoming, now that glory covered his fleece.

Harold flew to Houston to be with his clients for their Shamrock Hotel booking, the only time he could take away from the office. As soon as he arrived, Lee asked him to draw up a will.

Lee had just turned thirty-seven, had never owned more than a typewriter and a drawer or two of ill-fitting clothes, had no dependents, had been starving two years earlier, and suddenly was "into wills."

Lee certainly was taking success seriously.

He had come to recognize the value, far into the future, of song royalties.

Each time a song is played on the air, its writers share in royalties paid through the performance unions, ASCAP or BMI. For each record sold, writers receive mechanical royalties. Publication of a song in sheet music or a songbook earns publishing royalties. All these royalties are paid during the lifetime of the writers and to their estates for decades thereafter.

Few of the thousands of published songs become hits. Of those, most last only a brief season. The Weavers recorded traditional songs of proven durability. Their versions could be copyrighted if there was "substantial change," musically or lyrically. Since the Weavers substantially changed everything they sang, they quickly racked up dozens of copyrights. Their records and songs could produce many years of royalties for Lee and his heirs.

If he died intestate (without a will), his estate would by law be divided among his closest blood relatives, his three siblings. With a will, he could specify otherwise.

Lee, for whatever deep-down reasons, made mighty sure he always had an up-to-date will that specified otherwise. Every one of his wills, from the first through the last, named Harold as executor. His beneficiaries changed often, as friends who needed help became less needy, or wandered out of his life. But they never included his siblings or their children.

Said Sue Brown Hays, "Lee would sometimes write suggesting

that he now had a lot of money but that we were not going to inherit any of it. He wrote that to us more than once."

In May, during their one-month engagement at the prestigious Palmer House Hotel, they recorded "Kisses Sweeter than Wine" and "When the Saints Go Marching In" with the orchestra of Decca's Lew Diamond. Issued as singles, the discs quickly moved up the charts, two more Weavers hits for Decca.

At the same time, *Billboard* charts showed three Weaver recordings—"On Top of Old Smoky," "The Roving Kind," and "So Long, It's Been Good to Know You"—among the top coin machine plays in America.

How did these lefties keep escaping the net that had so effectively caught so many other performers?

As the Weavers prepared for a busy mainstream summer, *Counterattack* went to press with an article about the group's "red-front" activities.

One paragraph of that article became a ritual part of every subsequent newspaper exposé and every letter-writing and pressure campaign: "After Communist-inspired riots at Peekskill, N.Y. in 1949, the Weavers made a record, 'The Peekskill Story,' with Paul Robeson and Communist Howard Fast. All royalties from this record were turned over to People's Artists, which provides entertainment for Communist Party conventions, May Day parades, etc."

The issue circulated widely among veterans and religious organizations. Three groups—the American Legion, the Knights of Pythias, and Catholic War Veterans—took particular note.

In July, NBC's Dave Garroway announced that the Weavers would be among his guests the following week. The protest groups swung into action.

In the fire storm of the next few days, lawyers and managers worked to extricate the network without damaging the Weavers, whose representatives threatened lawsuits. They hammered out a press release stating that the Weavers "had asked to be relieved of their TV commitment because of conflicting rehearsal schedules." NBC conceded receiving complaints from the Joint Committee against Communism in New York "and other patriotic groups," but denied that the protests were responsible for the cancellation. Nobody believed them.

From here on, controversy stuck to the Weavers like a tar baby, eventually driving them to disband.

Yet July also had its high points. They were booked into New York's Cafe Society, a club with the feel of the Village Vanguard, only classier. Lee, Pete, and Fred wore midnight-blue dinner jackets; Ronnie, a filmy blue-and-white gown. (Rarely did the press take note of what the men wore; with maddening regularity, reviewers made mention of Ronnie's outfits. "Always what I was wearing, always," she recalled later. She bridled at reviewers' references to her as "the girl," "the chick," "the thrush," or "the distaff.") *Newsweek* ran a gee-whiz piece on the group, noting that their salaries had zoomed from $200 a week at the Vanguard to $4,000 a week at Cafe Society, "all on the strength of four Decca records— Irene, The Roving Kind, So Long, Old Smoky."

Their peaceful interlude ended with the announcement that they would perform at the Ohio State Fair, opening August 25.

Members of the American Legion quickly mobilized an army of protesters, all of whom sent letters and telegrams quoting *Counterattack*'s words about the Weavers. The fair's organizers, caught by surprise, floundered about, unsure how to handle the incendiary situation.

In Harold Leventhal's apartment, 1951, Lee and Leventhal expressing an affection that, with one glitch in 1964, lasted lifelong.

Ohio's Governor Frank Lausche acted. He wrote to the FBI on August 9 (reports David Dunaway, on the basis of what he found in the FBI files) asking for confidential information on the Weavers. Because the law makes it illegal for anyone, even a governor, to inspect FBI files, Lausche promised not to reveal his source. At the same time, he offered to slip the material to reporters.

In New York, Pete Kameron visited the editor of *Counterattack* and asked him to relent, assuring him that in the future he would refuse any left-wing bookings. (The Weavers blew up on learning of Kameron's pledge. If they had to seek approval from *Counterattack*, they'd be conceding the field to the red-hunters.)

As the story built in Ohio, hopes of the Weavers' singing at the fair sputtered out. But for contractual and legal reasons, the group flew to Columbus on the booking date, August 25, acting for all the world as if they expected to sing that night.

They didn't. "Weavers Banned at Fair; Union to Decide Fee Split," ran the headline in one Columbus paper. Officials of the fair gave a check for $3,850, the Weavers' contracted fee, to the American Federation of Musicians Union. Let *them* decide what to do with the money in this unprecedented situation. The union gave the money to the Weavers.

On the same day, August 25, the *New York World-Telegram and Sun*'s most dogged pursuer of lefties, Frederick Woltman, published a five-column article headlined "Melody Weaves On, Along Party Lines."

"From 'People's Artist' for the Communist party to a smash commercial success in television, the record industry and swank night clubs throughout the country may seem like an insuperable jump," wrote Woltman. "Especially when accomplished in almost no time flat.

"Not so for Pete Seeger, founder, director and member of the Weavers, that folk-singing quartet which has practically revolutionized music publishing by popularizing such hits as 'Goodnight, Irene,' 'Sweet Violets' and 'On Top of Old Smoky.' "

Woltman recounted the *Counterattack* charges, the Garroway show cancellation, the Ohio State Fair ruckus, the history of People's Songs, Pete's part in the Henry Wallace campaign, the antiwar songs of the Almanacs—much the same information as Dunaway found in the FBI files.

"At this point," Dunaway's biography of Pete notes, "Senator Pat McCarran (D-Nevada) joined the hunt. The FBI turned over a basketful of informer reports and clippings to his Senate Internal Security Subcommittee. . . . The McCarran Committee actually investigated whether the Weavers had violated Title 18 of the U.S. Code, sections 2383–85: Rebellion, Insurrection, Advocating the Overthrow of the Government, and Seditious Conspiracy. The Weavers may have been the first musicians in American history formally investigated for sedition."

Booking agents who had sought them a year earlier tossed their publicity material into the circular files. Who needed that kind of trouble?

But Weavers records were still selling, still being played on radio stations. Their pursuers would not rest until they obliterated the sound of the Weavers.

Members of the American Legion "and other patriotic groups" launched a letter-writing campaign, urging stations not to play Weavers songs, urging shops to refuse to handle their records.

Lee, deeply concerned, wrote to Decca, "For nearly two years we have been proud to record for Decca. And now we understand that there have been certain rumors and allegations about the Weavers.

"We feel that you might like to hear the facts directly from us. We would like to tell you that we have never in our lives knowingly participated in nor contributed to any action or cause disloyal to this country; that we are not engaged as individuals or as a group in any activity of any kind, whether professional, artistic, organizational or personal, that is unrelated to our main business of singing.

"To put it another way, we are singers who make recordings of the best American folk songs we know, who appear in theaters, clubs and television. We collect and arrange songs, and we write new ones. And this is all we do.

"Through our association with you and our friends at Decca, we believe you know that we have always sung the best songs we know. We think that not one line nor word of any song we have recorded for Decca can be construed as harmful to our country—indeed, we believe that our songs have helped Americans in these troubled days to know themselves and understand the great traditions of our country.

"We have been fortunate in being able to work with Decca. Folk songs were a risky experiment only a year or two ago, and the results have proven that the experiment was worthwhile. Surely the more than 4 million persons who have bought our recordings have found nothing objectionable in them. We are proud that so many of our fellow citizens have liked our songs.

"We often wonder whether the persons who have questioned us have ever honestly listened to our songs. We would like to invite them all to listen, and to sing with us. If they did, we think they would have more faith in this country.

"P.S. As the fellow says, 'We deny the allegations and defy the allegators!' "

Lee loved making those records with Gordon Jenkins, his orchestra, and chorus. "There is something immensely thrilling about being in a studio with a big ensemble that made me feel stronger and more professional and more powerful than anywhere else," he said in his memoirs. "By powerful I mean personal, physical, bodily power, the ability to use voice and all given talent to the fullest. . . .

"One time we were in a Decca Studio with Jenkins doing a recording with a huge orchestra and perhaps twenty singers, all backing up this greenhorn quartet. After working for a couple of hours, in accordance with union rules Jenkins said, 'Take five.' I was standing near the podium, and I took the notion to stand up and say, 'Wait a minute, I want to tell you a story.' And I took an old story I'd heard somewhere and turned it around so it came out like this:

" 'I had a dream last night. I was in a recording studio; Gordon Jenkins was conducting. There were five thousand musicians, the best in the land; four thousand choral singers; three thousand tenors sounding exactly like Pete; two thousand women singers sounding just like Ronnie Gilbert; one thousand singers sounding just like Fred Hellerman. After a while Jenkins tapped on the stand and brought everything to a halt; he turned to me and said, 'Not so loud in the bass please, Mr. Hays.'

"It was very effective if I do say so, and on Gordon Jenkins's

The Weavers as themselves. (Photo by Sonia Handelman)

photograph he wrote, 'May you always be a little too loud in the bass, Mr. Hays.' "

The Weavers had no bookings at all in September.

October brought another ruckus, this time in New York City. The owner of the Icelandic restaurant, at 1680 Broadway, told the *New York Journal-American* that he had canceled a Weavers engagement after receiving protests from the Catholic War Veterans. The newspaper reprised the Garroway incident, the Ohio State Fair episode, and the standard paragraph about Peekskill and the Weavers' record.

"That kind of thing," said Fred, "began to happen with great regularity."

"Life became hard," noted Ronnie. "Very hard."

In November, they flew to Cleveland to sing at a benefit for a local disc jockey. (Lee made no attempt to get his brother Reuben up from Cincinnati. Reuben surely had followed the Ohio State Fair incident, which must have caused him some embarrassment among his Republican banker friends.)

Later in November, they played the Blue Note in Chicago, not through any efforts of Pete Kameron but through those of their old People's Songs friend Bernie Asbell, who now handled the club's public relations.

Asbell had taken the owner of the Blue Note, Frank Holzfeind, to the Palmer House in May to hear the Weavers sing. Now, with the blacklist doing its worst, Holzfeind booked them into the Blue Note. It was a step down from the Palmer House, they agreed, but at least it gave them a place to sing in Chicago.

They wound up the strange, troubling, ominous year with their second annual Town Hall concert, which they again sold out.

One of the many requests Lee had made of Harold Leventhal while on tour was that of finding him a new apartment. He would settle "for a very large studio maybe 100 feet long with a love seat and television, at no more than 60 bucks a month." Lee also enlisted his old People's Songs roommate, Harold Bernz, in the search.

The two Harolds found a place that Lee moved into at the end of the Weavers tour. For $60 a month, Lee sublet half of a floor in a Brooklyn Heights brownstone from the Earl Robinson family, who paid $150 a month for two floors of the building. The Robinsons needed help with their rent.

Earl was about as big a composer as you'd find on the Left. His credits included "Joe Hill," "The House I Live In," "Ballad for Americans," and "The Lonesome Train."

He'd been doing well writing music for Hollywood films until the blacklist cut off every possibility of work in the sensitive industry. When the money ran out, he returned to the East Coast. There he would find a chorus to lead, students to teach. In Los Angeles, a blacklisted artist felt a terrifying sense of isolation. The Robinsons had many friends and relations in New York. One needed plenty of warmth at a time like this.

Lee had known Earl since Almanac days, when Earl wrote "The Lonesome Train" with Millard Lampell of the Almanacs. He liked the prospect of moving in with the Robinsons. He didn't know that they would be his family for the next nine years.

It just seemed that, the way things were going, Lee and Earl both would have plenty of time to write. Since Lee wrote lyrics and Earl music, mightn't they develop into a team?

Alas, events so agitated Lee that he couldn't begin to focus on songwriting. Who'd sing his songs? Where?

In January, the Weavers played Daffy's Bar on the outskirts of Cleveland. Daffy couldn't care less about the blacklist. But while they sang at Daffy's, another storm cloud gathered.

The Cleveland Press Club organized a telethon to benefit the Cleveland Area Heart Society. Invited to appear, the Weavers accepted. As soon as their names were announced, the by now expected happened. Protests poured in. The press club, upholders of freedom of speech, refused to cancel the Weavers. Politicians and other performers scheduled to appear on the telethon called in sick, or to say their cars had broken down. Protesters jammed the switchboard, so that pledges for the Heart Fund couldn't get through.

On February 6 and 7, Harvey Matusow testified before HUAC, swearing under oath (falsely) that Pete, Fred, and Ronnie were members of the Communist party and that Lee had been, but quit.

Matusow's testimony delivered the coup de grace.

The American Legion intensified its campaign to eliminate Weavers records from circulation.

By 1953, Decca had not only stopped recording the Weavers but also deleted their old records from its catalog. Later, in folk boom times, Decca reissued the records, profitably.

Odds and ends of bookings trailed through the remainder of 1952. In February, they sang in a little bar in a dumpy hotel in

Philadelphia, where customers shouted them down.

In March, there was a concert on the campus of Oklahoma A & M, their first concert outside of Town Hall. What a relief after nightclubs and hotels! God, if only they could do concerts instead of clubs! Ironically, the hated blacklist eventually gave them that wish.

Also in March, they played a little club in New Jersey and another round at the Blue Note. Then came weeks and months of nothing.

On June 24, they sang at a private party at the Indianapolis Country Club, honoring the president of an Indianapolis steel company, a fan of their music. Lee saved the program, a brochure entitled "Papers from the Life of C. Harvey Bradley," with reproductions of his birth certificate, Marine Corps honorable discharge, his diploma from Yale, his marriage license, and so on, plus the menu, from green turtle soup through baked Alaska, and the names of the entertainers—Lilly Quartet and the Weavers. The program made Lee chuckle, but the memory that this party was their sole June booking was enough to make him wince.

In August, they played a club in Elko, Nevada, and a small club in Los Angeles. Nothing else followed until late October, when they sang at an Omaha club named Angelo's, a small club in Detroit, and a beer convention in Detroit.

They had no other bookings until their year-end concert, their last, at Town Hall. After that they had to take a sabbatical, said Lee, which turned into a "Mondical" and a "Tuesdical."

12

"If I Had a Hammer"

1952–1955

> If I had a hammer, I'd hammer in the morning,
> I'd hammer in the evening—all over this land;
> I'd hammer out danger,
> I'd hammer out a warning,
> I'd hammer out love between my brothers and my sisters,
> All over this land.
>
> —Words and music by LEE HAYS and
> PETE SEEGER

*T*he ironies of the McCarthy era abound. On the government side, McCarthy's special turf, the real target was New Deal liberals, people described as "soft on communism"—damning words that ruined unnumbered lives and careers. In the arts, the House Un-American Activities Committee's favorite arena because it led to splashy headlines (on which congressmen run), many 1930s lefties had long since lost their esteem for the Soviet Union and more were turned off every day by recurrent stories about new purges in Russia and the Soviet satellite countries.

But if the Soviet Union's polar opposite was American democracy, what could be said about lists of un-American organizations, lists of government workers "soft on communism," loyalty oaths, floodlit hearings, insistence on crawling and name-naming to cleanse oneself, loss of jobs, blacklists?

Americans whose careers and lives were ruined by McCarthy, HUAC, and the private business loyalty enforcers felt the same sickening terror that victims of a dictatorship know.

In time, Soviet actions managed to alienate just about every old believer. But the early 1950s made it a lot easier for some to say, "A plague on both your houses."

No blacklisted American was ever found to have been engaged in plotting the overthrow of the government. None was found to have been a spy. Actors, working in movies, plays, soap operas, spoke the lines of their roles. Screenwriters wrote for studios that paid them well for scripts aimed at the mass market; no script was sacrosanct, scripts being then as now subject to change by producers and directors. And musicians—well, is there subversive music?

In perhaps the greatest irony, the next time the government uncovered an American spy ring working for the Soviets, the ringleader turned out to be an extreme right-wing American ex-navy man, in it for the money. About the same time, another American went on trial for spying for the Soviets—an FBI agent derailed by a passionate love affair.

What was so threatening about the music of the Weavers? They didn't sing their protest songs and union-organizing songs at the Palmer House or the Nicollet, or on the Decca label.

On the contrary, they practiced what Fred called "a certain kind of self-censoring, as much aesthetic as political." "It's one thing to sing Aunt Molly Jackson at a hootenanny," he said, "and another to sing it at the Vanguard. We were essentially a musical group. That we *came* from a certain place, out of People's Songs, is secondary to one's consideration of the group. First comes the music. If the music wasn't good, the rest is shit."

To the red-hunters, the music was important only because they had such a hard time shutting it up. The main question was where the *singers* came from, where they'd been before Snooky Lanson started performing their songs week after week on "Your Hit Parade."

And in fact, once Snooky Lanson started singing "Tzena, Tzena, Tzena" on the hit parade each week, it began to sound like one more novelty song. If the Weavers hoped that "Wimoweh," an African tribal song, or "When the Saints Go Marching In," a black American song, would somehow improve racial understanding, they must have felt some disappointment. Instead, their rousing performances turned the songs into commercial hits, pop songs.

The Weavers playing Ciro's, or the Strand, or Las Vegas had drifted into the role of entertainers.

Ironically, the political persecution of the Weavers eventually led to their revival as something quite different: the musical embodiment of bravery under fire. Their songs would once again sound true and resonant and full of hope and love of mankind. And for a while, every concert would be an epiphany.

Out of business, the Weavers went their separate ways. Ronnie and her husband moved to the West Coast. Fred picked up several small music-teaching jobs. Pete and Toshi targeted a potential audience beyond the range of the red-hunters' vision—small colleges and churches. They prepared a brochure and mailed out hundreds of copies. For the next few years, Pete covered the country like Johnny Appleseed, singing $25 and $50 bookings, pioneering the college circuit.

Lee, hunkered down at the Robinsons', entered 1953 vowing never to be a performer again. Perhaps he could write television plays (pseudonymously). First he'd have to watch a lot of TV. He settled in to watch, with cans of beer and a notepad.

As for the man who in publicity releases had sometimes been called the fifth Weaver—their manager, Pete Kameron—he quickly put as much distance as possible between himself and the four pariahs, an act they never forgot or forgave.

Soon after Lee moved in, the Robinsons had called a family meeting. Their resources were about gone. Helen, Earl's wife, said she'd look for a job if the others would do the housework. Lee volunteered to cook. The Robinson sons, Perry, fourteen, and Jimmy, five, agreed to do the dishes. Earl would make the beds in the living room, his and Helen's, before getting on with his composing. He was working on a folk opera about the Irish laborers who dug the Brooklyn–Battery tunnel. (*Sandhog*, with words by the blacklisted Hollywood writer Waldo Salt, opened on November 23, 1954, at the Phoenix Theater for a six-week run.)

The Robinson establishment, at 11 Cranberry Street, near the foot of the Brooklyn Bridge, might have been a musical version of the Lowenfels household or the Williams manse. People wandered in and stayed into the night, talking familiar politics, Earl

Earl Robinson, composer of
"The House I Live In" and
head of the family Lee lived
with for nine years, in front
of the Brooklyn Heights
brownstone they shared.

at the piano trying out a new song or accompanying anyone who
wanted to sing an old song, Helen and Lee serving up tea and
Lee's famed home-baked bread.

Pete would come around with his banjo; Woody, visibly deterio-
rating from the effects of Huntington's chorea, would stagger in.
Other visitors included old friends from Almanac days, singers
from the choruses Earl had led, blacklisted Hollywood screenwriters, Harold Leventhal, Harold Bernz, Helen Robinson's psychia-

trist brother and his family, and Perry Robinson's teenage jazz combo. Nobody telephoned ahead; everybody was welcomed warmly.

They joked that the FBI had a camera trained on the front door; they believed it. They took for granted that their telephone calls were tapped and their letters opened and read.

Occasionally, an FBI agent rang the doorbell and asked Earl if he had anything he cared to discuss. Earl, who at forty still had freckles on his wide and boyish face, would say, "No, I don't think so," and the FBI man would respond, "Well, that's too bad," and leave. Then Earl would look in the bathroom mirror and wonder how he'd remained so calm.

Once, when Earl wasn't home, Lee answered the door to an agent. The episode quite unnerved him.

The tensions of surveillance, of the blacklist, of subpoenas expected every day, did little good for Lee's hypochondria and for his vows not to seek solace in the bottle.

And so when the Lowenfelses bought a house in May's Landing, near Great Egg Harbor, in New Jersey, Lee quickly accepted their invitation to help clear brush. He'd done plenty of that at Pete and Toshi's place in Beacon. In early spring of 1953, Lee wrote Harold Leventhal and described the property: "There are five acres here, set off in the woods, no neighbors close by, a self-contained little house with an electric water pump and an outhouse, much sand all about, and growths of pine and weeds. In two weeks we have cleared a whole acre about the house, burned great piles of brush, disced the ground, limed it and planted pounds of rye grass seed. I have prepared the ground for a garden and have already planted the peas, beans, onion and radishes. I will add things like squash, cucumbers, peppers, sweet corn, etc. . . ."

In the same letter he conceded, "The transition from a Weaver's life to a more sedentary—and lonelier—life has been hard as the devil to make. I think I have been through a kind of nervous collapse, and only things like the TV set and my own work have kept me more or less in line."

After a detailed accounting of why he needed fifteen dollars a week from the savings account that Harold managed for him, Lee concluded, "One more point: I feel fairly sure that this is the year when we may be called by some group or another. I don't know how to tell you by mail the experiences I had during your absence, when some persons came around asking leading questions. If I, myself, ever get that piece of paper, I want to be in the best possible physical and emotional health to meet the new problems. . . ."

Several severe emotional blows lay just ahead.

In April, Lee's mother, who had never recovered from her breakdown in 1927, died.

He'd seen her only once in all the years she'd been in custodial care. He remembered she wore what he called a "shimmy," or chemise, a loose, straight-hanging dress, and that she looked at him with large, unrecognizing eyes.

He told Bill and Sue that she'd died for him a long time ago. But in the quiet of his room, he scribbled these notes on yellow legal paper:

"I hope that in my posthumous works I may tell truly of that beautiful woman whom I called Mama.

"She died this year. I got the news in a cranberry bog in New Jersey. . . .

"The house I promised to build for her. . . ."

And on another page, an afterthought:

"I have had some remarkable encounters with women, and some, if not all, of these meetings have left me sad. . . ."

His posthumous works. Post-humous, Lee pronounced it, always getting a laugh. He'd borrowed the phrase (though not the pronunciation) from Walter, who generously told Lee he needn't return it.

"Yes, it used to be MY POSTHUMOUS WORKS," Walter wrote to Lee. "You can have it. I am beginning to publish them so don't need the title anymore. . . ."

For thirty years, Lee fended off questions about his activities by responding, "Been working on my post-humous memoirs." People laughed, but they also believed. They'd read his columns, treasured his anecdotes. Wouldn't his memoirs be something, after all he'd seen and known and done, south and north, top of the heap and bottom!

But apart from perhaps a dozen hours with a tape recorder, Lee never seriously pursued the project. In a taped message he sent me on March 17, 1977, he finally admitted that he never would.

"It's six o'clock in the morning, and once again I haven't been able to sleep. I recently became sixty-three while my back was turned, and that doesn't help. During the course of this long night, I've had an insight which I have to share with you, which has brought on a very critical decision. I'm faced with the sad fact that this project of producing memoirs has made a shambles of my life. I haven't been doing it well. I've felt guilty about it. As is obvious, I've been extremely disorganized and disoriented with the material. Even to think of it and some of the history that I would like to relate tears me up emotionally, suspends all objective judgment, gives me nightmares. . . .

"I think the truth that I haven't faced is that I don't even want a book with my name on it published in my lifetime. I've been living a very private life. . . . If a book came out with some of the things that would have to be discussed, if it should be successful enough to be reviewed and read about by my friends and neighbors, I would be embarrassed and horrified. . . .

"The things that upset me are primarily the resentments, the memories of tensions, of life among the Weavers and the Almanacs, and the growing realization . . . that I've survived not so much by my own efforts as by the generosity and kindness of associates who have included me in, and made it possible for me to share in the good things that I've had. . . . [But Lee minimized "the whole sense of a human being, his personality, that made others *want* to include him," Harold protested.]

"The strange and powerful influence of Pete and Toshi on my life leads me to many dilemmas, much gratitude and much resentment. . . .

"Anathema comes with the thought of memoirs. . . ."

Memories of Walter, too, brought pain. Something had happened to change their relationship. Earl, head of the family that supplanted the Lowenfelses in Lee's life, never knew why, but he noticed that Lee put Walter down whenever his name came into a conversation.

In the summer of 1953, while Lee was working a job he'd sworn he wouldn't take, that of emcee at the leftish Schroon Crest camp, he learned that the FBI had swooped down on May's Landing and arrested Walter in the middle of the night.

Earl later remembered the self-referential joke Lee made: " 'I was flushed out of the mountains like a bull moose,' said Lee. He came down from the camp at once and went to Philadelphia to lend support. So his loyalty to Walter overcame his anger."

Walter had supplanted Claude as Lee's surrogate father, and Walter had been "negated," a word Lee used to describe a process he considered part of growing up. Lee once wrote to Pete that he'd gone through such a process with Claude, overturning his leadership in order to find himself. "In the same way," he went on, "I have had to negate my family, and to a small degree you, and so many of the factors of adolescence, before I could arrive at any mature view at all. . . ."

Negating, in fact, was one of Lee's most frequent activities.

Nonetheless, Walter had been like a father, and the FBI had burst in—in the middle of the night!—and taken him to jail, just as an earlier surrogate father, Claude, had been jailed for political reasons.

The government charged Walter and eight other Philadelphia Communists with sedition under the Smith Act. Because Lillian had been diagnosed as having a prestroke blood condition, a judge granted Walter release on bail until his trial in 1954. The trial ended in conviction; Walter went to jail for three months, during which he wrote a slim book entitled *Letters from Prison.*

Lee couldn't sort out the conflicting feelings of fear, anger, guilt, and old loyalties to the family that had been so generous to him.

So deep and fresh were the wounds that Lee turned for relief to material from the past. He enjoyed a developing correspondence with his sister, Minnie Frank Mosely, eleven years his senior and very unhappy maritally and professionally. Lee later described her as "a frustrated southern lady writer."

For Minnie Frank, the renewed relationship with her baby brother let some air into a life stifled by a rigid, humorless husband. Lee encouraged her to tell hilarious anecdotes about their family. Through him, she felt a connection to the glamorous world of show business and the dangerous world of left-wing politics. She wrote Lee not just faithfully but prodigiously, feeding him information about the family, about southern modes and manners and speech patterns, about outlandish local incidents that Lee might turn into an anecdote or short story.

Lee felt he'd fallen into some personal research library, which left no request unanswered. He especially wanted to know about ancestors. They might come in awfully handy in a meeting with HUAC. Minnie Frank herself belonged to the Daughters of the American Revolution, a good credit to cite, should the opportunity arise.

Something about her spirit, her indomitability in the face of personal misery, her perseverance in submitting her little poems to local newspapers, opened Lee's eyes to the wasting of his talents.

He started to write short stories again. He sent one off in November of 1953 to Robert Mills, the editor who had bought his earlier stories for *Ellery Queen's Mystery Magazine.* Flinching in recollection of Mills's enthusiastic words back in 1949, which promised *EQMM* readers that they'd be hearing more from Lee Hays, Lee wrote a modest cover letter. He wasn't sure this was a story for *EQMM*, but he'd value an opinion. He added, "I am spending a lot of time writing these days—feel like a beginning amateur all over again, which indeed I am. . . ."

"Banquet and a Half," won an *EQMM* short-story award and was reprinted in anthologies in the United States and Britain. The story, the editor said in introductory comments, is one "of great power, yet it is tender, subtle, understanding, evocative, and packs enormous sociological implications. It is, to quote the author himself, a tale 'of human need, of human misery, of unsung little people in trouble.' . . ."

Lee told Mills about the genesis of the tale.

"In the late thirties two Negro boys . . . were executed in the electric chair at Tucker Farm, near Little Rock, Arkansas. They had appealed their case and fought for their lives for about three years after their conviction. That they kept going so long was due to the efforts of their lawyers and also to the labors of several white ministers who had become convinced of their innocence. It was an ordinary case, of the classic kind that happens too often in the South; a white woman accused the boys of raping her. She said the rape took place at a certain spot along the roadside, on the steep banks of a drainage ditch. Defense evidence was introduced to show that the ditch was full of water at the time she stated—not unlike the evidence of the almanac which A. Lincoln used to free the Armstrong boys.

"I got into the case in a very slight way when one of the ministers [presumably Claude] asked me to write a one-act play about the case, which I did. It was mimeographed and sent to churches in East Arkansas, where it was either performed or read from the pulpit. . . .

"When all efforts had failed, the execution date was set. . . . The newspapers had their usual morbid accounts of the execution. The *Gazette* really undid me; I stood reading it on Main Street crying, for I was so shocked at the cruel story they printed. The reporter had obtained a list of the foods the boys had ordered for their last supper and it was a big joke—they had ordered things they could not have seen, ever, but only heard about; and they had to die to get all the good things. . . .

"The little story of their last supper ["Banquet and a Half"] is only a tiny part of their agony. The story is not literally true, but is as true as my imagination can make it."

EQMM unhesitatingly used Lee's byline. Would any of their readers make the connection between Lee Hays the blacklisted Weaver and Lee Hays the short-story writer? How many people even *knew* the names of any of the Weavers, anyway, possibly excepting Pete?

Well-known blacklisted writers routinely used pseudonyms in that period. And with the loyalty enforcers going over names, by-lines, casts, faculty lists, and the like with a fine-tooth comb, it seemed foolhardy to send out new material under one's own name. Lee, too, began using pseudonyms.

One name he wrote under belonged to an ancestor, Christian Reinhardt, who'd fought against the Tories in the Battle of Ramsour's Mill. To Christian's byline, Lee appended a pseudoaddress, that of his sister, Minnie Frank, in Greensboro.

(Certain names stuck to Lee's ribs. Back in the mid-1930s, when he and Alan Hacker were shooting the sharecropper film, they signed off one report, "Write to us as C. Reinhardt, Box 5215, Memphis, Tennessee." And Minnie Bell, a name he favored for southern girl characters, had been borrowed from Claude Williams's mother.)

In 1954, he began to write "bawdy stories" under the pseudonym of Mordecai Jones. Most were adapted from *The Satyricon* or *Arabian Nights* and were told in the cadences of rural America. A Brooklyn Heights neighbor who published "nudie" magazines bought the stories for thirty-five dollars each.

Lee very much resented the financially secure neighbor who went out of his way to tell Lee he was prostituting himself, "but thirty-five dollars was very helpful in those days."

Nor did Lee sign his name to a long review he wrote of six recently published homosexual novels, all of which failed, in his opinion, because of their "subjective defensiveness." What is needed, he wrote, is "not defense but understanding, not deceit and protection, but struggle for human rights. Homosexuals need better advocates than these writers. In life they need more than the clan which, till now, is mother and family to these; they need to relate themselves to the human family, wherein they are neither cursed or blessed.

"If they do not find themselves in humanity, they must accept the Fascism they are helping to bring."

Although he received little for his writings, and worried much about falling back into destitution, at least minimal royalties did continue to come in. Harold put the royalties into a savings account against the needs of an unknown future.

Soon enough it would have to cover the costs of a lawyer.

For all the negative publicity the Weavers received, two of Lee's siblings (brother Bill and sister Minnie Frank) had no intention of abandoning the fraternal ship. Bill and his wife, Sue, lived in Washington, D.C., now, Bill working as district manager for B. F. Goodrich. They had come up to visit Lee at 11 Cranberry Street with young Bill. Given Lee's bohemian propensities, Sue warned young Bill, Jr. not to be surprised at what they might find or whom Lee might be living with.

When they arrived, Helen Robinson answered the doorbell. Does Lee Hays live here? "Oh, yes, he lives with me," said Helen. Then, upstairs, Lee introduced Perry Robinson as "his boy."

Bill, Jr., found it all to be "as unexpectedly expected."

In January of 1955, several years into the well-publicized blacklisting of the Weavers, big Bill procured an "employee's discount privilege card" for "Lee Hays, Brother," entitling Lee to substantial discounts on Goodrich products. Big Bill didn't worry about surveillance.

And Minnie Frank, in a letter on the day of Lee's interrogation by HUAC, wrote in her usual insouciant style, "I have been glued to the radio. Here things went off very well, on the whole; I have been cut dead once by a rather stupid dame whom I considered quite stupid to begin with, and called many times, and threatened by what sounded like an old female bat. We rather expected fiery crosses in our yard, but I was not bothered, spent the week-end by myself while Bob went fishing, and oddly enough was worried and concerned only that the jugheads with the cross might get it in the wrong yard and worry the neighbors. . . ."

After receiving Lee's account of the day, Minnie Frank replied, "I was glad to hear from you, and of course, glad the business is all over. . . . Of course I can't discuss the business, as I really don't know anything about it, in addition to which, anything I say might be used against you. . . ." The fear of letters being opened had been transmitted to Minnie Frank—fear for him, if not for herself.

And Minnie Frank always showed the Hays family sense of humor: "Dear Lee: Well, when everything is cleared up for you, plan to come down to see us. In the meantime, as soon as I can get hold of enough shekels I'll plan to come up. At the moment I am in a sad state, financially speaking, as I remind myself of Sue's father, of whom her mother often said, 'Dear Alfred was so impractical, he ruined himself paying his debts.' . . ."

The subpoena, signed by Francis E. Walter, chairman of the House Un-American Activities Committee, and dated July 1, 1955, was delivered to Lee Hays at 309 West Eighty-second Street, New York City—the wrong Lee Hays. The committee apologized to the wrong Lee Hays, an actor, and made sure the right Lee Hays got the notice.

Lee appeared before the committee on August 16; Pete, on August 18. The lawyer Paul L. Ross accompanied both. On Ross's advice, Lee took the Fifth Amendment in response to all questions about his associations, his beliefs, and his personal, private convictions.

Pete resolutely declined that legal advice and insisted, rather, on his First Amendment rights as an American—"I am not going to answer any questions as to my associations, my philosophical or religious beliefs or my political beliefs, or how I voted in any election or any of these private affairs. I think these are very improper questions for any American to be asked, especially under such compulsion as this."

The Fifth Amendment gives Americans the right to refuse to testify against themselves. That was okay with HUAC. Witnesses who fell back on that constitutional right immediately found themselves labeled "Fifth Amendment Communists" by the public— unemployable, ostracized. That, after all, was the point of the exercise. So, after testifying and taking the Fifth (HUAC mission accomplished), they were off the hook legally. The matter ended there.

Lawyers whose HUAC-subpoenaed clients had no desire to grovel and name names (the only way to "cleanse" oneself) could rely only on the Fifth. Earlier targets of HUAC had placed their faith in the First Amendment. "Congress shall make no law . . . abridging the freedom of speech . . . or the right of the people peaceably to assemble." A long and honorable tradition of dissent rested on the First.

But in a 1948 Circuit Court of Appeals case, *Barsky et al. v. United States*, Judge E. Barrett Prettyman ruled, "Congress has power to make an inquiry of an individual which may elicit the answers that the witness is a believer in Communism or a member of the Communist Party." A few months later, the Supreme Court refused to review the case. The First Amendment would not apply to HUAC's probes. A stand on the First would therefore result in a citation for contempt of Congress, and in a trial and, probably, a jail sentence.

Pete, knowing all that, refused to take the Fifth.

He didn't want to cast any aspersions on people who had used the Fifth Amendment, Pete wrote in his book *The Incompleat Folksinger*. "I simply did not feel that I wanted to use it myself," he said, "As my lawyer explained it to me, using the Fifth Amendment is in effect saying, 'you have no right to ask *me* this question'; but using the First Amendment means in effect, 'you have no right to ask *any* American *such* questions.' Since I felt I was in a strong enough position to make a broader attack upon the committee, I chose the second course."

That was Pete, just naturally doing the heroic. Those who took the Fifth could only look on with awe and a touch of shame, acknowledging they were of lesser mettle. About the best one could do as a Fifth taker was try to hang on to one's dignity, responding as Lee did, openly to nonincriminating questions, unquaveringly to questions about one's associates and beliefs ("I firmly believe that under the Fifth Amendment I have a right not to be a witness against myself"). Lee didn't feel brave. He felt frightened. But his voice didn't betray him.

Many of the questions HUAC asked both Lee and Pete had to do with the Hays-Lowenfels song "Wasn't That a Time!"

During Lee's testimony, a committee member described it as the song that "deals with Valley Forge, Gettysburg and Bunker Hill" and added, "It sort of ridicules them, doesn't it?" Another asked if it had been written "for the purpose of extending comfort to those who were convicted under the Smith Act case, the 11 who were tried and convicted in Foley Square." Chairman Walter asked, "Did you write that song?" Replied Lee, "I will decline to answer that question, sir, under the privilege of the Fifth Amendment."

Pete was asked again and again whether he'd sung the song at this fund-raiser or that. Pete said he'd be glad to sing the song right there, though he didn't know how well he could do it without his banjo: "I am proud that I have sung for every American, Americans of every political persuasion, and I have never refused to sing for anybody because I disagreed with their political opinion, and I am proud of the fact that my songs seem to cut across and find perhaps a unifying thing, basic humanity, and that is why I would love to be able to tell you about these songs, because I feel that you would agree with me more, sir."

The committee declined Pete's offer, not graciously.

"I'm sorry you are not interested in the song," Pete insisted. "It is a good song."

When the interrogation ended, Pete sang "Wasn't That a Time!" to the assembled reporters and television cameramen, who filmed it for the nightly news.

Harold Leventhal told Pete and Lee it was a hell of a way to get a song on the air.

"It's Almost Day"

1955–1957

There was a dairyman who had a sign in his office, "All that I am I owe to udders." All that I am I owe to the Weavers and to the work I was allowed to do with them and, of course, to the money that accrued from that period and without which I doubt I would have survived at all.

So I am not sympathetic to blasts against "commercialism" or "going commercial," which usually means selling your wares on the open market instead of maintaining the pure life of the artist, starving in a garret.

—LEE HAYS, *taped memoirs*, 1976

*L*ee returned from his HUAC appearance to an empty house. The Robinsons were vacationing on the West Coast.

The usual crank calls alternated with supportive calls from friends. In the days that followed, appreciative letters heavily outnumbered hate mail.

"Mr. Hays, I'll never understand a person like you. Why are you trying to sell us to the Commies, can you honestly believe in the rubbish they tell you? How can you be so stupid? . . ."

"Hi Stupe: What comes over people like you anyway—do you think for one instant that Russia wants a traitor to his or her own country? . . ."

On the other hand, from Allentown, Pennsylvania, came a card thanking Lee "for defending the American way of life and for standing up to Congressman Walter and his—in truth—un-American committee!"

From Manhattan: "My dear Mr. Hays, I wish to tell you I think that your behavior at the hearings was most admirable, and how much I hope that there are more like you. God Bless You."

A postcard: "Dear Mr. Hays: Just to inform you that you did a commendable job at the hearing. You acted like a real American and your efforts to keep the Bill of Rights alive are admirable. More power to you. The American people are behind you."

From the secretary-treasurer of the Socialist party in Nassau and Suffolk counties: "Dear Mr. Hays: Warmest congratulations for your fine defense of freedom before the UnAmerican Committee. The Theater and indeed all who treasure civil liberties owe a very great debt to you for the courage you've shown. . . ." The writer urged Lee to attend the group's annual picnic; Norman Thomas and Bayard Rustin would be there to discuss civil liberties.

Wires and letters poured in from friends around the country.

Earl wrote that Pete's singing on TV "must have been at least a minor sensation." He continued, "Well more power to you, man! I have had many twinges of conscience at being on a vacation and enjoying myself out in God's country while you guys were going through the ordeal. But no doubt my time will come. The old subpoenas-envy again. . . ."

Lee relished a letter from the wrong Lee Hays. The Weaver Lee had written to the actor Lee after the HUAC mix-up, enclosing a picture of himself and giving family data—might they be related? The actor Lee replied that he'd been proudly showing Lee's letter all over town; it was one of the nicest things that had happened to him in many moons. He enclosed two snapshots of himself, family information (they were not related), and a recap of his career. If the Weaver Lee thought he could take the chance and step into the big city without being picked up by the gestapo, maybe they could meet for lunch some day.

Coping with the mail took several weeks.

And then "the long-awaited" was over for Lee. For Pete, an extended aftermath—citation for contempt of Congress, indictment, trial, appeal, the possibility of jail—was still to come.

Despite all the encouraging words, Lee couldn't keep himself from falling into torpor and lassitude. He plunked himself down in front of his TV set, with cans of beer delivered by the nearby mom-and-pop store, and watched until the channels signed off with their sermonettes and, to the music of "The Star-Spangled Banner" or "America the Beautiful," their shots of warplanes, warships, exploding bombs, waving flags.

Among the people who dropped in and watched TV with him were the members of the new family upstairs: my husband and I and our year-old baby, Jeff. We'd just returned to the United States from five years abroad. My husband, Milt, worked for International News Service. He'd been transferred from the post of news editor of the London bureau to that of feature editor of the whole shebang. I did free-lance assignments for newspapers and trade magazines. While out of the country, we'd missed the rise and fall of the Weavers; we'd never been into hoots and folk music or dissident politics; everything about the Robinson menage seemed exotic. So perhaps did we, a Hearst editor and his wife, seem to them. But we loved their music and spirit, and Lee, always fascinated by the media, adopted us at once as his latest "young people." We talked endlessly about news events and their coverage. I became "Sister Doris," Lee's confidante on Robinson household matters. We spoke of perhaps collaborating on article writing.

Eventually, Lee and I would make four albums together, as half of a quartet called the Babysitters, possibly the only children's albums ever recorded in a beer-filled bed–sitting room.

"Uncle Lee" with Tinya, Pete and Toshi Seeger's daughter, at the Seegers' hand-built cabin in Beacon, New York, 1955.

For Lee, the year 1955 dragged unproductively, depressingly on.

Harold Leventhal, worried about the individual Weavers and sick and tired of the blacklist's effects on his friends, hatched a plan. He would get the group together again for a Christmas concert in Carnegie Hall. Every one of them would say no, of course, but if he told each of them that the other three had already said yes . . .

Why did he bring the Weavers together again, Lee asked in an exasperated letter written in 1957, when many of the old tensions and aggravations had resurfaced? Harold sat down and typed out four reasons:

"1. I felt that the group could continue to make a great contribution to our entertainment and musical scene. And I now believe that our concerts and LP have proved this correct.

"2. I knew that all of you wanted to get together again—this was to be the one stimulant, especially for you, Freddie and Ronnie—that would take you out of the depressed inactive state that all of you floundered around in for several years. Yes, this stimulation gave the three of you confidence and assurance that all of you, even on your own, could be productive. . . .

"3. Certainly you and Freddie needed the extra money—in fact the monies earned in the past year have been the only sizable amount that you have earned in many a year. This cannot be discounted.

"4. I felt that even if on a limited scale the Weavers could undertake certain projects, as concert tours and additional recordings. Out of this will come added enthusiasm and new fields for all of you to work as individuals. THERE IS NO CREATIVITY WITHOUT WORK, AS LIMITED AS IT MAY BE."

The Carnegie concert sold out almost as soon as the tickets went on sale. The concert itself was a smash. After the opening number, "Darling Corey," the audience cheered so long the sound could have taken up one side of an album.

They were back; the Weavers were wonderfully, gloriously back. For all the efforts to stamp them out forever, they had overcome, their voices triumphantly ringing out their right to sing, and the audience went crazy with the excitement of it all.

And Lee, who only two years earlier had written Harold that he detested performing so much that it was "almost an obsession," handled the interim comments with his old professionalism.

"Oh, for the good old days when all we had to fear was fear itself. . . ."

"The main thing is to be optimistic. Like the little old lady who didn't have but two teeth in her head. She didn't complain. Said, 'Thank the Lord they're hitters.' "

"Yes, you've got to look at the bright side. I always do. I've been bowled out and balled up. Held down and held up. Bulldogged,

Poster for the 1955 Christmas concert that relaunched the Weavers after three fallow, blacklisted years.

blackjacked, walked on and walked over. Cussed and discussed, lied to and lied about. Boycotted, blacklisted, talked to and talked about. Worked like heck and been worked like heck. Lost all I had and part of my furniture. And friends, the only reason I'm even bothering to stick around is just to see what in hell is going to happen next."

What happened next was decidedly on the bright side. That didn't stop Lee from finding things to bitch about.

The day after the Carnegie concert, Harold's phone began to ring. When would the Weavers sing again? Where would they sing again?

Of course, Harold meant to keep them singing, though Ronnie didn't intend to move back from California and though Pete was ensnarled in post-HUAC legal problems, planning with lawyers how to deal with his inevitable contempt-of-Congress citation.

So clearly did the concert presage new successes that Pete Kameron "reappeared and wanted back in." "We said forget it," Fred recalled later.

Harold booked Carnegie Hall for a spring concert, then began a search for a record company that would produce an album from the concert tapes. He found a willing management at the Vanguard Recording Society, known at that time primarily for its Bach Guild label.

At 11 Cranberry, the energy level rose dramatically. Young musicians who'd attended the Christmas concert came to see Lee as they would a guru. Some, encouraged by Lee, eventually formed groups of their own. Mary Travers, of Peter, Paul, and Mary. Alan Arkin, whose first success was as a member of the Tarriers, singing "The Banana Boat Song."

Downstairs, Earl sat at the piano for hours each day, composing a score for (of all things) a General Motors industrial film, *Giants in the Land.* Under his own name. Hired by the writer of the film, a man Earl didn't know. It was Earl's biggest job in the 1950s. (When the film was screened at GM's Motorama in Chicago, an FBI man spotted Earl's name and questioned a GM executive. The executive, head of GM's industrial films, told the FBI man that he knew nothing about Earl except that he was "a good composer.")

Lee and Earl finally collaborated on a song, "Study and Learn

Together, Side by Side," based on the U.S. Supreme Court decision outlawing segregation in schools.

Lee and Earl and little Jimmy and the black woman who cleaned once a week, Marian Hicks, a powerhouse alto, performed the song at teachers' conventions. Lee introduced Jimmy as his favorite "jubilant delinquent."

Small events became news in the struggle against the blacklist. One such was a recording session where Lee and Fred sang solo verses for a hillbilly tune composed by a musician who once did some work with the Weavers.

"Although it is just a paid job—i.e. no royalties—"Lee wrote to Helen Robinson, "it was so thoughtful of him to think of us. . . . Such small breakthroughs, we think add up to a small change in climate, if only of a degree or two.

"I went into the session with a feeling of suspicion but it all went so well, and musicians and all were so friendly, that I stopped looking around for boogers and concentrated on the job at hand and, I must say, this is the profession for me. . . ." That week, anyway.

Was the climate of oppression beginning to lift ever so slightly?

Having relaunched the Weavers, Harold Leventhal turned his mind to the troubled financial affairs of Woody Guthrie, by now an incurable patient in Brooklyn State Hospital.

Early in 1956, a meeting was held at 11 Cranberry with Harold, Earl, Lee, Pete, Marjorie Guthrie, the International Paper Workers Union leader Lou Gordon ("We always tried to have at least one union leader involved in all our projects," said Harold later), and several others. Still charged by the success of the Weavers' concert, they decided on a benefit concert to raise some money for Woody's children.

Joe Klein, Woody's biographer, described the event:

"The concert, held on March 17, 1956, at Pythian Hall in New York, proved memorable. Millard Lampell prepared a script that interlaced Woody's songs and autobiographical writings, and managed to convey—for the very first time—the awesome diversity of his work. But more than that, the concert was a reunion of sorts—of the Almanac Singers, and the People's Songs gang and the rest of the left-wing music community. For the first time they were all out in the open and celebrating one of their heroes. More than a thousand people filled the hall that night and the program closed with the entire cast singing 'This Land Is Your Land.'

"As the last verse ended, the spotlight swung suddenly to the balcony and settled on a spidery little man with salt-and-pepper hair who struggled to his feet and saluted the audience with a clenched fist—a perfect gesture, quite in keeping with the defiant spirit of the evening. Pete Seeger, tears streaming, began the first verse of 'This Land' again, and now the entire audience was up and cheering the man in the balcony, and singing his song.

"Years later, Seeger and others would look back on the evening as an important moment in the rebirth of the folk music revival. It was more than that, though: it was the beginning of Woody Guthrie's canonization."

After that, "This Land Is Your Land" had mythic meaning, and the Weavers rocked a sell-out audience with their version in the spring concert at Carnegie. (The song led off the Weavers' third album for Vanguard, *The Weavers at Home.*)

From that triumph, they headed for Chicago and a booking that proved that their troubles were far from over.

Variety headlined the event "WEAVERS STINK-BOMBED IN CHI; NEAR SRO 5G" and under a May 22 dateline reported, "A stink bomb that exploded a few minutes before curtain time delayed slightly a concert present Friday night (18) by the Weavers, folk singing quartet, at Orchestra Hall. Group drew a near-capacity 5,000. . . .

"Weavers Peter Seeger and Lee Hays were the subject of an open letter sent out the week before by Edward Clamage, chairman of the anti-subversive committee of the Cook County council of the American Legion. Letter was addressed to the Kemper Insurance Bldg., under the mistaken impression the group was appearing there in the Civic Opera House."

Incompetence can be a form of grace.

On July 26, 1956, the House of Representatives voted 373 to 9 to cite Pete and seven others, including the playwright Arthur Miller and the economist Otto Nathan, for contempt of Congress. Waiting for the next shoe to drop, Pete kept on singing with the Weavers. Their schedule was far from heavy, thanks to Lee.

"After the '55 concert," Fred said, "there was much demand for us. But largely due to Lee's nature, inclination, hypochondria—well he's too tired, whatever— . . . the Weavers would work only on weekends. We'd go up to Kansas City and do a concert on a Friday night, then to Detroit for a Saturday night concert, and then fly back to New York.

"In a way, that's kind of nice, in that you weren't away long enough to collect much dirty laundry, and so you didn't *feel* you were out on the road. But the fact is you can't make any money. The only ones who make money on that are the airlines."

That miffed Fred. Harold had other Lee-generated problems with the Weavers back in action.

"Lee required a lot of extra attention when he was on the road," said Harold. "Check up on the flight—is it air pressured? Maybe he wants a wheelchair when he gets somewhere—he feels tired. [This was twenty years before Lee *needed* a wheelchair.] When I would be on the road with the Weavers, I kind of turned into being his valet.

"The syndrome of the hotels, which he really loved. At some points, it was amusing; at some points, a pain in the ass. And yet I felt this is part of my duty, to take care of the Weavers. Some needed it more, some less. Lee always needed it more."

As for rehearsals, they were something else.

When Lee did come to rehearsals, he'd be there early, said Harold. "Very patiently, he'd stack up the medicines he was taking at the time. Slow. A lot of side talk. Ronnie would say, 'Let's get on with it.' Lee would give all kinds of cockamamy explanations about the medicines.

"Many times, Lee would call me the last minute to say he wouldn't be coming to rehearsal. Half the time, he'd show up anyway. Then there would be rare times when he'd want a special rehearsal called—he'd thought of new material. Very erratic."

One day, years after the Weavers broke up, Lee told Harold about a recurring nightmare—the so-called actor's dream of being unprepared when going onstage. That prompted Harold to say, "My recurring nightmare is that I'm back on the road with the Weavers."

On Tuesday, March 26, 1957, a federal grand jury indicted Pete on ten counts of contempt of Congress. On Friday, he pleaded not guilty before a judge and was released on $1,000 bail, having had no prior offenses. The judge forbade him to travel outside the Southern District of New York without notifying the district attorney where he was going and how he planned to get there.

He had to hurry to notify the district attorney that he would be going on a Weavers tour that started on Saturday in Toronto.

"The Weavers' Reunion Tour," patiently assembled by Harold Leventhal despite Pete's court appearances, Ronnie's baby-sitting problems (her daughter was three), and Lee's complaints, was the kind of tour the group used to dream about. No nightclubs this time. Just concert stages, in cities or at universities. They played to rapturous audiences.

The *Los Angeles Times* reported an "amazingly large crowd of fans that filled Philharmonic Auditorium to capacity." The group's style, it noted, "is marked by a great deal of vigor, and they have their repertoire perfectly and professionally in hand. . . . It took no time at all until the audience joined in a song and soon after began spontaneous hand clapping as the rhythmical accompaniment for some ditty everyone seemed to enjoy. In an atmosphere like this it was easy for the Weavers to maintain a high pitch of acclaim whether they sang work or railroad songs, blues or familiar and unfamiliar folk songs old and new. . . ."

In San Diego, "their audience was with them all the way."

In Salt Lake City, where they wound up the University of Utah's Lecture and Artists Series, they "performed to one of the season's most enthusiastic audiences," said the *Salt Lake City Tribune.* The reporter, clearly not a folkie, disputed the adjective *authentic* in the Weavers' billing: "This swingin', informal, easy-going combo represents top box-office entertainment of the sort one expects in the night club circuits of Las Vegas, New York and Hollywood. The crowd ate it up, and I with them, as sheer entertainment. No one could resist the tuneful, rhythmic, exhilarating performance they brought off."

Even less steeped in folk was a Toronto reviewer, who admitted, "Until last night, when the Weavers weaved their spell over [Massey] Hall and filled everybody with a wonderful sense of informal fun, I had never cared too much for folk-songs, real or spurious. . . . [However,] the Weavers bring a freshness, imagination and spontaneous charm to their work which is downright irresistible.

"One fellow played guitar most of the night and another played the banjo. A stoutish man did most of the introductions and sang bass in the quartet; and a young woman with a rather deep, resonant voice sang solos and in the ensemble. . . ."

The *San Francisco News* reported, "A completely different cross-section of the music-loving public—mostly young people—turned up at Nourse Auditorium last night to hear the Weavers. The show was as extraordinary as the audience. . . . From the moment the four bounced onto the stage and went into their jiggling and vocalizing routine, the audience was with them. Feet were heard tapping out the rhythm. Auditors joined in the singing, by request. Smacked their hands, too—when the music called for such—and loved every minute of it. . . ."

Reviewers and reporters complained that no printed programs were provided, which accounts for some of the vagueness about who sang what. "The senior member of the group, who claimed to be an ex-minister, announced numbers," the San Francisco newspaper noted.

By the tour's end, Harold had enough enthusiastic press clips to produce a hard-selling flyer he mailed to concert halls and colleges across the country.

Vanguard finally released *The Weavers at Carnegie Hall* in April 1957. It became an instant classic, as the Christmas concert itself had become an instant legend.

By September, it ranked third among album best-sellers as listed by *Variety*, behind Decca's sound track of *Around the World in Eighty Days* and Capitol's newest Sinatra album. *Variety* got its numbers from "Sam Goody's, leading New York disk retailer whose global mail order operation reflects not only the national market, but internationally."

Vanguard's management wasn't used to best-selling albums. It looked for more from the Weavers.

"We achieved a real breakthrough with the first album," Lee wrote to Toshi Seeger in late May, when the reunion tour ended, "and Manny [Maynard Solomon, Vanguard's head] is most proud that he helped us to reassert our leadership in our field. Naturally he wants to follow up, now, while the job can be completed. To do this he needs another album of concert tapes, which he knows

The Vanguard Recording Society issued the Weavers records after the 1955 reunion concert. Lee with Vanguard's heads, Seymour (*left*) and Maynard Solomon.

will not be as good as the first one but which will still be a good item. But he also needs a studio-recorded album, a prestige album which can really break through; and he would like to have further albums for release during the year. These would give us a good equity for the future, but of course would still be far from full time work for any of us. . . . If we did some first rate recording, records might even take the place of a tour next year. I thought Pete might like this idea; it would certainly give us a minimum program and cut out the hassle of touring, which seems to be such a drag all the way around. . . ."

Lee was sulking. He couldn't get the others to care as much as he did about producing albums. Solomon wanted—in addition to a concert album and a studio album—perhaps a children's album and certainly "personality" albums, solo recordings from each of the Weavers.

The other Weavers would only agree to work that summer on four singles!

Lee kept pressing various Weavers in notes and letters. In a note to Harold, he finally concluded, "This is the last memo I shall write the Weavers on any subject, and this is why: It doesn't pay. Consider: [a list of particulars on the others' refusal to work on more material to record] As a matter of fact, I doubt whether it is worth my time to go to Beacon for four days, just to work up 4 songs. The whole project begins to get rather boring. Let the other three work up the songs and tell me what to sing, I'll be glad to oblige."

Pete, coping with his legal problems on top of tours and recordings, responded with a tinge of weariness:

"The only sensible thing to do is realize one's limitations, and not try and do everything. Actually, if we can put aside all recriminations, *really* put 'em all aside, I feel we can have a most productive two weeks at least, the four of us. If we can accentuate the positive and eliminate the negative, we can not only prepare six sides for singles, but a Lee Hays Album . . . and perhaps a children's album, though this is more of a moot point.

"I am in favor of rehearsing and recording just as much as we can. I want to dive in with enthusiasm and spend these two or three weeks thinking about nothing but Weavers' work. Eating, sleeping and drinking nothing but Weavers' work. We can make up some new songs, if we can stay on the same track and not get derailed, we can make up some new arrangements.

"I guess you know that the Music Inn concert is going to be the most crowded affair Lenox has ever had. Whole busloads of campers are coming in from miles away for it. So if we really do right by them, there is no reason we can't do right by some recordings. . . ."

The Weavers "did right" at the Lenox, Massachusetts, Music Inn concert in August; they returned for an encore concert in September.

The concerts provided Vanguard with sufficient tapes for a second album, *The Weavers on Tour*.

Of the "Weavers' personality albums," only Ronnie completed

hers. Lee did a great deal of work on one, according to Maynard Solomon, "but in the end he felt the material was not worthy, and scotched the whole thing."

And since he couldn't get the Weavers interested in a children's album, Lee simply started another group, the Babysitters.

If you were around Lee long enough, you couldn't help singing. You were bound to discover music in everything, bound to start making up lyrics to whatever you were doing.

Baby Jeff was served up lyrics with his mashed peas, his bath, his diaper changes.

Lee waited on the second-floor landing for our return from the playground and sang, "Jeffie take a one step, one step, one step/ Jeffie take a one step, he's going home." That got Jeff up the first step. "Jeffie take a two step, two step. . . ."

Jeff, enchanted, began to fill in the last words of each line sung to him by, among others who visited 11 Cranberry, a young musician named Alan Arkin and his wife, Jeremy.

Perhaps, Lee suggested, the Arkins and he and I could tape some of the homemade songs we sang for Jeff. He'd like to try them on Maynard Solomon at Vanguard. Jeremy and I took a giggling fit, the idea seemed so ludicrous; we couldn't sing more than a stanza before breaking up. But Maynard recognized something fresh and real in the tapes and offered a contract for a full album of songs. Jeremy and I continued to giggle and break up each time we stood before the microphone (in Lee's bed–sitting room, equipment supplied by Vanguard)—how could *we* possibly be recording? Musically, I didn't know a third from a seventh and could carry only the simplest tune. ("Doris is the one who makes it sound like real parents singing to real children," Alan said later.) This had to be a figment of Lee's imagination. Lee patiently kept us at it, assigning songs, writing lyrics, coming up with new ideas, trying out songs ("market research") on Jeff and other Brooklyn Heights kids.

The album, accurately described by a Vanguard staffer as "a miracle of engineering," won loving reviews. "Charming," said the *New Yorker;* "uninhibited fun," proclaimed the *New York Times;* "soft sell as a lullaby and just about perfect for the just-out-of-the-nursery-set," wrote *Time* magazine. Nat Hentoff, writ-

In the garden at 11 Cranberry Street, "Uncle
Lee" bouncing Jeff Kaplan, the baby around
whom the Babysitters albums grew. 1956.

ing in the *HiFi Review*, judged it "one of the most successful
and charmingly informal albums of folk songs directed to children."
A reviewer for the *Catholic Messenger* stated, "This is easily the
most popular record, so far as this reviewer's children are concerned,
that has come into the house."

In time there would be three more Babysitters albums. Three
of the four remain in print, still get press.

From the August 1985 issue of *American Baby:* "The Babysitters were a well-known musical group in the sixties. . . . Their three albums, consisting of upbeat and lively songs, are still very popular today. . . ."

Newsday, February 16, 1986: "The Babysitters provided a model for children's music."

And that's what being around Lee could do for you.

It didn't take much looking to find the bright side now. Vanguard was preparing to issue Weavers and Babysitters albums. Leon Bibb, a popular black singer, recorded "Seven Daffodils," a ballad Lee wrote with his sister, Minnie Frank, during her visit to Brooklyn. The Weavers had even managed to sing on television. They'd appeared, along with Mahalia Jackson and Richard Dyer-Bennett, on "Hour of Music," a local Chicago show. The influential *Chicago Sun-Times* columnist Irv Kupcinet wrote that the hour had been "a folk-singing delight . . . worthy of replay on a network." (Needless to say, no network picked up on the suggestion.)

Now something else exciting came up—an "opportunity" to record a jingle for an L&M cigarette commercial! A TV producer at a major advertising agency had sought them out. What a crack in the Great Wall of the blacklist! On behalf of all blacklisted artists, one must put aside one's feelings about commercials and do it, Lee argued. (As for cigarettes, Lee, Ronnie, and Fred all smoked so much they could hardly see one another across a rehearsal room.)

Pete, who had defiantly stood alone on his principles before a congressional committee, was hardly the man to see merit in singing for a cigarette commercial. He argued against the proposal, lost in a majority vote, and stoically recorded the jingle with Lee, Fred, and Ronnie.

He then invited them to join him at Harold's apartment, where he announced he was leaving the Weavers for good, and would have nothing more to say on the subject, ever.

"Around the World"
1957–1963

We can't get everything right these days,
and what's more, we never did.

—LEE HAYS

"*Y*ou may remember the dreadful night I came home after Pete resigned, after doing the cigarette commercial he disapproved of—although that wasn't the total reason for his resignation. I was in tears. You and Milt passed me on the stairs and later came down because you figured I needed company, which was certainly true that night," Lee said to me in 1976.

Fred later thought that too much was made of the commercial, that Pete was beginning to find the Weavers intrusive. "But it *was* a cigarette commercial," added Fred, "and his mother-in-law was dying of lung cancer. By the way, we never did get rich from the commercial."

(They received a recording fee, but their version of the jingle never played on air. Leventhal blamed the blacklist. And indeed, no advertising agency at that time would have jeopardized a major account by producing commercials with such recognizable black-listed voices. More likely, the agency wanted to tape their musicianly version of the jingle. If it worked, the agency could rip it off by recording it with nonblacklisted singers.)

In an interview for this book, Pete said, "The commercial may have been the specific thing that led to my resigning, but for a couple of years I felt I just couldn't keep on going. I had a family, and my own singing was going fairly well, and I was teaching, too, and to also sing in a quartet was impossible. I wasn't giving it my full attention and didn't feel particularly happy about just coasting along. Maybe if we hadn't been blacklisted it would have been different. . . ."

Lee came around to believing that, once the Weavers were successful, Pete felt he'd proved a point: "Pete had said there's something that makes you want to compete and see if you can do as well as the next fellow. Having proved it, he was ready to go on to something else.

"It came out in the guise of going ahead to do something pure and noble, which had the effect of making the rest of us feel guilty as hell for going on, as if we were doing something wrong, as if he were telling us we were doing something wrong. It took quite a while to get over that hump. He just walked out on us, and it was a terrible blow. I was dissolved to jelly the night it happened. I hadn't expected it, and he refused to discuss it."

(In a continuation of his pique, Pete signed over 50 percent of his "royalties" on the commercial to *Sing Out!*, the left-wing folk magazine. Presumably, Pete meant residuals. Either way, the expected gusher turned out to be a dry hole.)

It constantly irritated Lee that Pete acted on his anticommercial principles so righteously and at the same time built such solid success in the marketplace.

Pete had his own following. None of the others did.

There was something else that only Pete had.

"It's my theory," said Lee, "that one essential element made the group something no other group was: Pete's enormous knowledge and experience and his fantastic accumulation of songs. When I first met him, he made up a list of songs he knew—I was astonished—he knew as many as three hundred, enough songs to keep a dozen quartets in business for a lifetime. An invaluable element, his ability to trot out a song. . . .

"So when Pete left, he took away with him much of our stock in trade, as was his right to do. . . . But there was extreme bitterness all the way around, which could be said to be a result of seeing our meal ticket vanish or possibly realizing that from now on we would have to work ten times as hard to accomplish the same goals. . . ."

For years, Lee brooded about this third, and most public, break with Pete.

In 1976, he had a dream about talking to Pete: "In my dream, I said to him, 'You know, the Weavers never amounted to a damn after you left.' And he paused and thought about it and said, 'That's true.' "

Not everybody thought that was true. The Weavers had five more productive years ahead, touring, turning out albums, turning on new young audiences, pushing the folk music revival forward, inspiring new groups.

Fred thought the characteristic stamp of the Weavers came from Lee, not from Pete. "When Pete left," he said, "we were able to get a replacement and maintain the Weavers. We couldn't have maintained the Weavers without Lee. Of the four of us, only Lee was irreplaceable."

Pete's departure created an immediate problem—the completion of the Weavers' third album for Vanguard. This would be the prestige studio-recorded album that Maynard and Seymour Solomon wanted so badly. An album's worth of songs with Pete had been recorded, but they didn't program well. Additional songs had to be done.

Pete proposed Erik Darling, a twenty-three-year-old banjo player who with Alan Arkin formed two-thirds of a young folk group called the Tarriers. Erik's high tenor voice and dazzling banjo technique might add an exciting new element to the album. Pete was right. Lee, Fred, and Ronnie were sufficiently happy with Erik's work on *The Weavers at Home* to invite him to join the group permanently. (But the album cover showed the four original Weavers; Erik got a mention as "guest artist" on the back cover.)

Like many young banjo players in America, Erik idolized Pete. He could hardly believe that Pete had nominated him as his successor. A daunting assignment, stepping into Pete's shoes.

Musically, Erik worked splendidly.

A superb musician, a demonically hard worker, a perfectionist, with much new material to contribute, Erik brought a whole new vitality to the group.

Years later Don McLean, in taped conversations with Lee, his mentor, talked at length about the Weavers' role in American music. He assessed Erik's contribution as follows: "Good new material, everything from 'Jerusalem' to 'The Virgin Mary,' foreign songs, wonderful banjo breakdowns that Pete couldn't handle, because Pete didn't play that way and Erik could. . . . The group snapped to attention a little bit. There was a sense of real shock harmonies. The group . . . didn't have the heart that it had before, but it had a lot of that heart and a lot more bite."

Fred called some of the records made with Erik "marvelous, absolutely wonderful. There were certain tensions with Erik, but musically he was wonderful."

Philosophically, Erik couldn't have been a greater mismatch. Even though the Weavers sang more gospel than protest at this stage, though time and events had somewhat frayed their radicalism anyway, where they came from was essential to the spirit of their music. Erik's musical idol might be Pete Seeger, but his philosophical idol was Ayn Rand, the apostle of superman individualism versus "government interference" in citizens' lives. Politically, that translated into hard-core conservatism.

Well, that mattered offstage, not onstage. The Weavers, the idea of the Weavers, represented something terribly important to their young college audiences, just emerging from the miasma of the Eisenhower years, just realizing the appalling dangers of the McCarthy years. This group, this terrific group, which couldn't get on the air, was blacklisted, and went right on singing—God, wasn't it something?

Every performance ended with a standing, shouting ovation, the kids' eyes filled with tears of excitement and gratitude and pride. Everybody just knew, as young Don McLean knew at the time, that "the Weavers lived the life they sang about."

Not that any of them felt guilt about earning money. Really, none of them ever had, outside of Pete. If anything, they worried about not earning enough. Their albums remained blacklisted, hobbling royalty payments. The weekend flights and hotels cost almost as much as they received in booking fees. Working as a Weaver limited other earning possibilities. Ronnie had split from her husband; every one of the group had bread-winning responsibilities.

"I had no strong opposition to making money doing a cigarette commercial or any kind of a commercial," Lee owned.

Although the L&M commercial hadn't gone anywhere, Lee still felt that any assignment from an advertising agency helped under-

Philadelphia, where customers shouted them down.

In March, there was a concert on the campus of Oklahoma A & M, their first concert outside of Town Hall. What a relief after nightclubs and hotels! God, if only they could do concerts instead of clubs! Ironically, the hated blacklist eventually gave them that wish.

Also in March, they played a little club in New Jersey and another round at the Blue Note. Then came weeks and months of nothing.

On June 24, they sang at a private party at the Indianapolis Country Club, honoring the president of an Indianapolis steel company, a fan of their music. Lee saved the program, a brochure entitled "Papers from the Life of C. Harvey Bradley," with reproductions of his birth certificate, Marine Corps honorable discharge, his diploma from Yale, his marriage license, and so on, plus the menu, from green turtle soup through baked Alaska, and the names of the entertainers—Lilly Quartet and the Weavers. The program made Lee chuckle, but the memory that this party was their sole June booking was enough to make him wince.

In August, they played a club in Elko, Nevada, and a small club in Los Angeles. Nothing else followed until late October, when they sang at an Omaha club named Angelo's, a small club in Detroit, and a beer convention in Detroit.

They had no other bookings until their year-end concert, their last, at Town Hall. After that they had to take a sabbatical, said Lee, which turned into a "Mondical" and a "Tuesdical."

try. When the money ran out, he returned to the East Coast. There he would find a chorus to lead, students to teach. In Los Angeles, a blacklisted artist felt a terrifying sense of isolation. The Robinsons had many friends and relations in New York. One needed plenty of warmth at a time like this.

Lee had known Earl since Almanac days, when Earl wrote "The Lonesome Train" with Millard Lampell of the Almanacs. He liked the prospect of moving in with the Robinsons. He didn't know that they would be his family for the next nine years.

It just seemed that, the way things were going, Lee and Earl both would have plenty of time to write. Since Lee wrote lyrics and Earl music, mightn't they develop into a team?

Alas, events so agitated Lee that he couldn't begin to focus on songwriting. Who'd sing his songs? Where?

In January, the Weavers played Daffy's Bar on the outskirts of Cleveland. Daffy couldn't care less about the blacklist. But while they sang at Daffy's, another storm cloud gathered.

The Cleveland Press Club organized a telethon to benefit the Cleveland Area Heart Society. Invited to appear, the Weavers accepted. As soon as their names were announced, the by now expected happened. Protests poured in. The press club, upholders of freedom of speech, refused to cancel the Weavers. Politicians and other performers scheduled to appear on the telethon called in sick, or to say their cars had broken down. Protesters jammed the switchboard, so that pledges for the Heart Fund couldn't get through.

On February 6 and 7, Harvey Matusow testified before HUAC, swearing under oath (falsely) that Pete, Fred, and Ronnie were members of the Communist party and that Lee had been, but quit.

Matusow's testimony delivered the coup de grace.

The American Legion intensified its campaign to eliminate Weavers records from circulation.

By 1953, Decca had not only stopped recording the Weavers but also deleted their old records from its catalog. Later, in folk boom times, Decca reissued the records, profitably.

Odds and ends of bookings trailed through the remainder of 1952. In February, they sang in a little bar in a dumpy hotel in mine the blacklist. Thus he gladly agreed to write jingles for other products when asked by the producer of the L&M commercial. The fees started small but promised to increase substantially if the commercials went national.

And so, with Erik on some assignments, with Alan Arkin on others, with me occasionally—Lee wrote singing commercials for Gold Medal flour, Betty Crocker pancake mix, Old Manse syrup, Red Star flour, Falstaff beer, and Chock Full o' Nuts new frozen doughnuts.

Of course, jingle writers aren't credited publicly, so who would know? However, for fear and trembling, advertising agencies take the cake. The producer did take some risk, hiring blacklisted talent to work on his agency's biggest accounts. Lee in return crafted each jingle as caringly as he did his songs.

As Pete used to say, there's something that makes you want to compete and see if you can do it as well as the next fellow. That applied to commercials too, in Lee's book. Alas, none of his jingles "went national." Few do.

One notices that Lee, during the blacklist era, kept upping the ante on his religious background. In biographical material, he rises from "son of a Methodist minister," to "itinerant preacher," to "former Methodist minister," to "following his father, a bishop of the Methodist Church, to many of the church assemblies throughout Arkansas-Missouri regions."

Lee would sometimes tell the story of a visiting preacher, arriving at a country home, who was urged by the good woman of the house to take some food. The preacher kept saying, "No thank you, sister, I never eat before I preach." He wouldn't even eat supper before they went to evening services for his first sermon. On the way home, somebody asked the woman how she liked the sermon. She replied, "In my opinion, he might just as well have et."

And for all the good Lee's religious citings did in blacklist days, he might just as well have et.

Lee looked on writing commercials as an exercise in craft; "selling out" applied to quite different matters. He drew the line some yards beyond Pete's line, but he drew it firmly.

One night (in the post-Pete era), Jack Paar announced that the

Weavers would guest star on his show the following night. The switchboard, as they say, lit up. Protests swamped NBC. Paar considered the situation and decided to let the Weavers come on anyway, *if* they signed loyalty oaths.

Lee later said, "It seemed so ridiculous. If we were truly subversive we'd have signed anything."

Don McLean, sixteen at the time of the Paar incident, subsequently told Lee, "The next night, it was announced you wouldn't be appearing, and there was a little Associated Press release that went out that you had refused to sign loyalty oaths. I was so looking forward to seeing you on that show. And then you were going to play at the College of New Rochelle, and you were also canceled out of that. The father in a Catholic girls' school said, 'Wait a minute, we know about these people. They're not going to corrupt our kids.' So whether Pete was in the group or not, the group itself was going through the same experience."

In 1959, for the first time since the McCarthy era, the government eased up on the issuance of passports.

Then how about an international tour?

Out of the past came Pete Kameron, now in business as a booking agent, waving proposals for concerts and recording sessions and broadcasts abroad. The Weavers swallowed hard and accepted Harold's hardheaded assessment that such a tour would bring fresh honors, new audiences, additional recordings, a welcome boost to the exchequer, and a splendid opportunity to junket in Europe and the Middle East. (As for Harold, he meant to use his brand-new passport to visit India instead.)

And so Harold and PK sat down to talk about logistics. They settled on an end-of-May departure for England, following the Weavers' first post-Pete Carnegie Hall concert.

Meanwhile, the Weavers maintained a busy weekend schedule. In March, for example, they flew to Cleveland (sponsored by the Cleveland Opera Association) the first weekend; to Toronto, where they packed Massey Hall, the second weekend; to Troy, New York, where Skidmore coeds filled the auditorium, on the third weekend. Wherever they sang, they brought the audiences to their feet.

Between weekends, Lee recorded commentaries for a weekly show sponsored by Vanguard Records on station WBAI-FM, choosing material from Vanguard catalogs and writing scripts to introduce the singers and the songs.

What would happen to the show when he went abroad? Lee proposed to Maynard that Alan Arkin take over as host. Alan could produce very exciting shows, Lee promised. If his own name had value, the show might go on as "Listening with Lee Hays," with a statement from him like this: "This is Lee Hays, all right, but I don't know where I am at the moment, could be Tel Aviv, Istanbul or Llandudno. But I left some records at home and while I'm gone my partner Alan Arkin is going to be listening to them. . . . Alan is an actor, singer, writer, husband, father, and chief Babysitter. . . ."

Lee hoped to keep his franchise. But most of Vanguard's artists had already been featured on the show, and the company was ready to wrap it up. Lee, always ready with self-criticism, feared he'd lost the show's audience because his commentaries were riddled with long and frequent pauses. Here was another small failure to brood about. For years, people had told him he ought to be a disc jockey. He'd never thought so, he told Maynard, and his experience on WBAI made him sure of it.

Nonetheless, 1959 was one of the busiest years of Lee's life. Tours, the WBAI series, albums, and writing, writing, writing. Songs, commercials, press material for the tours, an introduction to a Weavers songbook that Harper's would publish, a major article on folk music for *The Elektra Folk Song Kit* (an Elektra Records softcover aimed at the exploding market of young guitar pickers), a regular column in the local *Brooklyn Heights Press*.

And, for good measure, several short stories yellowing with age were bought by Lee's old fan and *Ellery Queen* editor, Bob Mills, who had changed jobs and now edited *Mercury Mystery Magazine* and *Bestseller Mystery Magazine*.

Lee had sent his "Little Sam and Opal" stories to Mills back in the *Ellery Queen* days. Mills had returned them with a letter saying they were the best stories ever to come across his desk, but they violated existing taboos and he could not publish them. Little Sam, a girl, and Opal, a boy (reflecting common southern practices in nomenclature), were murderously amoral children.

"There had been a number of stories about child murderers,"

said Lee in his memoirs, "but they always got caught, and mine didn't. They got hauled off to the arms of a psychiatrist, and mine didn't."

Times had changed. Mills printed them as written, though he wished Lee would inject a "fantasy gimmick." Lee declined. "The stories are fantastic enough," he wrote to Mills, "being extrapolations in which children carry out to most logical, if murderous, conclusions, the very attitudes of the adult world in which they lived and from which they took their mores." In any case, he continued, "the very act of heightening bare facts is an act of fantasy; and if I am honest, I have to say that I never told a story in my life in which I did not elaborate upon the facts. Because if there is one thing I have learned during my tours of duty with the Weavers in nightclubs, on records, in theaters and concert halls, a song or a story or any work of art does not exist, has no entity or being at all, until the artist has delivered it to an audience of seeing eyes and hearing ears and perceiving minds, to be translated into personal experience and thereby joined to life."

Lee showed the stories to some young neighborhood people in the 1970s and reported, "The kids can't make head or tail out of them because they are a little bit obscure, not always clear as to who killed who and how, which of course is the point of the exercise."

Grown-ups, including Mills and Fred Hellerman, have tended to think of Lee's "Little Sam and Opal" stories as classics.

On top of everything else, Lee had to move himself and his few belongings out of the Robinson household. The family needed his space for Pop Wortis, Helen's old father, recently widowed and growing senile. Lee chuckled every time the old man addressed him as Leo. Nobody chuckled when Pop Wortis wandered to the front door, muttering that the FBI had a car out front, waiting for him. "All the old worries came up again," said Earl.

The Robinsons were Lee's last live-in family. Neighbors took up some of the slack. Lee briefly lived in cramped quarters on the third floor of a rickety wooden house on Middagh Street, in Brooklyn Heights. A young CBS reporter named Charles Kuralt lived on the second floor with his wife and young daughter. Their neighborliness would one day result in the Weavers' appearing on network television, thirty years after being blacklisted. If it hadn't been for Lee's interval on Middagh Street, that would never have happened at all.

Billboard, reviewing the spring concert in Carnegie Hall, reported, "The house was packed with so many stage seats that there was hardly room for Lee Hays, Fred Hellerman, Ronnie Gilbert and newcomer Erik Darling. The predominantly teen-aged audience responded warmly to the 'Folksongs Around the World' format. . . . The group's vitality seems to increase with time."
The Weavers, minus Pete, were doing just fine.

Dashing off an introduction to *The Weavers' Songbook* before the group departed for its international tour, Lee wrote, "As we end our first ten years of work we feel that we are just beginning. Decades to come cannot be more exciting and rewarding than the first one."
Indeed, the decades to come were *not* more exciting and rewarding than the first one.
The songbook introduction also spoke of the Weavers' expectations for the tour: "It will be a musical trip part way around the world, at least, and we will visit the home grounds of many of the songs we sing. We have learned that in some of the places we shall visit, such as Israel, our songs are already known, and that American folk songs have a greater audience in Europe than ever before. . . ."
Lee's forecast proved only partially right. As for the group dynamics, Lee's almost daily letters to Harold tell the story:
May 27—"We have been here a day and a half and already half the group detests the other half, so everything is normal. . . . I hear we are to do 6 songs on the radio Saturday in a show with a fairly bad local reputation. . . . I don't know why PK has to come here at all, unless he has other business; we can do the songs and fly to Israel without any further coaching or direction. . . . I am sure there will be few if any rehearsals. . . ."
May 28—"Haven't seen the Weavers as a group for days, it seems. . . ."
May 29—"There is a rehearsal this morning, and it is about time, but I wish it had been scheduled earlier. . . ."

June 1—"We did the radio show this morning. We sang fairly well, but learned that the show is a two hour melange of rock and roll, which is hardly the setting for our music. Some of our folk song friends were dismayed that we were on the show at all. . . ."

June 3—"We have begun work on the ep [extended play] recording and have discussed the 13 week series for Radio Luxembourg. It seems to me that such a series is almost impossible; but the others view it as a snap. . . ."

June 4—"PK has persuaded us to take on a tour with [Lonnie] Donergan in Sept., on the grounds that we are so unknown that we need Donergan's pull. . . ."

June 8—"We had lunch and a visit with Ron Bell today and learned how little known we are. . . ."

As dates fell into place, Lee realized that the Weavers would be abroad all summer and into the fall. How much trouble would it be for Harold's office to mimeograph a weekly newsletter to a list of about forty-five or fifty people? He was eager to share his sightseeing experiences with everyone he knew.

Harold immediately arranged for publication and distribution to Lee's friends of "A Newsletter From LEE HAYS," consisting of comments on the tour (or The Tour).

Here are excerpts from two of the newsletters, for the flavor of their stay in Israel:

". . . We are headed for the Ein Gev kibbutz, and to get there we turn around the lake and go north on a narrow strip of concrete through fields of tobacco, under the Syrian Hills not a hundred yards away. On the top we see the Syrian army buildings from which they fired down on the kibbutzim. We come to a sign: WARNING. BORDER. DO NOT PROCEED. And we turn into the Ein Gev.

"Ein Gev is an outpost. Here a handful of people stood against an army. . . . We see bomb shelters, twenty rooms under heaped-up earth, a surgery still equipped, a newspaper room, school, nursery. Here these people survived planes, cannons, snipers. . . . Now there is a fish cannery, and boats which go fishing when it is safe. . . . But the amazing thing about this little community on the shores of Galilee is that it has become a music center, and there is a music shed modelled after that at Tanglewood holding

Lee at the Tower of London during the Weavers'
international tour in 1959.

3000 people, with room for 2000 more outside! Symphony orches-
tras come here. Bernstein gave the first concert and has returned.
Koussevitsky was here. . . . Here are the names of Marian Ander-
son, Isaac Stern, European artists—and now the Weavers. We are
so near the Syrians that the cars and buses coming in from the

kibbutzim might alarm them, so they have to notify the army that the Weavers are coming. They do this through the UN commission here, members of which also attend from Jordan and Syria. The Israel army is in attendance, with jeeps, walkie-talkies, guards at the door. We are told that the Syrians are up there listening, and my only regret is that we do not know a Syrian song. The huge audience is just sensational, though there are fewer English-speaking people than in the cities, as I can tell at once when some of my jokes fall flat. And it is hotter than the hinges of hell. . . ."

". . . We are doing lousy performances, but the audiences get more demonstrative. The audience likes a song, applauds, then decides it likes the song very much, whereupon out of nowhere comes a rhythm to the handclapping, as stunning as anything I ever heard, and with no Pete Seeger to lead, either. . . ."

Fred remembered their two months in Israel, averaging one concert a day, as "a marvelous, triumphant tour. After all, the Weavers' hit record, 'Tzena, Tzena,' based on an Israeli song, had kind of given international validation to Israel soon after independence. So the Weavers were heroes in Israel."

Even Lee, in his personal letters to Harold, couldn't find anything to grumble about: "Hal, we did two great shows in Jerusalem. . . . Restores the faith a bit. My ad libs improve as we go along— many good laughs. The Weavers are almost human at times. . . . Joan D. [Erik's wife, with him on the tour] improves. Erik performs better each day. PK is relaxed—pockets full of money, why not? Fred is very funny—offstage. Ronnie is Ronnie is Ronnie. . . ."

After Israel, they headed for Italy; a newsletter from Lee dated August 4 tells a desultory story: "My first news is that there ain't any. This is not exactly a triumphal tour through Europe, due to circumstances within our control. So we wait, and wait, and spend money, and wait, and go broke quickly while waiting for pick-up jobs here and there which may or may not come through. . . ."

Pretour assurances of bookings in Italy and France proved will-o'-the-wisps; the Weavers discovered they were not at all known in those countries.

Harold had urged them to return after the Israel tour. Lee had insisted they hang on in Europe while waiting for September bookings in England. He had prevailed over those Weavers who argued

that the September bookings weren't worth waiting for. Their attitude, if not their words, now proclaimed, "I told you so."

"I would like to have a chance to reconsider that decision,"
Lee wrote Harold from Milan, "but facing Ronnie on this point,
in her vile mood, is too much to ask for. . . . I am sorry that the
others have not written you so that you could get a better picture
than I can give you. I do not move in the circles that attract half
of this group, both by choice and lack of invitation, so I can't
really say what Fred and Ronnie think about anything much. . . ."

In late September, they played two weekends of concerts with
Lonnie Donergan, having been jobless in Europe through August
and half of September.

The British concerts were okay, said Fred, "but we didn't set
the country on fire, as we did in Israel."

A splendid surprise awaited Lee on the Weavers' return to New
York at the end of September. Harold Leventhal and friends had
found him a new Brooklyn Heights apartment, at 19 Pierrepont
Street, and furnished it for him, simply but comfortably. They
then topped the gesture by getting him a brand-new Smith-Corona
electric portable typewriter—"so much fun to operate that I am
like a kid with a toy," Lee told friends.

To hail the heroes who had conquered Israel (and to ease the
pain of the European fiasco), Harold rented a big black Cadillac
for the Weavers' first concert of the new season, at the University
of Vermont in Burlington.

Lee described the event in his year-end newsletter to friends:
"You can imagine the reaction among the campus folkniks when
we arrived. You could hear the whispers going down the line:
Weavers—Cadillac—Cadillac—Cadillac! Made me think of the
whorehouse madam who, one Sunday morning, said to the girls:
'Let's put on our best gowns and hire a buggy and drive right
past the Methodist church!' Funniest bit was when we stopped
for gas and Harold, who was driving, couldn't tell the man where
to put the gas in at. Took them five minutes to find the hole. . . ."

Lee expressed a new concern in the newsletter: "We rehearse
every week, some weeks. Almost every week we have a college
concert and they are the best kind. But the group is not as productive
as it should be, and we work too slowly. I begin to wonder, as

we grow older and relatively more successful, whether it is true that the best group is the hungry group. I would not like to re-live the hungry years of my life; but sometimes I think they were more creative."

Picking up on this theme, Don McLean told Lee later, "One thing I'll say for Pete is that he's tried to stay hungry even when he didn't have to be. I've often wondered why anyone would do that. But I can see why, from his perspective, it's very important."

Lee's demons were at it again, some self-destructive inner com-pulsion that drove him to bitch about the productivity of the Weav-ers when he was the one who made rehearsals impossible.

"These are laughable things when you're removed from them," Fred said, "but when you have to live with them . . . when you have a rehearsal scheduled for nine o'clock in the morning, and at eight-thirty you get a call, 'Well, I can't make it today,' and he's obviously just hung over, and when more than half the rehears-als were called off because of that . . . well, I began to lose patience with that."

Erik lost patience sooner. As a perfectionist, he took pride in the way the Weavers' songs were "worked like a piece of fine steel." But he hadn't the proprietary interest in the Weavers that Fred and Ronnie had. He threw in the towel in 1962.

The Weavers had replaced Pete, and they probably could replace Erik. Though (deep collective groan) what a pain to have to break in someone new.

They sifted candidates and selected a young Chicago folkie, Frank Hamilton. Oriented toward purist folk music, Hamilton simply didn't fit in with the Weavers' way of reworking songs to make them their own.

The new vitality Erik had inspired began to drain away.

Lee could still excite an audience, make them feel part of the struggle, by singing "Wasn't That a Time!" and bringing them news of Pete's post-HUAC activities.

Pete had been tried for contempt of Congress in March 1961, found guilty on ten counts, and sentenced to a year and a day in federal prison. In May 1962, a court of appeals dismissed the case on a technicality. Pete was free, but without toppling HUAC's right to probe a citizen's political beliefs. Nonetheless, his battle for his principles raised Pete to heroic stature, especially among college students.

Pete, he of what Lee sometimes called the *meshuggeneh* ideas and actions, kept on climbing higher in the esteem of those whose esteem one would want. And though he came out of the Almanacs, out of the Woody Guthrie and Leadbelly times, Pete was as contemporary as Bob Dylan and Joan Baez.

The Weavers, meanwhile, were beginning to just go through the motions.

Out of the hospital for an afternoon in 1962, Woody Guthrie is entertained by a gathering of his friends at One Sheridan Square, the old Cafe Society Downtown, in Greenwich Village. *Left to right, standing,* Arlo Guthrie, Will Geer, Cisco Houston, Lee Hays, Millard Lampell; *seated,* Woody Guthrie, his daughter Nora, and Blind Sonny Terry.

Frank Hamilton, another kid who idolized Pete, lasted a year. In the Hamilton period, the Weavers did some fine recording— "every bit as good as anything they ever did with Seeger," in Don McLean's opinion. They added some new songs, such as "Get Up, Get Out," "Brazos River," and "Yerakina."

Bernie Krause, who replaced Hamilton on Lee's recommendation, simply didn't work out at all.

But early in 1963, the Weavers didn't suspect that Bernie wouldn't make it. They planned to introduce him at their Carnegie Hall concert in May. Erik and Frank agreed to join them in performance. So did Pete.

Tickets for two nights of "The Weavers Reunion at Carnegie Hall" sold out in a day; to those who hadn't scored, getting tickets became an obsession.

For the usual emotional and political and musical reasons, the concerts were bound to be an event. Then a new development fanned the flames. An article in *Variety* on April 11, 1963, tells the story:

" 'Hootenanny,' a weekly folk music program that began April 6 on the ABC television network, might be greeted with some sense of gratification that at last the music is reaching a mass audience. But the show has sour undertones which put it out of harmony with its title. Pete Seeger, the Weavers and others are to be excluded because they are on a blacklist.

"Television was born during the Cold War and came by the blacklist congenitally. Hundreds of performers, writers and directors have been excluded from the networks because their names appear on a list of persons whose present or former opinions might offend the American Legion. Despite some easing of the blacklist in movies, it continues in force on TV. There is a particular irony in Seeger's case. He and Woody Guthrie resurrected the word 'hootenanny' from the folk lexicon (it's not in the dictionary) and used it as the title for folk music jam sessions.

"Also, Seeger has been the inspiration for about every teenage banjo picker in the last 20 years. He is to folk music what Charlie Parker was to modern jazz.

"In the entertainment business, the blacklist is denied in public and deplored in private, but nobody does anything about it. The 'Hootenanny' case may be an exception. . . ."

All the Weavers who ever were came together for the May 1963 "Weavers Reunion at Carnegie Hall." *From left*, Bernie Kraus, Erik Darling, Frank Hamilton, Ronnie Gilbert, Lee, Fred Hellerman, and Pete Seeger. (Photo by Norman Vershay)

The writer, Robert E. Light, went on to report why the show might be an exception. Joan Baez had refused to perform on learning of Seeger's exclusion. Numerous other folk singers and musicians planned to protest. Student groups (the show was filmed before student audiences) organized boycotts.

After weeks of press coverage, protests, and negotiations, the producer of the show called a press conference to say that he couldn't hire everyone and that he'd decided after listening to Pete's records, "He just can't hold an audience."

And so, here the Weavers were, reunited, still blacklisted, Pete having walked barefoot over the live coals of the HUAC experience, the "Hootenanny" business a fresh wound. Every song stirred with new meaning. This concert, the impassioned audience knew, was the stuff of history.

Don McLean later described it as "a stirring and fabulous event that made [him] want to devote [his] life to music. It was the overwhelming sense of life as music on the stage."

No more than the Weavers themselves did he realize that the group was nearing the end of its run.

"Lonesome Traveler"

1963–1965

I am a lonely and a lonesome traveler,
I am a lonely and a lonesome traveler,
I am a lonely and a lonesome traveler,
I've been a-travelin' on.

I traveled here—and then I traveled yonder,
Well, I traveled—here and then I traveled yonder,
Well, I traveled—here and then I traveled yonder, well,
I've been a-travelin' on.

I traveled cold—and then I traveled hungry, well,
I traveled cold—and then I traveled hungry, well,
I traveled cold—and then I traveled hungry,
I've been a-travelin' on.

Traveled with the rich, traveled—with the poor,
Traveled with the rich, traveled—with the poor,
Traveled with the rich, traveled—with the poor,
I've been a-travelin' on.

One of these days I'm gonna—stop all my travelin',
One of these days I'm gonna—stop all my travelin',
One of these days I'm gonna—stop all my travelin',
I've been a-travelin' on.

Gonna keep a-trav'lin—on the road to freedom,
Gonna keep a-trav'lin—on the road to freedom,
Gonna keep a-trav'lin—on the road to freedom,
Gonna keep right on a-travelin' home.

—Words and music by LEE HAYS

"*D*unaway makes Pete into a Hamlet figure, which is not the Pete I know," Lee wrote to the filmmaker Jim Brown on the publication in 1981 of David Dunaway's biography of Seeger. "I see no point in what's called 'psycho-history' and dwelling on the frustrations of life; it's the bright side of the mirror that does the work."

Pete quickly wrote to give "eternal thanks" to Lee "for that great line, 'it's the bright side of the mirror that does the work.' "

Unfortunately, it's the dark side of the mirror that can play havoc with one's work.

Was Lee, in criticizing Dunaway, concerned about Pete's image (which Pete himself has never worried about, and which—therefore?—seems to grow ever more heroic), or was he letting us know how he would like his own life presented?

But how, omitting "psycho-history," can one explain the end of the Weavers? And weren't the same forces at work within Lee at the time of the Almanacs, and in the argumentative days at People's Songs, and during the besotted absences from the Village Vanguard? And later, when Lee wouldn't stop smoking after he'd lost a toe to blocked circulation, and then a leg, and then the other?

How could anyone fail to see a pattern of self-destructiveness?

Only much later would the pattern be presented as something quite different.

The person who would feel the most betrayed, the most bereft, the most fearful of the future, in the Weavers' end, was Lee. And yet the person who most surely caused the end to come about was also Lee.

His inability or unwillingness to be on the road for longer than a weekend severely limited the earning power of the group. Fred and Ronnie turned to other projects. Fred worked successfully as a record producer, arranger, recording musician. Ronnie had reimmersed herself in an earlier passion—the theater. Lee resented their unwillingness to give all their attention to the Weavers. ("Some of us were too busy with other matters to give time to the work of the group," Lee angrily wrote Harold.) Was that behind his tormenting Fred (and the others, but Fred had the least patience for this) by phoning fifteen minutes before rehearsal to say he couldn't possibly make it? Over and over again?

Fred told Harold he absolutely could bear it no longer. He had no interest in giving it another chance. The final nail was the way Lee, who'd suggested Bernie in the first place, turned on him when he didn't work out. Why try to go on?

Harold had held the group together with baling wire and funny little comments that made them feel like asses any time one threatened to quit. Now even he saw that the Weavers should ring down the curtain while the audiences were still cheering. He didn't worry about Fred and Ronnie; they had youth and health and energy and superb musicianship, and they hadn't blown it. They would find new directions, and they wouldn't be burdened psychologically with guilt. Lee had never been young; the only time he'd made a living was as a Weaver; he would surely feel remorse for having exacerbated group tensions.

Harold decided to bill their scheduled bookings as "farewell appearances." Before he sat Lee down to tell him that the time had come for the group to disband, he gave thought to a number of projects he hoped Lee would embrace. Lee hardly listened to Harold's suggestions, so stunned was he by the news.

He turned on Harold.

It seemed clear to him (he wrote to Harold in November, from Los Angeles, where the newspapers and radio were announcing the farewell appearances) that the dissolution had been decided months earlier—that Harold's mind had been "made up sometime in August or before." He was irate that a press release had gone out attributing the dissolution of the group to *his* retirement. That was "a damned lie," and he was saying so to concert audiences. He regretted having gone into rehearsals after Labor Day "on the false premise that we were planning to continue." He would be pleased if illness forced the cancellation of all future concerts. That was harsh, he said, but it was a "true statement" of his "resentment over the almost total collapse of morale in the group, for who can ride a dead horse?"

The projects Harold had suggested, Lee went on, interested him not at all: "Only one thing interests me now, trying to learn how to plug my songs without paying tribute to Sanga [Harold's music publishing house]. . . . Why should I not become my own publisher?" Moreover, Harold's "constant bridling at even the slightest criticism of [his] staff and office procedure" suggested that Harold must have "some sizeable problems there, or [he] would not be so sensitive and defensive." Not that it mattered. Their working relationship in the future would be "minimal." And so on, "love, Lee."

On reading the letter, Harold reacted as always—with a shrug, a grin (Lee would be Lee), no rancor, amusement at the concept of Lee's becoming his own publisher. Lee could no more be his own publisher than he could be his own doctor. Harold wouldn't respond to the letter, wouldn't even acknowledge receiving it. Let Lee's anger blow over. He would quickly enough recognize that he couldn't go it alone. And Harold would be there for him, always.

By February of 1964, Lee had sufficiently cooled off to write a newsletter, circulated to Lee's mailing list by Harold's unvituperative office.

Nineteen sixty-three, Lee related, "was a year when I had another career shot out from under me. I refer to the dissolution of the Weavers. No, that's the wrong word; *that* took place earlier. I mean the official ending of the group. We have had so many notes of condolence that this is the only way I can answer them. There are a number of opinions as to why we quit. One paper said that I am ill and have retired, which ain't so. Pete Seeger wrote from Tanganyika (that's just like him, too) to say that singers do get hoarse but 'the pressing plants will keep us golden-throated on the turntable, at least.' One writer mentioned Gresham's Law, which I don't understand. Another quoted what the lady told the judge: 'It was a great profession before so many amateurs got into it.' I shall leave such pejoratives to others. I think, if we had a point to make when we started, it has been made; and was made during the first few years of work with Pete. Some of our work with Erik Darling will endure. There is no law requiring fine musicians like Ronnie Gilbert and Fred Hellerman to spend their working lives with one group. But I wonder if the artist-in-gallery principle may be true, after all. Is the best artist necessarily the hungry artist? . . . Perhaps some of us may have the chance to find out, again."

The image of the hungry artist seemed to express some of Lee's deepest anxieties. It evoked his fears of hunger and homelessness, fears dating from the loss of his family and compounded by later losses—the Almanacs, his job with People's Songs, the departure of Pete from the Weavers. It reminded him that perhaps his hungry years *had* been more creative. (And yet, at the time, he had often blamed hunger for his inability to produce.) It made him reflect on the way Pete tried to keep himself hungry and on the irony that Pete scored larger commercial triumphs each year while sticking to all his anticommercial political principles.

In his heart, Lee continued to identify with the disinherited, the dispossessed. At the same time, he marveled at his escape from poverty, reveled in success and celebrity, grandly picked up the tab for old friends after concerts on the road (travel-and-entertainment, just like a corporate executive), and unreluctantly left the old audiences behind.

But no amount of success had tempered his insatiable need for paternal care (the endless stream of requests to Harold) or for testing his colleagues (by torpedoing rehearsals, in the latest case) to make sure they really loved him. Pushing, pushing, until they gave up, and then saying, "See, they don't really love me."

Fearful of losing what he had gained, Lee was unable to keep himself from behaving in ways that led inexorably to that end.

On March 14, 1964, a few weeks after the Weavers, barely speaking, wound up their farewell tour, Lee reached the age of fifty, having had his last career "shot out from under him."

The rest, professionally, would be postscripts, addenda, and an unexpected, glorious finale.

Ironically, Lee earned more money in the first years after the Weavers' end than at any other time of his life.

Peter, Paul, and Mary had recorded "If I Had a Hammer," the song Lee and Pete Seeger knocked out during a People's Songs executive board meeting in the 1940s. The trio's exhilarating arrangement shook the torpor out of young people formed in the 1950s, renewing the force of those suspect words: *freedom, justice,* and *love.*

The song, intended by Lee and Pete to warn of threats to liberty as the red-hunting gathered force, now climbed the charts, and soon was being recorded by dozens of other artists in the United States and abroad.

BMI performance royalties for air plays, and payments of mechanical rights from recording companies, rolled in.

"Lee literally lived off the royalties of 'Hammer,' 'Lonesome Traveler', 'Kisses Sweeter than Wine,' " said Harold. "Fifteen years, they continued to earn money. 'Hammer' still earns several thousand dollars a year for his estate."

That the message of "If I Had a Hammer" can be read in many ways is evident from some of the requests for permission to use the song: for a Save the Children Federation public-service television spot; as the theme for a civic campaign to modernize the government of Harrisburg, Pennsylvania; for a National Film Board of Canada documentary; as a campaign song for Kenneth Monfort, running for the Democratic nomination for U.S. Senate from the state of Colorado.

By 1973, the song had so woven itself into the fabric of the nation that Senator Sam Ervin recorded it in his heavy southern drawl, with stirring passages of "America the Beautiful" as background.

Among the numerous projects Harold Leventhal had put forward to Lee, three seemed most accomplishable: Lee's long-promised "posthumous memoirs," a third Babysitters album, and a book based on what came to be known as the Cisco tapes.

Of the three, only the album became a reality.

The Babysitters should have followed up the first two albums, both still selling well, long before this. Alas, the outwardly ideal marriage of half of the quartet, Alan and Jeremy Arkin, had split like an oak struck by lightning, taking down smaller trees called friendship and singing groups as it fell.

By 1964, traces of that disaster had been covered by new and exciting growth. Alan had captivated Broadway with his performance as the autobiographical son in Carl Reiner's *Enter Laughing*. Movie contracts were pending. And he was in love, with the sweet, blond, wholesome young actress who was playing Honey in the national company of *Who's Afraid of Virginia Woolf?*—Barbara Dana. I, after four years as a columnist for the *New York Journal-American*, two years with an advertising agency, and two more babies, had moved to Washington, D.C., and worked part-time at the *Washington Post*, while my hus-

band worked time-and-a-half as head of a national news agency.
May 1964. Alan wound up the San Francisco run of *Enter Laugh-*
ing and flew to be with Barbara. Happily, Barbara's show had just
started a run in Washington, D.C. Surprisingly, Barbara's singing
voice had the same endearing, little-girl musicality as Jeremy's.
Miraculously, our next-door neighbor, Day Thorpe, former music
critic of the *Washington Star*, had Ampex studio recording equipment at home. We were more than welcome to record there.

Lee forgot how much he hated motion, and lumbered into Washington for five days of writing and rehearsing and recording in
two big old Cleveland Park houses (the Thorpes' and ours). We
even had three built-in children (mine) to sing with us: Jeff, ten;
Pete, seven; and Dan, four. Alan would dub in special effects and
his own children later in the year, but basically the project was
done—quickly, professionally (no girly giggles between Barbara
and me), and no beer until nighttime.

Anything was possible with a little organization and a whole
lot of coincidence.

Harold knew his man. Lee soon forgot his rancor and threats
of becoming his own publisher. Instead, he began sending Harold
friendly notes about his progress on projects Leventhal had encouraged.

A note on April 29 regarding projects reports that with a young
helper hired for the job, he had already "sorted and catalogued
about ¼ of the papers, books, songs, photos and letters in [his]
files; . . . corrected much of the Cisco manuscript, timed portions
of the Cisco tapes. . . ."

The phrase "posthumous memoirs" recedes for a time; Lee thinks
he has found a way around the painful recollections. Instead, to
put together a "Lee Hays' Commonplace Book," a collection (traditional in earlier American times) of whathaveyou—in Lee's case
songs, poems, anecdotes, thoughts, recipes, essays, articles, short
stories, letters, photos.

Thus the sorting and cataloging.

Harold was to gather all People's Songs material, lead sheets of
every song Lee "ever wrote or had a hand in," "whatever writing"
Harold might have that might belong in the book. And photos.
Harold was also to explore ways of reproducing photos, "including

framed ones, in cheap enough fashion," so that they could be studied and selected from.

A few years later, the concept seemed less wonderful.

"What would be the spine of such a book?" asked Lee. The songs and poems and short stories and anecdotes by themselves did not, disc by disc, build a spine. And without a spine, a book (or song or movie) wouldn't hold.

But if the spine were a creative personality in his historical context, then it wouldn't be a commonplace book, would it? Still, the songs and poems and stories would have impact only if printed within the context of the times and politics and conflicts.

Back Lee's thoughts went to his "posthumous memoirs," until 1977, when he gave them up for good.

On the Cisco tapes, Lee never gave up.

In 1961, living at 128 Willow Street, in Brooklyn Heights, an apartment made available when Alan and Jeremy left each other and it, Lee asked Cisco Houston to come over to his place and talk onto tape about the good times and bad, and about knocking around the world with Woody Guthrie.

Cisco, Woody's closest friend and singing buddy, and one of Lee's favorite people, was dying of cancer at the age of forty-two.

Lee wanted, as much as he ever wanted anything, to capture what he could of Cisco and shape it into a piece of immortality.

Perhaps that would mean talking more about Woody than about Cisco; everybody would want to hear Woody stories. (Though friends also loved Cisco stories, such as his response to an acquaintance who asked to borrow a thousand dollars: "You caught me at a bad time. I've got it.") Through Woody's fame, Cisco would be remembered.

Lee had in mind "that people like Alan Lomax had taped whole books. He had interviewed Woody and others, asking rather organized questions." "But the fact that Cisco, my old friend, was dying," Lee said in his memoirs, "inhibited me from following a plan. So usually when he'd wake up and sit up for coffee, I'd turn the tape on and we would just talk."

Cisco had made his first appearance in Lee's life in 1940, resplendent in full epaulets uniform—as barker for a Forty-second Street burlesque house. A Californian who'd acted with Will Geer and

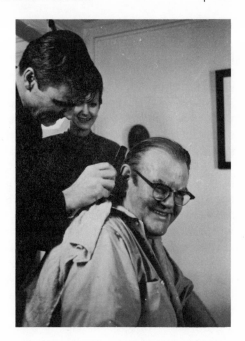

Cisco Houston playing barber to Lee, while staying at Lee's Brooklyn Heights apartment early in 1961 to make what came to be called the Cisco tapes. (Photograph by Richard Lukins, reprinted with permission)

sung with Woody Guthrie, dark, handsome, a ladies' man, warm, sweet, politically left, Cisco soon became a regular at Almanac House.

"It was always to my sorrow," said Lee, "that we had not included Cisco in the Almanac Singers, but he was blackballed by one of our members, so he hung around on the fringes of things and never really got anywhere as a singer until a year or two before his death when Harold took him over and began to get him jobs and he made eight and ten thousand dollars a year."

On the liner notes for Cisco's first solo album, after Cisco's big breakthrough at Gerde's Folk City, Lee wrote, "Cisco fits the scholar's definition of the wandering folk singer as well as anyone except Woody Guthrie, who was a sidekick of Cisco's for a long time. They travelled and sang together, and they both had close personal ties with Martha and Huddie Ledbetter, whose home was, at times, the only one they had. . . ."

Cisco had picked spuds in Wyoming at spud-picking time;

worked in a desert potash plant, in logging camps, in a pickle factory, in warehouses, and on a road gang. He'd played small parts on network television shows, on Broadway, in films, in commercials. He and Woody had served together on merchant marine ships in the war.

"Many of Cisco's strongest associations were with Woody," wrote Lee, "telling about their traveling together and their experiences in the Merchant Marines; traveling and singing in saloons, scraping up enough money to get them from one town to the next. Cisco lacked a certain ambition or drive; he always took a back seat to Woody. We can hear that on the records they made together. Woody always stood out in the foreground and Cisco more or less harmonized in the back. Although once in a great while Woody would let him come forward."

Here is Cisco's voice on that point:

"I was more than willing to be behind Woody, and if staying together meant . . . well, I enjoyed singing with him. I suppose that early on I could have said, 'I have to have more to sing or I won't work with you.' I never thought of it in those terms; I was more than willing to let Woody's talent shine out in front.

"It was certainly natural and normal for Woody to enjoy his new reputation and not want to be identified with anyone else. To say, 'I'm me and I don't need anybody else with me.' But as time went on, it became another matter. We toured a lot of colleges together. Woody often did great shows. But there were times when I had to pull his chestnuts out of the fire. Times when he just didn't feel like entertaining, where I had to carry the show and make it something. And later he would comment, 'Well, I guess I sort of fell through. I just didn't feel right, and you saved the day,' and so forth.

"We had our times together. We cursed each other. Battled each other. I had him get so mad at me on stage that he walked right off. People are people, and they can't live and work together without certain little conflicts coming about. Woody and I had ours."

Lee and Cisco talked and drank and taped for nearly four weeks.

What did it mean, knowing you're going to die?

"Just let me state it this way," replied Cisco. "When I spend time with Woody, and I see this broken man going in and out, back and forth from his hospital, trembling and shaking and at the end of all the good things in life, just sort of breathing and walking around . . . if I knew I'd have to struggle on for years and years like that, knowing there was no hope, I might not be as good at it as Woody is, facing it with tremendous courage.

"Being a terminal cancer case, as I am, happens to a lot of people in this world. Nobody likes to run out of time. But these are just mistakes of nature, things that eventually, some day, will be overcome. It's not nearly the tragedy of a Hiroshima, which could have been avoided.

"Anyway, there's no panic, there's no nothing. I plan to do the most sensible things I can possibly do in the next few months or however long it will be, and that will be it. I think it's sort of a privilege to know that you've got so much time. Other than that, what is it? It's a few more winters wishing it was spring, and a few more summers wishing they would last."

Although Cisco had died weeks after their conversations, Lee had not yet done anything with the tapes. Now, at last, in his April 29 project report to Harold, Lee said he hoped to do these things:

"Edit two sides of anecdotes for a 45 rpm record to submit to Vanguard. You are to clear the Cisco label and explore possibilities of mail order and other advertising.

"I hope to get an article together, based on the tapes, to submit to magazines, along with photos, possibly to serve as the basis of a Cisco book.

"I want to use portions of the material in my Commonplace Book."

Harold's interest in the project went far beyond make-work for Lee. Sure, it would keep Lee (client and friend) productively busy. It could also preserve the memory of Cisco, client and friend. And basically, it was about Woody, client and friend.

Moreover, the timing couldn't have been better. The canonization of Woody Guthrie, so impressively begun at the 1956 concert, had moved onto a national level, with Bob Dylan's idolizing "Song to Woody." Old Woody records were being released in new versions by companies lucky enough to own them. Elektra, in 1964, released a three-record set of Woody's Library of Congress interviews with Alan Lomax. Harold saw to it that some of Woody's unpublished

writings—a collection of poetry and short prose, and a novel—
got published. He commissioned a screenwriter to tackle a script
for a movie (eventually filmed as *Bound for Glory*, with David
Carradine starring as Woody) and opened discussions on an off-
Broadway show about Woody (produced in the 1970s).

The Woody industry boomed. The Cisco tapes could be a productive subsidiary.

Harold provided money from the Guthrie royalties (developing
into a gusher as every singer in America recorded "This Land Is
Your Land") to transcribe Lee's tapes, at a dollar a page for the
typist. When she finished, the manuscript came to 305 legal-sized
pages. A daunting pile.

But they didn't add up to a book, and mass magazines hadn't
been swept into the Woody industry. Moreover, *Sing Out!* wasn't
at all what Lee had in mind.

A rambling conversation between two old friends, about people
and events significant or amusing in the folk field, the tapes would
have been perfect for extended play on FM and college stations
around the country.

Alas, every segment is punctuated with hacking, racking
coughs—not from the terminally ill Cisco but from Lee. ("It was
only later that I found out I had pneumonia and didn't know it,"
said Lee in his memoirs.) As radio material, the Cisco tapes were
hopeless.

Yet Lee couldn't give up on them. Cisco had talked the length
of a book because Lee had asked him to. He must have hoped
Lee would use the material to advance the legend he, Cisco, wasn't
going to have time enough to ensure. The responsibility was, in
the primal sense of the word, terrible.

For the remainder of his life, Lee tried the Cisco tapes out on
writers, editors, and producers, hoping to find the key to publication
or production.

Perhaps one day technology will scrub the tapes clean of the
hacking sounds and leave only the good talk and laughter of two
old friends, a conversation many would be happy to listen in on.

Lee's stream of newsletters, started on the Weavers' international
tour, all but stopped (there'd be one more in 1966) with the group's
demise. He went back to one on one, a formidable job, given the

number of people he kept in touch with. The volume of mail from members of his family had grown over the years.

Minnie Frank wrote almost every day. Bill and Sue's son, Bill, Jr., and Lee had developed a special relationship when the boy took up the guitar and vowed to become a folk singer. Lee, flattered, had encouraged the lad. And vice versa. How could Lee not thrill to the last words in a 1960 letter from Bill, Jr.: "Keep singing— you give more to people than all the Hays family put together."

A year later, visiting Lee in New York, Bill, Jr., couldn't believe his good luck when his uncle got him a one-week job "managing" a folk trio during an engagement at Grossinger's. It was a disillusioning experience. Bill, Jr., saw the group as surly and colorless, playing not for love of music but to earn money. "This is fun?" he'd asked himself at the end of the week, promptly returned home, married, and gone into the tire business, following his father's line of work. But his closeness to Lee continued; he would name one of his daughters for Lee.

Bill, Sr., wrote rarely when well but frequently when ill, as he was much of the time from the end of 1962 until his death early in 1965. His letters were jaunty, brave, joking, and full of family news.

December 4, 1962: "Reuben phoned Sunday and I told him about your fete [a Carnegie Hall concert]. He is looking up the *N.Y. Times* article. I wish you two were closer together. He doesn't understand you and the fact that I am sure you have enjoyed life more than he has, and have done well by doing what you like to do and what comes naturally. . . ."

August 30, 1964, from the Touro Infirmary: "They have me grounded here with what is diagnosed as a 'coronary insufficiency.' A 59 h.p. motor trying to carry a 210 ton load. . . ."

October 1964: "M.F. [Minnie Frank] arrived by team Tuesday night unannounced and we were of course glad to see her. I have not been improving—my E.K.G. is worse. . . . I planned to write you a good long cheerful letter—excuse please. We are looking for you at Thanksgiving. [In vain. Lee didn't show up.] I will be well by then if I take care of myself."

December 11, 1964: "I'm so glad to know you phoned Reuben. He has way down deep a lot of sentimentality and a tender heart."

On Christmas Eve of 1964, Reuben at last wrote to Lee. "It

has been over 30 years since I believed I knew what was best for the world and you. . . . From what I read and learn from MF and Bill you have had some rough spots—and haven't we all? But during the past decade you have worn the laurels of success. If they have brought you happiness I am mighty glad. I judge they have for an article, I believe it was in *Time*, referring to the Weavers said, 'They sing—not so much for money but for the love of it—but the money rolls in.' I, who cannot carry a tune in a clothes basket, look on with pride and admiration.

"My course thru life has been quite different from yours. It was about the only one I could have followed. My talents, if they could be called that, were of another kind than yours. I have been reasonably happy and feel I have made the world a little better place to live, at least for some people.

"The banking profession has been good to me. It allowed me to accumulate enough to live on. Early this year I decided to retire and become a professor in the University—you see, I am still telling young people how to live—but not with the dogmatism of 30 years ago, I assure you.

"I appreciate your phone call the other night more than you know. It is one of the nicest things to happen this Christmas season. Nothing would please me more than to have our paths cross with time out for a good visit. . . ."

This time, the rapprochement took. From then until Lee's death, he and Reuben exchanged frequent familial letters, Reuben enthusiastically responding to Lee's many questions about the mother and father he too little remembered. Later, when Lee moved to the country, Reuben would pay for some needed improvements to the property. Often they wrote to plan a meeting. Somehow the plans never materialized.

Lee flew to New Orleans to visit Bill in February, shortly before Bill died. Then he found an excuse ("minor surgery—couldn't be helped") to avoid returning for the funeral. Lee avoided funerals, as well as anniversaries, birthdays, and holiday celebrations. Reuben attended the funeral but hadn't come to see Bill while he was still alive—had kept writing that he knew Bill would "make it." Minnie Frank did both.

Sue appreciated Lee's timing more than she did Reuben's. Odd the way someone so careless about his appearance (Sue was immaculate), so critical of the institutions and values on which her life was built, so intemperate in his consumption of food and drink, so blunt about his determination not to leave her family a dime, could nonetheless be the one in-law with whom she felt an affinity.

It came down to one thing, said Sue: "I could *talk* to Lee."

In time, she would become Lee's most elegant and cherished correspondent.

Just down the road, she would be the caretaker to whom Harold Leventhal would ship Lee, half pickled in alcohol under the strain of events, to dry out.

16

"Go Tell It on the Mountain"
1965–1980

I get up each morning and dust off my wits
Open the paper and read the obits
And if I'm not there I know I'm not dead
So I eat a good breakfast and roll back to bed

—Lee's verse in the Pete Seeger Song
"Get Up and Go"

A great and long-awaited movement was going on out there, and Lee sat immobilized on the sidelines.

Activism had wakened from a long, nightmarish sleep and had thrown itself into the struggle for civil rights.

Here was the cause closest to Lee's heart since the summer of 1934, in Paris, Arkansas, with Claude Williams. His songs, his film, his agit-prop plays, his short stories—all reflected his rage at the injustices borne by blacks.

But he wasn't a marcher any longer. Not at his age, and weight, and condition. So he didn't join in the March on Washington for Jobs and Freedom in 1963. He could feel all the old anger and hatred of the South after the explosion that killed four young black girls in a Birmingham church, but he had no forum, and nobody to sing the old freedom songs with. Well, new generations had taken up the battle.

Yet there was Pete, right in the fray. Returned in June 1964 from a year of traveling with his family through the Far East, India, Africa, Europe, and Russia, Pete had hurried south for the Mississippi Summer Project.

The project, sponsored by major black organizations, including Dr. Martin Luther King's Southern Christian Leadership Conference, aimed at registering blacks as voters in the most segregated, racist state in the union. Idealistic young people had come from around the country for the dangerous work. The least Pete could do was to back them up with his songs.

Pete was doing a concert in Meridian on August 3, the night word came that the project workers Andrew Goodman, Michael Schwerner, and James Chaney had been found buried in a dam. He led the weeping audience in "We Shall Overcome."

On March 24, 1965, Pete and Toshi flew to Alabama at the invitation of Martin Luther King, to join the final two days of the freedom march from Selma to Montgomery.

Television news covered the brave march, the hatred of the locals, and finally the murder of one of the participants, a Detroit woman named Viola Liuzzo.

Pete and Lee, Lee and Pete. They'd started as the young Almanac Singers together. The warp and the woof of the Weavers. Brothers, in some ways. That explained the resentments that Lee couldn't help mentioning in his taped messages. If your brother walks fearlessly into the jaws of redneck danger, you just can't help comparing yourself and, finding yourself wanting, being annoyed with him for making you feel less noble.

The songs the marchers sang were songs Lee had sung with Claude and Zilphia and John Handcox.

"We sang it first like this," Claude replied to a question from Lee:

I will overcome; I will overcome;
I will overcome one day;
And with Jesus Christ (subs. And with the union) as my
    leader
I will overcome one day.

"That must have been about 1936 in the New Era School in Little Rock," he added, signing himself "Preacher."

Lee responded, "I thought we knew it with the line 'Down on

my knees, I will sing and pray' which I am sure we did not sing but I forgot how we did sing it in the play."

Well, here the old hymn was, theme of the civil rights movement, so inspirational and powerful that President Lyndon Johnson wove the line through his speech to Congress on behalf of the Voting Rights Act of 1965. "We *shall* overcome."

That was the good news about the power of music.

The bad news was the *new* music.

Bob Dylan, having achieved stardom as a brilliant young folk singer–songwriter, moved on to rebellious rock in 1965, taking the youth of America with him, in the van of a wild, drug-saturated ride through the rest of the decade.

Fortunately, "If I Had a Hammer" had by then established itself as a standard. They weren't writing them like that after 1965. Or if they were, nobody was recording them.

Lee stopped thinking about writing songs.

Drinking made as much sense.

Something would have to be done about Lee, Harold saw. Apart from the new Babysitters album, Lee's energy had pooped out on the post-Weaver projects. His drinking had become serious, a real health problem. Also a social problem—friends stopped coming around, finding him sloshed so often. And the more alone he was left, the more he drank.

Lee admired Sue, his brother's widow. Perhaps having company would help Sue in the lonely aftermath of Bill's death.

Harold made all the arrangements, including paying for a sublet in the building where Sue now had an apartment.

Sue remarked later that Lee had no interest in going to restaurants for dinner; they always ate in. But they could talk. One night, Sue wondered whom God heard, the bird who asked for food, or the insect who asked not to be eaten. Lee said, "Let's write it."

They wrote "The Butterfly and the Bird":

Once a little butterfly, a pretty sight to see
Was flying in the garden praying "Lordy deliver me
I am too young a butterfly to lose my little head!"

But then a bird was also praying,
"Lord, give me my daily bread!"
Down flew the bird and according to his lights
Gobbled up the butterfly in two delicious bites.

And so it goes with butterflies and hungry birds and bees
And so it goes with almost everything right down the line
   to fleas;
For little fleas have other fleas upon their backs to bite
   'em
And the bigger fleas have bigger fleas and so ad infinitum
For that's the way of nature, red in fang and claw;
But we, being human, live by a higher law. . . .

Harold published the song, hoping Lee's collaboration with Sue would prove as successful as his teaming with Minnie Frank. (Royalties for "Seven Daffodils" still trickled in.) Hoping, really, not for the money but to jog Lee into a writing frame of mind again. Lee had so often longed for freedom from the burdens and tensions of rehearsals and concert tours, certain he would rejoice in the opportunity to focus entirely on writing.

Instead, it had driven him clear up the wall.

A newsletter from Lee Hays, New Year's Day 1966, reported, "You'd think a fellow as old and smart as me would stay home after having so many careers shot out from under him. So I stayed home for quite a spell and then I was taken by the idea of a long trip, a real swing around the country, with stops to visit family and friends. . . ."

(He'd intended to meet with Reuben, but didn't. "My Brother," wrote Reuben, "I have treasured the thought of your visit, deplore the change in your plans. . . .")

Lee told of his two weeks with Alan Arkin and Barbara Dana, now married, on location in California for the shooting of *The Russians Are Coming, the Russians Are Coming,* Alan's first movie job. Lee had stayed in the house they'd been provided with—"a magnificent artist's house on the coast, overlooking the wild Wagnerian tumult of the ocean, grottoes, seals, passing whales."

Lee and Barbara had written a song. "Or re-wrote an old poem by Southey, which we found in a copy of McGuffey's Fifth Eclectic

Reader," Lee's newsletter continued. "It is 'The Battle of Blenheim,' and the lines are so real for today that we tried to make a song of it. It tells of an old man sitting by his cottage door, when his grandchild comes to him with a skull. He says it is all that is left of some brave young fellow who fought on that proud day. 'For many a thousand men, you see, were slain in that great victory.' The child asks about the war and the old man says that what they killed each other for he never could make out. 'But people always did agree it was a famous victory'. . . .

"I hope someone sings it soon."

Having people to write with—that was key. Maybe the living alone, in Brooklyn, with his days and nights unstructured, was altogether wrong. That fabled Brooklyn Heights gathering place, the Robinsons', had gone into the memory books—the building had been sold out from under the tenants. A year or two later, Helen Robinson had died of leukemia; Earl remarried and moved to the West Coast. Alan and Barbara lived in Manhattan's Greenwich Village. None of Lee's working colleagues still lived in the Heights.

Manhattan might be less of an obstacle to future working relationships than Brooklyn. Manhattan people thought anyplace in Brooklyn was remote, inaccessible, and dangerous. Well, Lee would put himself within easy reach of productivity.

With hope and fanfare, Lee moved into a one-bedroom apartment in a hulking West End Avenue building at Ninety-seventh Street. Crews of his inevitable "young people" sawed and painted and set up audio equipment. Old projects were hauled out for a fresh look (especially the Cisco tapes and the posthumous memoirs). Lee's commercials producer friend sent him new assignments for jingles. A fourth Babysitters record went into the planning and writing phases. This one would not be "homemade." Stereo was a given at this point, and we recorded *The Babysitters' Menagerie*— our last and slickest album—in a proper stereo studio. F. A. O. Schwarz built a window display around it, replicating the album cover with their own stuffed animals.

Minnie Frank came for a long visit, and she and Lee tried to write more lyrics. She never stopped marveling at the royalties she'd made from "Seven Daffodils." (Her husband, on the other hand, never could get accurate numbers from her for income tax returns, and wrote pleading letters for the information to Lee, to Harold, to BMI.)

But if Manhattan brought more visitors and talk of projects than Brooklyn did, Lee's two years on West End Avenue only made him more anxious. He loathed every day after the week that an elevator breakdown isolated him, on the fourteenth floor, from the world. He took up every invitation for weeks or weekends in the country and wished above all for a country home of his own.

It was tiny and flimsy, the box of a bungalow at 4 Memory Lane, just off Mount Airy Road in Croton-on-Hudson. The gray tiled exterior had no distinguishing lines or features. Inside, a dreary little living room with yellow walls and brown linoleum floor, two small bedrooms, an unmodernized kitchen just large enough to cook but not eat in. Built as a summer place, it had no insulation, no storm windows.

What it did have was half an acre of grass and shrubbery and garden plots and dogwood trees. Land, blessed land.

Harold Bernz, Lee's old People's Songs roommate, called Lee as soon as the place came on the market, for $16,500.

Bernz lived in the neighborhood with his wife, Ruth, and their three children. Lee had often spent time in their big, comfortable house, writing songs with Ruth, a pianist and composer, and singing with Harold, now an affluent businessman. He hastened to Croton to see the property.

A quick look, and Lee knew, in every expansive inch he'd grown since his aborted childhood, that he could be happy in this little house, sitting in the sunlight, growing flowers and vegetables in the garden, breathing the clean air on a mountain that gently rose from the majestic Hudson River. He'd always felt a kind of oneness with the country—what *had* possessed him to imagine he could exist on the fourteenth floor of an Upper West Side apartment building, overlooking the walls of an even larger building across the street?

But could he afford to make this move? Harold Leventhal assured him he could. Leventhal had negotiated an annual $2,500 BMI guarantee for Lee; between that and the songwriting royalties that Harold had invested and administered, Lee certainly could afford the small down payment and monthly mortgage payments. Lee never quite understood how the money kept from running out.

"As a child of the depression," he wrote to Leventhal, "I have the recurrent nightmare of hunger and homelessness. It is almost impossible to believe that I shall reach my allotted three score and ten without knowing further depression and despair. As I enjoy my relative affluence—and wonder constantly how it came to be—I can never escape the fact that life changes constantly and that there are ups and downs to come. . . ."

Although he constantly urged others to look on the bright side, Lee could always manage to see darkness ahead. With ample reason, his friends learned later.

In the second decade of the twentieth century, Greenwich Village's avant-garde discovered Croton-on-Hudson, a sturdy blue-collar, Catholic town, populated by the families and descendants of Irish river workers and Italian masons.

The very rich, free-living, occasionally revolutionary Mabel Dodge sought solace on Croton's Mount Airy in the aftermath of a shattered love affair with the radical journalist John Reed. Later, Reed and his wife, Louise Bryant, bought the house that Dodge had rented on Mount Airy Road. The free-spirited Isadora Duncan alit on Mount Airy Road for a time, and Edna St. Vincent Millay came up from Greenwich Village to write her lyrical poems celebrating life, love, and moral freedom.

In the wake of the Village avant-garde came a new generation of unrestrained city dwellers—the lefties of the 1930s and the 1940s. The flavor and color of art and left-wing politics made Croton unique among Hudson River towns, not necessarily to the joy of the old residents, with their traditionalist ways of life. They referred to Mount Airy as "Red Hill." Croton men were well represented among the rock throwers at the 1949 riots in nearby Peekskill.

By the time Lee arrived, some of the bitter resentment against the "interlopers" had worn down. Townies who'd moved up from the low ground to the rustic hill were learning to live with the old lefties, many of whom had in any case given up on radical politics.

Among the residents of Mount Airy were two of the Lowenfels daughters, young women who had loved Lee since the years in

Philadelphia when he had been "another father" to them. Their parents had moved from Mays Landing to Peekskill in 1965 to be near them. Lillian had suffered a stroke in 1958; Walter had since taken care of her, full-time.

Now, with Lee living around the corner from Judy, perhaps the "family" relationship would resume? Instead, Lee set an icy distance between himself and Walter and Lillian. It prevailed to the ends of their lives. Why, no one knows for sure.

Money may have been a factor. Lillian had hoped Lee would take over a debt incurred during the financially desperate days of Walter's indictment and imprisonment. Lee angrily refused, "due to the well known fact that you can't get blood from a turnip." Yet Lee and Walter continued to write occasional letters as late as 1964.

Another consideration was song credits. "You, and possibly you alone," Lee wrote to Pete in 1977, "should know that Walter had absolutely nothing to do with the writing of 'Wasn't That a Time.' . . . I put his name on [it] as a sort of promissory note, to repay him for considerable money I owed him and, as it turned out, he was more than repaid. [It was] written in his house, but he lacked the ability to put songs together. Yet encouragement may be a form of co-authorship, for all of that." Pete was not alone in receiving this version of the song's authorship. More than once, Lee urged Harold Leventhal to remove Walter's credit, which Harold could not, would not, and did not do. Surely something deeper than royalties was involved. Lee, in other song-assignment sessions, would argue that anyone who contributed to a song, *even one word*, should share credit. Walter, a poet with a vast knowledge of American history, would doubtless have contributed a great deal more than one word to "Wasn't That a Time!"

Perhaps Lee's never-ending "need to negate" the authority figures in his life—his brother Reuben, Claude Williams, Pete—caused him to draw the emotional curtains when he found his old surrogate father Walter in his new neighborhood.

Or perhaps the simple pleasures of country living amid untroubled neighbors were too precious to be diluted with constant reminders of Lee's strife-filled past. Walter hadn't softened; he was an unreconstructed hard-liner. Lee, while remaining "some kind of socialist," had finally and irrevocably signed off on Russia in a letter (carbons to Pete and Harold) to the Soviet ambassador to the United Nations, on June 11, 1967:

"Dear Sir: As a citizen of the United States and a lifelong friend of the Soviet Union, I am deeply distressed by the charges you have made against Israel in the recent debates. Your equation of Israeli attitudes and actions with Hitlerism are shocking to the point of incredibility. What hurts the most is the painfully obvious fact that this charge is not true; and doubly painful because it is apparent that *you know it is not true*, yet went ahead and made the charge, time and again.

"There have been other representatives of nations, including my own, who have sacrificed personal morality by following instructions of their governments. Seldom have I heard anything so shameless as your vulgar charges against a tiny nation which is not without blame, but which cannot possibly be guilty of the monstrous charges you have made.

"You have demeaned the United Nations and yourself. You have lowered my respect for you and your country. It will be a long time before I can give trust to anything you do or say. As an ordinary citizen, I feel betrayed. Hope dies hard. Be ashamed, sir."

If hope was late and hard in dying within Lee, at least its expiration did not strangle his empathy with the dispossessed, nor did it spawn the need for a substitute faith. The old lefties who turned to spiritualists, gurus, and other otherworldly guides astounded Lee; his bred-in-the-bone patience and politeness in listening gave out when Earl Robinson told him he was communing with the dead.

Though hope died hard, Lee would remember its early years with full-bodied appreciation, as he did in a letter to Harold Leventhal after reading Joe Klein's book on Woody Guthrie:

". . . Joe is cynical altogether about the influence of communist and socialist thought on the arts—in fact he seems not to know much about it. He is cynical about . . . the Wallace movement, about our politics before and after 1939—we look like a bunch of puppets operated from Moscow, instead of living, working artists doing the best we knew how in a threatening world. We lived in a veritable renascence of art and letters, thanks to WPA and the various projects. The work of Steinbeck and Hellman and so, so many others was a direct result of the ferment of socialist thought that was going on all over the world.

"Joe has the facts; he dismisses those great days as chimera, illusion. He misses the soul of the times."

Among his old friends and associates, the consensus is that Lee was not a member of the Communist party. Their reason: Lee himself.

Temperamentally, Lee was nearly unsuitable for membership in any authoritarian organization. His entire life was marked by his negating authority figures, disrupting groups he was part of, questioning everything out of existence, and deep psychological inability to make a commitment.

But if he wasn't a member, he incontrovertibly had close ties to "the movement."

In a letter written after an interview about Almanac days, Lee told Pete, "We all had Communist friends and I certainly did, but I was never aware that any of them were giving me any orders. None of us were very good order-takers to begin with. If the Communists liked what we did, that was their good luck. . . . I suppose the most that I can claim is that I was a fellow-traveller."

That would have been claim enough in harsher political times.

Lee Hays of the Weavers was living on Mount Airy! The word went out among the guitar-strumming and banjo-plucking teenagers who'd grown up on Weavers albums. Would he be approachable?

Sure enough, the first time the high school jug band played at a picnic on the ball field a hundred yards from Lee's house, here came Lee with a lawn chair and some cans of beer, attended by a couple of next-door kids. Lee introduced himself to the players, and they talked about how the folk boom had revived jug band music—originally a black folk style, related to English skiffle music, popular in the South during the ragtime era. Before he left, Lee invited the young music makers over to his house, any time of the day or night.

"Lee's house became a hangout," recalled Jim Brown, guitarist in the school jug band then, and later the creator of a documentary film on the Weavers. "We could drink beer there when we were too young to go to bars. He employed many of us, gardening mostly.

He taught us a lot about gardening. He was concerned about environmental issues; very concerned about composting. He had an interest in our music, the music that was going on during that period, the social concerns that were being expressed in it. We met musicians there. Don McLean was around a lot. Pete Seeger was in and out.

"Most important, he reached us on an attitude that was ageless. We were talking to someone the same age as our parents, but he tuned into our concerns in a way that made him more like a contemporary, a well-seasoned contemporary who gave good advice. Lee was Croton's greatest human resource."

By 1968, music and drugs had begun to bridge the sociopolitical gulf that divided Croton kids into "Commies" and "greasers." If the "Commies" (anyone who lived on the hill) knew who Lee was, the "greasers" (the Italian and Irish workers' descendants) did not. Nonetheless, with Lee's encouragement, they too found welcome and employment at his place.

What they heard was the following: There's this old guy up on the hill who'll find work for you to do—gardening or running errands—anytime you need a few bucks. Weavers? What are they? But the old guy is amazing. He keeps a refrigerator full of beer and lets you drink some. Best of all, he has an ear. You can talk to him about problems you're having with your folks, about being messed up on drugs, about screwing up at school, about how much you hope you don't get drafted, about what you'd like to do with your life. He listens! He doesn't brush you off the way parents and other adults do—telling you to pull your goddamn socks up.

David Karpoff, one of Lee's ex-kids, said, "Lee was a completely nonjudgmental adult presence who offered much in the way of faith and confidence to a lot of sometimes-troubled young people. To many of their lives, his presence made a great difference."

Another, Charlie Maguire, remarked, "He straightened out a lot of kids."

Lee gave his young neighbors what he had always given young people—the sense that what they had to say was worth listening to.

(Alan Arkin, in a letter to Lee, said, "I think often of the years way back when, and how you were the first adult who ever took the time to talk to me, who felt that I might have something to

The bungalow on Mount Airy Road in Croton-on-Hudson, where
Lee finally found contentment.

say. It was a mighty important time, and I don't know how any
of the good things could have happened without that base. . . .")

Lee became an established figure in Croton. That he was content
with his new world comes through every image in his American-
pastoral description to Earl Robinson of his Croton life:
". . . The street is like a country lane, full of kids on bikes,
each house with its own little acre, trees and perennials. The greatest neighbors I have are establishment people, and we have a marvelous open relationship, swapping garden notes, books and tools.
Sunday I borrowed a scoop of bone meal; lady neighbor borrowed
my colander while making green tomato mince meat; another
came with bags full of shredded leaves and grass clippings for
my compost heap; three girls came in and made oatmeal cookies;
two neighbor college boys dug out some troublesome rocks; visiting
nurse bandaged my toe; high school kids washed my front windows
and hung up halloween cats and clowns; all the while my stereo

played Beatles and Stones and Babysitters and Walter Carlos and Weavers and avant garde stuff like that; a very beneficent Sunday. As my dreams of infantile security take me back to Commonwealth, Pete's, Cranberry Street, Highlander, and other such communes, there is a feeling of community here which is unlike apartment dwelling. Community but with privacy. My only problem is to maintain the privacy and enjoy the community without depending too much on it or asking too much.

"Once in a while a song comes out, but nobody sings them, so there isn't much incentive. That Hammer song still pays the mortgage, for awhile, anyhow, but I have no idea how to earn new money."

A key sentence in the letter: "Having a listed phone number with no fear of Trotskyite crank calls is a huge relief."

For the first time in his adult life, where he came from politically didn't matter. No crank calls, no knocks on the door, no concern about taps on the phone or subpoenas to come or stink bombs in theaters or protests by the American Legion.

Just sitting there, "trying to maintain a dignified silence." Not wanting to publish his "posthumous memoirs," because the things that would have to be discussed would cause him to be "embarrassed and horrified" around his neighbors.

Lee, the old radical, weary of strife and danger, aggrieved that the struggles of the thirties and the dreams of the forties had led to the front-page Weavers busting of the fifties—here was Lee, enjoying a kind of *Saturday Evening Post* life, surrounded by fresh-faced country kids, building up a compost heap, planning improvements to his house, and carrying on a lengthy correspondence with his sister about possible genealogical links between the Hays family and Molly Pitcher, of Revolutionary War fame.

If Pete contained a multitude of contradictions, Lee wasn't exactly simple to figure out.

Of course, none of Lee's old friends had any idea how atavistically he would fall into the rhythms of country living, how deeply he would become absorbed into the community, how much he would come to mean to its young people and they to him.

Some of those old friends worried that Lee was isolating himself from the possibility of future artistic projects. Not simply by virtue

Lee's bookmark.

of distance; Pete's house in Beacon was much farther from the city, but Pete lived on wheels; Lee could hole up in Croton and drink beer for the rest of his days. And he was only fifty-four. He should have fifteen, twenty, or thirty years left. For all his deadpan jokes about giving lessons on retiring and about posthumous memoirs, he had for decades lived and created in the ferment of politics and the arts. Mightn't sitting on top of a mountain result in a quick rusting out?

Harold Leventhal kept up a constant volley of suggestions—writing assignments, serving on judging panels for music festivals, musicology projects—most of which Lee politely but emphatically rejected for a variety of stated and unstated reasons.

But one Leventhal suggestion lured him off the mountain in November of 1968: a bit part in the film version of Arlo Guthrie's epic and hilarious antidraft ballad, *Alice's Restaurant.*

Harold, associate producer of the film, nominated Lee to play a heal-by-prayer tent preacher in a revival-meeting scene. The ministerial bass, the rolling sonorous phrasing. Perfect, said the director, Arthur Penn. Lee agreed. He relished the memory of the weeks on location with the Arkins for the making of *The Russians Are Coming, the Russians Are Coming*. And Arlo—well, he'd known Arlo from the time he was a baby, though never well.

Arlo's perspective on Lee derived from his childhood: "I was basically your average kid not knowing anything. I just knew that we knew Pete, we knew Lee . . . as a family group. We'd go someplace to hear them sing, or we'd go to their house to visit, but it was always my mom or someone who was doing the talking, and us kids just went out and played on the swings. . . .

"The things I remember most [about their concerts] were the humor onstage, Lee's stories especially. Punctuating lines, timing, those kinds of things . . . have become a part of me—I learned them as a kid. Watching the group onstage."

Lee had spent a few hours with Arlo when Woody's son was fourteen and hoping for a summer job at Schroon Crest Camp. Lee had found him a "very sociable, humorous, talented boy." He wrote to Harold, "I don't know whether [the camp owner] would consider anyone his age, but was impressed by his interest in outdoor work. . . . Joady [Arlo's brother] may make the larger contribution in later years, being the troubled one, but Arlo's affability and poise would lead me to recommend him."

Arlo, at sixteen, had been invited by Lee to help a crew redecorate his West End apartment. "He stayed for the weekend, but he didn't do a lick of work," Lee related later. "He spent the entire time sitting on a stepladder with his guitar making up a song about what everybody else was doing. 'All Lee does is sit and yammer, while Billy's working with his hammer . . .' and so forth, describing all the activities that were going on while he was having a ball sitting there and playing the guitar."

As a master of sitting there while others did the work, Lee doffed his cap to Arlo's charming and creative method of doing the same thing.

At eighteen, Arlo, with one musical shaggy-dog story, *Alice's Restaurant*, had become the folk-singing embodiment of anti–Vietnam War sentiment, spreading, in his humorous way, more dissent than Woody had ever managed to do. Without ever being troubled!

Now the song was to be a film; Lee couldn't quite imagine how. After receiving the page and a half with his scene, he asked to see the entire script.

Arthur Penn, the director, stalled, Harold Leventhal recalled, "and of course never meant to send it to him. Lee's pay was scale—$125 a day, and the scene would only take a day. But Lee came a week ahead and checked into the Howard Johnson's where the crew was staying. He got a room with a kitchenette and proceeded to cook up a storm for everyone. He waited for Arthur Penn to meet with him—and waited, and waited. Eventually, the night before his scene, Penn did.

"The hotel bill, the room service, the cost of the food he cooked, et cetera came to more than he made. But he had a great time; it was a way of keeping him going."

It also launched a close friendship with Arlo. From then on, Arlo would drop around whenever he was in the area, and always on the weekend of the annual Croton Festival. Arlo named his daughter, Annie Hays Guthrie, for Lee.

Before the winter snows melted, Lee would watch for the first crocuses and snowdrops, announcing the coming of spring. He and his helpers would soon start working on the gardens, preparing the soil with organic compost. They would plant lettuce, beans, peas, peppers, summer squash, tomatoes, cucumbers, herbs. When the crops came in, the kids would crowd into Lee's kitchen to shell and pare and slice, absorbing lessons in "putting up" vegetables.

Lee had thought very poorly of gardening as a child, he said in his memoirs. He had done his young utmost to escape the gardening chores that his father expected of him. Perhaps his own late love of gardening, he mused, was expiation.

Whatever the reason, Lee seemed to find comfort, solace, even faith, in the cycles that nature so reliably rolled out each year, turning the mountaintop half-acre garden into a metaphor for life.

Lee sensed the onset of his own life's winter long before most of his friends gave credence to his forebodings. They joked that he would probably outlive them all.

Only a few grasped the significance of the amputation, in May 1972, of the little toe on Lee's left foot. Certainly, there seemed nothing ominous in the "Elegy" Lee wrote and mailed to friends on his return from the New York City hospital where he'd had the operation:

> Farewell, little toe,
> I loved you so,
> For we were so attached.
> We'll dance no more,
> Nor wade by the shore,
> For we have been detached.
>
> In the long, long years of a happy life,
> You were closer to me than friend or wife,
> And all that we shared of love or strife
> Ended with a whack of the surgeon's knife.
>
> As I go lopsided and grieving
> Through this vale of tears and woe,
> How sad it is to be leaving
> My valiant little toe.
>
> How loyally you took me
> Wherever I wished to go;
> Nothing ever shook me
> Like the loss of my little toe.
>
> In that great foot bath up in the sky
> I hope you'll always know
> I never will forget my
> Irreplaceable little toe.

Often that's how diabetic gangrene begins, with the removal of a toe. That doesn't solve the problem, but it gives the patient time to absorb the shocking news that the leg may soon follow.

Lee's big body had long harbored "two very insidious illnesses, which if you don't stay alert all the time can creep up and snatch you," said his doctor, Percy Brazil, when the need for confidentiality had passed. Either illness, diabetes or tuberculosis, could have accounted for the traits that aggravated the Almanacs and the Weavers—Lee's moodiness, his crankiness, his malingering.

Nobody had seen it that way. They didn't pay much attention

to Lee's talk about early tuberculosis; Dr. Brazil found evidence of the disease in Lee's system. The diabeties hadn't been diagnosed until the 1960s, but Dr. Brazil believed it had been with Lee long before that.

Through the years, people had dismissed Lee's chronic complaints as hypochondria or as a cover-up for a drunken night. That's how it had seemed to Pete and the others.

"Pete is the very opposite," said Dr. Brazil. "He's big and strong and goes out and chops wood and builds houses and sings songs at the same time. Nothing seems to faze him."

And therefore he might have little patience . . . ?

"And understanding. Because that's not the way life is. . . . It doesn't correspond to the life experience of somebody like Seeger. These things so often are genetically determined. Pete was blessed by nature in the sense that Lee was not blessed by nature."

"Wasn't That a Time!"

And now it's time to say so long
We're feeling young and fine
Before we have to end our song
Let's sing it one more time.

> —LEE HAYS singing the last verse of
> the last song, *"Goodnight, Irene,"*
> at the last WEAVERS concert

*L*ee, talking with Jim Brown, one of his ex-kids and now a documentary filmmaker, got down to a matter he'd been mulling for days: how to participate in a Weavers reunion without leaving his house.

He hadn't left Croton since his second leg was amputated, in 1978. He hadn't gone to New York City since the toe surgery in 1972. There'd been one awful health crisis after another. Below-the-knee amputation of his left leg in 1975. Multiple abcesses developed, necessitating three stays in the hospital (Phelps Memorial, in North Tarrytown) in 1976. During the second stay, surgeons implanted a pacemaker to maintain the regular rhythm and beating of his heart, weakened by diabetic cardiovascular disease.

In October of 1978, Lee returned to Phelps with a gangrenous *right* leg. Surgeons amputated below the knee, hoping to save the joint that might enable him to walk eventually with a prosthesis. No luck. A month later, they had to amputate again, above the knee. One week after that, they removed Lee's prostate.

"I'm Lee Hays, more or less," he took to saying.

Pete—vibrantly healthy, unflaggingly energetic Pete—had been shaken to his depths, watching his old friend giving up his body,

Lee and Pete, Pete and Lee. Brothers, in some ways. (Photograph by Philip Pocock)

piece by piece. The many times he'd been impatient! He'd do it differently if he could do it over! He *had* done it differently from the time of Lee's toe surgery—talking about Lee to his concert audiences, quoting his anecdotes, performing his songs. He stopped by Lee's house frequently, bouncing his *meshuggeneh* and not so *meshuggeneh* ideas off him. Cards and letters flew between them.

Lee found time had changed their relationship: "We chat like two old cockers—do you remember 37 years ago?—etc."

Whenever Lee was hospitalized at Phelps, Pete would visit. Lee's stock with the nurses hit record highs after each Seeger appearance.

In the kind of coincidence one expects only in a Russian or a Charles Dickens novel, Walter Lowenfels was brought to Phelps, dying of cancer, while Lee lay one floor above with an abcessed stump and a new pacemaker; Pete reached Walter's bedside as he died, then carried the news to Lee's sickbed. The impact on Lee's emotions of this conjunction—Walter's death under the same roof, Pete's bearing the tidings, Lee's memories of his closeness and rendings with both men, and the mutilations to his own body— can only be surmised. Remembering that day, Lee would shake his head in astonishment.

That worst of years, 1976, had sharpened Lee's visions of mortality, stirring him into brief activity on the "posthumous memoirs" front. In September, Lee taped the first of a dozen or so hours of his remembrances, some pithy, some rambling and far removed from any possible "spine." He asked Don McLean to talk on tape with him about the significance of the Weavers in the history of American music—a subject McLean had given far more thought to than had any of the Weavers. Their conversations transcribed into thirty-one legal-sized typewritten pages.

The effort and the memories overwhelmed Lee. He signed off on the project on March 17, 1977, with a final tape to me, relieved that his participation in creating a bit of immortality for himself had ended.

But as 1979 wound down, Lee contemplated the new technology and reconsidered.

Pete, Ronnie, and Fred had sung together again on Pete's latest album. None of the old tensions had resurfaced. The three had mellowed. They'd been through the fire, as a group and as individuals. One residue was a profound respect for one another's talents. It was wonderful, singing together. Pete invited Ronnie and Fred to join him the next year in his annual Thanksgiving concert at Carnegie Hall. They'd sing some of Lee's songs. He'd be with them in spirit.

Lee brooded. He wanted to be with them more concretely than that.

He asked Jim Brown for technical advice. Could he become a physical and vocal presence at the concert on videotape? A current shot through Jim's large body. He'd long wanted to do a filmed portrait of Lee. "But there was enough darkness in his past," said Jim, "that he never embraced the idea. Now he seemed to know

he had very few years left, and all of a sudden cracks opened up—
he was thinking about doing something public."

As they talked, Jim introduced the idea of putting the four Weavers on film, to screen at the Carnegie reunion. For that matter,
why not a full documentary on the Weavers? The group could be
filmed at Lee's place, reminiscing about the past, their music
heavily lacing the sound track. Call it a thirtieth-anniversary
reunion—the perfect peg.

That made sense to Lee, as against a filmed portrait of himself.
What would be the spine of a film about himself? He'd never
even been able to find a spine for a Lee Hays solo album.

No question that the Weavers' story had a strong plot line, a
sense of history, and a moral lesson.

Moreover, wasn't that the time he'd most like to be remembered
for? Mightn't this be the long-promised posthumous memoirs?
With at least three advantages a book could never have: the sound
of the Weavers' music; the brevity of a film, precluding a "warts
and all" approach; and, most appealing, the promise that the bulk
of the work would be done by others. "Lee was lazy," said Jim.
"No question about that."

And who more trustworthy or better qualified to do the job
than Jim? A tall, open-faced, apple-cheeked young man who had
lost his own father at the age of ten, Jim had adopted Lee as his
surrogate father in 1968, when he was sixteen. Later, he'd learned
documentary filmmaking from a master, George Stoney, at New
York University's Institute of Film and Television. Stoney had
become his mentor, his friend, and his employer. They'd made
many films together, including eight for WNET's "The Fifty First
State," on the actions of environmentalists to clean up the Hudson
River. The person who had done most to popularize that cause
was Pete Seeger. Jim and George and Pete had worked closely
and with good results on the Hudson River films. Pete and Lee.
Lee and Pete. With both of them on your side, what obstacles
could remain?

Stoney, listening to Jim talk his concept, felt little initial enthusiasm. A gentle, white-haired southerner who, like Lee, was the
son of a minister, he had found Lee "a bit of a chore" in their
social visits, "very cantankerous, very opinionated."

"When Jim said he was going to build a film around Lee," Stoney related, "I didn't tell him, You're nuts, here's a sick old man, a grouchy old man—how are you going to make a grouchy old man with no legs the center of your film? Instead, I said, You've backed me up in the past; I owe it to you. But I never saw what Jim saw in him until much later."

Stoney worried about how they would handle Lee and his legs. "This is something that is much more shocking on film than it is in person," he said later. "The audience has to get used to it. What can you do . . . how is *he* going to take it when he sees himself on the screen . . . all of that." Stoney suggested making a videotape of Lee, to test his tolerance for a camera and his reaction to seeing his truncated self on screen. Jim added a spin. Why not a videotaped letter to Lee's old friend Fran Dellorco, who was dying of cancer in California?

"This was a wonderful idea," said Stoney, "because it required Lee to be 'up,' since he was talking to a person who was dying. And also it gave him an excuse to use his wheelchair to show Dellorco how his neighbors had helped him modify his house to accommodate his wheelchair. So the wheelchair became part of the story—the ramp, the shower that he could wheel right into, and so on. And in the middle of this a neighbor, Harold Bernz, came by and they started singing. When it was over, I said to Lee, 'You want to see it played back?' And he said, 'Aaahh, I don't want to see it.' Well, we cut it into an hour and a half to send to Dellorco, which he saw a week or so before he died. I'm sure this introduction had a lot to do with Lee's attitude towards the Weavers film."

Jim wrote up a proposal to send to the Independent Documentary Fund for Public Television and other funding sources. His film would document the musical contribution of the Weavers, culminating in a "living room reunion" of the four Weavers, filmed "in vérité style to capture the spontaneity as the Weavers discuss and sing their own story."

Within weeks, the filmmakers had promises of sufficient backing to proceed. And Lee had an exciting project in his life again.

Jim thought that Lee had, for a long time, been "suicidal almost— the doctors had told him to stop drinking, stop smoking, cut out sweets—and that would just spur him to another carton of cigarettes, and a ten-pack of beer, and a little container of candy next to his chair. It seemed he was using these elements against himself, up to the time of preparation for the film." Then Lee stopped smoking, did push-ups, exercised his vocal cords, practiced memory training.

And he covered pages and pages with background material for the filmmakers, and thoughts about the project for the other Weavers.

Lee, the remains of a once mountainous, powerful man, drained of the old bitterness, sifted his memories of the Weavers:

Ronnie, he wrote, "gives energy to her understandings—her letters to me are like a good workout for the mind and soul. . . . As for Ronnie's voice, it goes right to my backbone and makes my neckbones rattle. Sometimes on stage I had to shut down my emotional dampers for fear that her singing would unplug my tear ducts. There are only about three singers that have affected me this way, and she's two of them. . . ."

On Fred: "We didn't hold auditions, but of all the dozens of young guitar pickers available at the time I am convinced, and grateful, that we found the one guy who had the sensitivity to make his enormous contribution to what is called the Weavers' sound. Fred is a good de-bunker, too, and his mordant tongue made it hard for any of us to stay stubborn for too long. . . ."

On Harold Leventhal: "He's a world traveller and can always tell me which side of any given political crisis I'm on. Every one of us can say what we owe to Harold as, in my case, my life. He touches people. He helps people to touch each other. He is always ready to make house calls, to come to our hearts and lives when we need him, and we love him."

Pete "is a geological force who moves mountains and tides and changes the seasons. He is eclectic, taking the best he finds in all music and art and literature and putting it to work in the service of the human race. Maybe it's his Puritan ancestry that drives him on and makes him uncomfortable when he isn't running down the line full steam ahead. He has more ideas and projects and concerns than any one genius is entitled to. . . . He has always pushed me forward when I needed a push and backed me up when I needed a back-up; his banjo will ring in my ears and in my soul until the day I die and I trust for some time afterward, due to an advanced case of tinnitus I enjoy.

When I get to Heaven tell you what I'll do
I'll tell the angels "I'm warning you,
You better get ready to sing and shout,
You'll learn what singing is all about.
Tune up your harps, let the banjos ring,
When Pete gets here, Godalmighty's gonna sing!"

About himself, Lee said, "I have tried to maintain a dignified silence lo these many years and so there isn't much to say about me. I have no ambitions and few expectations. As soon as this current fuss is over I expect to sink quietly back into my little pond like an old moss-covered log that has been unexpectedly fished out, examined briefly and tossed back into blessed obscurity."

Ronnie Gilbert considered the film proposal as it stood, as well as copies of an exchange of letters between Lee and Fred, then typed four double-spaced pages to "Lee (and Jim, Pete, Fred, Toshi— whoever has to do with the project)."

"I think," wrote Ronnie, "the whole thing could be thought of as a film about the Weavers coming together from hither and yon to take part in Pete's concert in November. . . . Maybe, with Pete's permission, some of the concert could be filmed. In any case, I certainly think we ought to think about opening up the rehearsal process to the camera—that might be a lot more alive than sitting around in unnatural conversation trying to say what we recall about how we used to, twenty or thirty years ago, arrive at our arrangements. . . ."

Of course, Jim had conceived the living room reunion out of the recognition that Lee was unbudgeable. Ronnie wasn't willing to be constricted by that fact.

"I admit, Lee, I am thinking of you as part of that rehearsal situation in November. But even should you not feel able, I don't see why *you* couldn't be filmed making comment on what we're doing, referring it to the past, dredging up the anecdote or two— quite as you used to and I don't doubt still do, between operations."

Ronnie then unleashed some resentments she'd felt on reading Fred's reply to a question about the way the Weavers used to work. Fred had written, "The word that keeps popping up in any answer to this question is 'marriage.' ('Being in the group was

like being married to three other people . . .') But that means a
lot more than spending a lot of time together, travelling together,
sharing hotel rooms and getting into arguments. . . . A good marriage (and I consider that The Weavers did have a good marriage
for a long time, notwithstanding arguments, differences, hurts,
etc.) goes further than that. It implies a sharing, an intimacy, a
reservoir of common viewpoints, attitudes, secrets, private jokes
that allows for a great deal of unspoken-ness. It involves the kind
of intimacy that allows for a glance, or perhaps not even so much
as a glance, but a sureness of common attitude that allows one
party to say or do something *knowing* that it represents the other
party or in this case, parties. It's getting up from the table at a
dinner party and announcing that it's time to go *knowing* that
my wife feels the same. . . ."

Ronnie saw it quite differently: "Well, I suppose our disagreements are interesting: for example, while the quote in Fred's letter
about being married to three people is probably mine, I no longer
think 'marriage' is a very apt metaphor, one's views of 'good marriage' having undergone some alterations with time. For instance,
I hate to say it, Fred, but your description of how you leave a
dinner party reminds me of nothing so much as how pissed and
pained I used to feel at your unilateral decisions and pronounce-
ments. They in fact rarely represented my opinions, wishes or
needs . . . although you used to seem to think they should. I
hasten to add that YOUR fury and frustration over being forced
to submit to group discussion and decision on every niggling question must have been just as painful to you as mine over the other.
. . . We all had our pet miseries, to be sure, along with the pleasures
and joys. It's that old 4-blind-people-describing-an-elephant syndrome. To Fred it was our 'togetherness' that was exceptional
and significant. To me it was our diversity.

"My god, what a lot of difference that thing called THE WEAVERS
represented, when you really look at us—in temperament, social
background, musicianship, life experience, expectations, even political outlook, for all our generally being leftists. We were certainly
not 4 kids from the same neighborhood who'd listened to the
same records and fought in the same street gang. . . . Yet we
managed to coexist for a respectable amount of time through several
phases, musical and otherwise."

Pete circled the last few lines of the paragraph and penned his own comment: "History gets made when people come to the same conclusion from different directions."

That was Pete, molding specifics into historical generalizations. But they were all, in their ways, summing up. Lee again considered The Question, or Big Question—which by now had settled down to this: Was it possible to be good (that is, make a difference to the world) *and* commercial?

"I believe that the work of the Weavers," wrote Lee to Pete, "while you were in the group, was an immense political, social and musical contribution. If we would not and could not sing Joe Hill to middle America, we did push out a kind of consciousness that had never been known before. . . ."

Later, Pete would say about The Question: "Well, we thought we failed, but my guess is that we succeeded more than we thought. It's just that we had such extreme ambitions, that because we didn't see world peace and plenty for every human soul, why we felt we failed. The way probably a number of artists have felt they failed when they aimed very high."

Finding a time when the Weavers could come together took several months. When would Ronnie be in New York, when would Pete be free, when could Fred make it over? Finally, they settled on a date in May and hoped for good weather. The format had changed to a reunion picnic in Lee's yard, the catering provided by the filmmakers, with friends and neighbors invited to enjoy the food and the music.

Two nights before the picnic, George Stoney got a call from Lee.

"George, I don't think I can do it. I'm not up to it."

"Okay," responded Stoney, "but we invited a lot of people, and I'm not going to sit on top of the hill and tell them to go home. They're going to be knocking on your door."

Said Lee, "Okay, you son of a bitch."

Stoney, sensing Lee's inability to commit totally to the project (how could he be sure it would be good enough?), had taken a "hard-assed producer" approach. It brought Lee into line.

* * *

Warming up for the Weavers reunion picnic at Lee's house in Croton-on-Hudson, Pete Seeger and Fred Hellerman tune their instruments, while Lee goes over lyrics.

When the Weavers began singing at the picnic, said Jim, "it was magical. With a few exceptions, they fell into the old harmonies. They were still very vibrant. And all of a sudden it was clear that this would be a film about surviving, and overcoming obstacles, and celebrating life . . . and Lee became a physical metaphor for that."

All of a sudden, it was clear to Pete that there *had* to be a reunion concert at Carnegie with the four of them. Not only because they still sounded so good together but also for the dramatic situation.

"Lee's voice is half shot, but he can do it," said Pete. Lee was not at all convinced. Should he really try to go through with a concert?

It would be so easy, Pete responded, for Lee to say, Let people remember me when I had legs and a good voice. But seeing someone doing his best in your situation, he told Lee, would be "an object

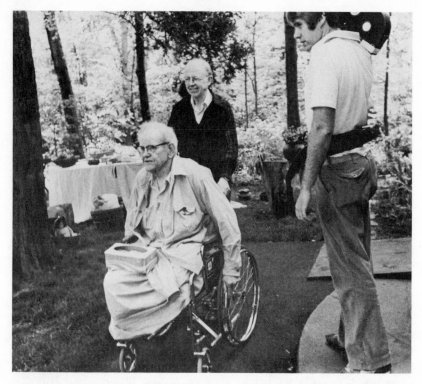

The documentary-film makers George Stoney (pushing Lee) and Jim Brown preparing to shoot the reunion picnic.

lesson to everybody else. That you don't give up. That you're still in there pitching. That's inspiring."

(Jim knew that such a situation could also be maudlin on film. He counted on Lee's "cracker-barrel humor" to spike any drift toward oversentimentality.)

After the reunion picnic, Lee wrote to Stoney and Jim Brown, "It was a once in a lifetime event, as you know. When the Weavers started to sing their first chorus my pacemaker almost stopped out of pure jubilation, and you may well believe we shared a tear or two. Going back 32 years was a powerful experience for all of us. . . .

"Pete is already looking ahead to a Carnegie reunion in November. I was not sure we could do this, but Thursday's experience makes me feel that we can survive Carnegie, if only for a brief appearance. . . ."

Pete promised they wouldn't have to prepare more than fifteen minutes of music. Well, maybe thirty minutes. By the time of the concert, they had two hours of rehearsed music in the bag, from which to create a one-hour program of new songs and old favorites, solos and duets and group numbers, changes in keys and moods and spirit, building, soaring, the way Weavers concerts always had. If they were going to do this, they were going to do it right.

Between the picnic and the concert, Jim Brown would film individual interviews with the Weavers, and maybe some joint ones. Lee wrote to Pete, Fred, and Ronnie, suggesting, "Each of us should ask him/herself: what do I want to say in this film?"

"I myself," Lee continued, "am interested in the contradictions of being a part of commercial show biz life while not really being a part of it. I still remember a couple of vaudevillians telling me that we were snobs. They were working for a living; did we have some nobler purpose? . . .

"And anecdotes. The blacklist. To this day I don't know what happened with two of us and HUAC—I only have the transcripts of my own testimony, which is sort of funny. Now."

(Fred had been called up well after Lee and Pete, among a group of educators—he taught music classes. The process servers never could find a Ronnie Gilbert, never looked for a Mrs. Weg.)

Lee hadn't much liked talking about the HUAC, but interviewers always asked him about the experience, and this *was* a summing-up time. He'd even been questioned about it by his great-niece, sixteen-year-old Lee Hays, for a term paper. He described it to her as he had described it to no one else, and she used his words in her paper:

"When I walked into the hearing room I passed two huge Irish federal marshals standing at the door. As I passed, one of them said, 'I'd like to take them all out in the courtyard and shoot them.' During my testimony the chairman asked how I felt about immunity. That is, if they gave me immunity against incriminating myself, would I then testify? They almost trapped me because I knew so little of the law, but my lawyer saved me by whispering that immunity was not the law and the question was hypothetical. But I could have got into big trouble by somehow agreeing to immunity voluntarily. This immunity device is now used in grand jury proceedings, thanks to Nixon and Mitchell, and is one of the biggest threats to civil rights the country has ever known.

"I didn't feel any better at the hearings when my attorney whispered to me that there was a bug under the table to pick up everything he might say to me.

"I don't think I have ever felt so damned alone as on that day. I had a good lawyer, who wasn't allowed to speak; reporters were obviously on my side, but I was nervous and shaken. When I got home my heart hurt and I place the beginnings of my heart trouble at that day. It was like having to walk a tightrope, to follow the legalities of the 5th Amendment."

Knowing her nonpolitical upbringing in New Orleans, he was touched by the words that followed.

"The feelings expressed by Mr. Hays," wrote young Lee, "are probably very similar to those of other witnesses who had to fight against HUAC or another congressional committee for their unalienable rights. Those who succeeded in keeping their pride and their values intact suffered greatly but emerged as heroes. In the words of Mr. Hays, 'If it wasn't for the honor, I'd just as soon not have been blacklisted.' "

Lee delighted in this third-generation family tie. Young Lee's writing (old Lee told Sue Brown Hays, the girl's grandmother) proved that "the good old Brown-Hays designer genes" were holding up. Not that he held with those who believe that genetics is destiny, "but sometimes pure acculturation doesn't seem to account for our family talents."

Sue's high-born Mississippi epistolary style enchanted Lee.

Another Lee Hays. Lee's
nephew's daughter Lee (*left*) and
her sister Catherine in 1974.

"Once again," he told her, "and I repeat myself every time I write you, I am overwhelmed with your elegance and style—even your symptoms are more elegant than mine. . . ."

Sue wrote often. She'd taken up the slack after Minnie Frank— Lee's sister—died in 1973. Minnie Frank's only child, Robert, had informed Lee of her death by mail, a week *after* the funeral, a casualness Lee never forgave.

Reuben wrote frequently from his condo in Delray Beach, Florida, a healthy old affluent Republican passing along jokes about Democrats, about aging, about inflation. The two survivors—a rural Arkansas Methodist minister's oldest and youngest sons, who had achieved success and prominence at diametrically opposed and violently hostile political poles. Their blood ties had overcome their differences. Reuben bought Lee a large-type IBM typewriter when his vision dimmed from diabetes; Reuben paid for a new asphalt runway to accommodate Lee's wheelchair.

"Reuben," wrote Lee in 1978, "thanks for your constant attention."

Jim Callo thought he would plumb wear out in 1980. And Jim was a healthy twenty-six-year-old, Lee's most devoted Croton kid.

He'd come up the hill in 1969 as a summer substitute for a high school friend who regularly mowed Lee's lawn and weeded his garden. He and Lee "adopted each other from the first," Jim remembered. Lee was his "Buddha." Jim worked his way up to "head overseer" on Lee's "estate," supervising Lee's "sharecroppers," the other kids who pulled weeds.

While Jim was unpacking his gear for his second year of college at New Paltz in 1975, he learned that Lee had lost a leg, and without missing a beat he repacked and returned to Croton, knowing Lee would need help.

Lee couldn't be left to live alone after the second leg went. Jim moved in permanently, occasionally spelled by his older brother Joe.

Lee had settled down emotionally after the loss of the second leg; he had little more to lose. The rhythm of life at 4 Memory Lane followed the seasons, the garden. Now, suddenly, the house transformed into the hub of the universe.

The film crew would come up to shoot some footage of Lee. Local reporters finally discovered the celebrity on the mountain and called for interviews. Academics writing papers on the agrarian Left of the 1930s picked up trails leading to Lee. Bob Sherman broadcast three hours of Weavers music on his weekly New York WQXR show, "Woody's Children"; Lee's delightful postcard comments, read aloud by Sherman, inspired more requests for interviews.

"It was wild," Jim Callo recalled. "The film crew kept moving furniture, putting gel on the windows, blowing fuses. This went on for a few months with additional things such as CBS-TV coming up to film Lee for the Charles Kuralt show. And more damned journalists and radio people coming and going. I'd have to come home from work, take care of Lee's necessaries, and act as host. Finally, he was asked to do the Joe Michaels show, 'Prime of Your Life.' I said, 'Forget it, Lee, you're exhausted, I'm exhausted. Tell them next spring.' "

In the middle of the night, when press interviewers and film-makers had gone, Lee thought often of death, and wrote of it. Being Lee, he couldn't play it straight.

IN DEAD EARNEST

If I should die before I wake
All of my bone and sinew take
Put them in the compost pile
To decompose a little while

Worms, water, sun will have their way
Reducing me to common clay
All that I am will feed the trees
And little fishies in the seas

When radishes and corn you munch
You may be having me for lunch
And then excrete me with a grin
Chortling, there goes Lee again.

'Twill be my happiest destiny
To die and live eternally.

Lee sent the sonnet to a fellow gardener, Pete's wife, Toshi. Pete set it to music, retitled it "Immortality," and sang it, to "explosive and sustained laughter," as the capstone of a long segment on Lee and his music, in his new season of concerts.

"Sometimes," wrote Lee to Pete, "I get the feeling that my time ain't long, so if I don't get to Carnegie you will have to speak and sing for me. You have been doing that a long time anyway. I am somewhat bone-weary these days. The pain of the world is too much with us. The dreams of youth were so sure and certain. The trouble is, they ain't all spent."

The closer time moved to the concerts, the more certain Lee felt that he could not possibly make his rashly promised appearance. He so informed Harold, Pete, and Jim Brown, frequently. Jim never fully believed he'd show up.

Was he willfully keeping everyone off balance, as he had during the late Weavers days—would he turn up, wouldn't he turn up? With all that everyone knew about amputations and such, no one

Rehearsing for the final Weavers reunion concert at Carnegie Hall.

could cry hypochondria at this stage; still, the familiarity of the pattern tended to dilute sympathy. Toshi Seeger stepped in, finding businesslike solutions to each of Lee's valid fears about the logistics of the operation—right down to the question of how he and his wheelchair could negotiate any bathroom but his specially reconstructed own.

Pete wasn't sure they could really carry it off. To him it felt like a basketball team thirty years later trying to run through its old plays.

Ronnie thought perhaps people should remember them as they were. But her own memory of "how wonderful it was to sing with those guys" won out in the end. "One more moment, one more possibility. . . ."

Harold Leventhal placed the first ad in the *New York Times* on Sunday, October 12. When he called the following Tuesday,

And yet the film, after all, would stand as his posthumous memoirs, so Lee honed every voice-over comment to its Haysian essence:
"I'm Lee Hays, more or less. . . ."

"I enjoyed the Weavers, and I still do. And I'm still trying to
get them to do things the right way . . . my way."

(Over a shot of Lee in his garden, with two young helpers.) "I
spent a good many years of my youth trying to liberate the sharecroppers, and now I've got some of my own."

(Listening to the recording made by Pete, Ronnie, and Fred.)
"They all said they missed the bass. If they had asked me, I would
have mailed the bass part in for that song."

(At the picnic reunion, a song concluded.) "We made it, by God!
We will now pass out among you. . . ."

(Rehearsing for the concert.) "There are quite a number of new
songs. Fortunately, the other Weavers will have to sing them. All
I have to do is sing bass, and you can always fake it. That's one
of the greatest advantages of singing bass—you don't have to learn
too many new words."

And so on. Flavor by Hays. The film was shaping up just fine.

Fred, producing the concert album, sent tapes of his work-in-
progress to the others, instantly reigniting some of the old Weavers
tensions.

"What's the chain of command on this here project?" Lee angrily
wrote to Fred, with copies to Harold, Pete, and Ronnie. "Who is
supposed to make final decisions on whether to use bass or not,
for example? . . ." Et cetera. Two pages of criticism of what Fred
had done, and what Lee, having played the tapes for friends and
neighbors, felt Fred ought to do.

"Somebody has to be in charge," responded Fred, on the boil,
with copies to Harold, Pete, and Ronnie. "Somebody has to make
certain decisions. . . . Perhaps it would be better to give it to
the engineer to put together or Ronnie or a committee of your
friends and Leventhal neighbors and let them make the literally
thousands of step-by-step technical and aesthetic decisions that
need making. That would be perfectly all right with me. But in
all fairness, such a decision should be made fairly quickly.

"If I am to withdraw from a producer function, I really don't
relish the idea of spending weeks up in Boston presiding over the

he was told that both concerts were completely sold out. "Then
things began to mount," said Harold, "people calling up for tickets
from all over the country. As there was more press attention, I
had calls from Chicago and Boston, Washington, D.C., Los Angeles
and San Francisco wanting to know if they could have a Weaver
reunion in those cities. But of course that was impossible. The
Weavers were not going to go and get together again, and we left
the concert and the reunion just for the city of New York."

From the moment Pete wheeled Lee out onto the stage of Carnegie, the experience of the Weavers' reunion was as different from
a concert as an epiphany is from the morning news.

The audience—a surprising audience, with more young people
than gray-heads—rose and cheered, and cheered, and cheered.

"We came out and stood there helplessly," Fred wrote to Lee
afterward, "for what seemed forever while the audience did *their*
number on us. . . . [The event] was an emotional feast that was
almost too much to bear. And when it was over, after feeling
drowned in this tidal wave of love, I must unashamedly admit
that I really had to get upstairs very quickly where I would finish
going to pieces in the privacy of my dressing room. I don't think
I ever admired the Weavers as much as I did this time around
nor was I ever prouder to be associated with you, Ronnie and
The Saint."

How much of this was due to the music, and how much to
what they stood for? Larry Josephson, producer and musicologist,
in his jacket notes for the concert album, wrote that "without
their *music*—and the sheer talent and energy that support it—
none of the folk musicology or the political history surrounding
the Weavers would be worth more than a footnote. . . ."

But without the political history?

"Considering the problems we had as a group," Ronnie said
later, "what we did and what we sang and what we represented
transcended all that. Four more oddly assorted people you could
never hope to find. Each with very strong opinions. Very different
backgrounds. Class differences. And there was a lot in the dynamics
of our relationships that none of us really understood.

"It was always clear to us that we had something Lee used to
say was 'greater than the sum of our parts,' a cliché but really

true. There was something about what we were doing, something in what we believed, something in how we touched one another and related to the audience. . . .

"I believe all public people are a kind of screen on which an audience projects itself and its wishes and desires. And there was something about us that let that audience project their sense of what could be possible when disparate people decide to be together. . . . Thank God for film, and for Jim Brown, because to be able to see that on film, to see what the audience saw, to feel what the audience felt, was an astonishing thing."

"The Reunion," Harold Leventhal wrote to Lee, "was above all a triumph for *you*. You made it possible, otherwise it would not have been THE WEAVERS.

"I know what you went thru . . . uncertainties, doubts, concern . . . but with all these problems you stayed with it and *you made it.*

"It was an experience and an event that 5,400 people will never forget . . . it was a celebration of Love, Respect & Admiration . . . and it was a great musical event.

"Above all, Lee, I am proud of you and love you more for the great joy you gave us all.

"And now I will officially recognize your 'retirement.' "

So transcendent was the audience emotion at the concert's end that it seemed it could transport a recipient soul up to the heavens. For good. Especially one in fragile health.

But the film remained to be shaped, a concert album to be produced. Lee put his mind to the work ahead.

Jim Brown and George Stoney felt they had the makings of a wonderful documentary. "The characters were great," said Jim, "it was a historic occasion, it told an important story, it had a metaphor. So much of making documentary films is having the right material; this happened to be a project that had all the right elements."

Lee felt far less sanguine.

"I have been telling Jim Brown that the film, like any work of art, should have a beginning, a muddle and an end," wrote Lee to Pete, "a thought hardly original with me but worth considering: like the Indian woman asking 'where's the melody?' it's fair to

The Weavers in 1950 (*insert*) and in 1980. (Photograph by Da⌐

ask 'where's the plot?' Conflict? Tension? Movement? Re⌐ Short of working toward a triumphal finale at Carnegie⌐ so far, only a rather flat declaration that a group has had ⌐ Maybe when we describe the slings and arrows of fo⌐ reunion will be seen as resolution and conclusion enou⌐ tension, there might be some doubt as to whether I ⌐ Carnegie; maybe there's the drama. Or whether you wi⌐ day's rest before the event. We need a story line. . . ."

Pushing, doubting, questioning. What are we trying t⌐

Again George Stoney noted Lee's caution about tota⌐ ment to the film. Again he attributed it to Lee's fea⌐ disappointed.

birth of a camel. [Camel: a horse created by a committee.] Indeed, if such is the case, I pledge that I will completely refrain from any suggestions, comments, complaints or what-have-you—not out of pique—but out of a firm conviction that a 3-humped camel is better than a 4-humped one."

Of course, Fred completed work on the album. But the episode reminded them why the Weavers had broken up in the first—or rather the second—place.

The pace simply didn't let up. While work continued on the film and on the album, and interviewers came and went, Pete began to push for yet another Weavers appearance, this time at the annual Croton Festival in June. Lee balked, protesting his voice was half or more shot. Pete took another tack.

"My own voice is at least a quarter shot," he wrote Lee. "My fingers are slowing down on me. But I've got to keep on trying. I don't want to sing with just Ronnie and Fred, good musicians though they are. I believe that two of the biggest mistakes I ever made were in asking you to leave the Almanacs in 1941, and in asking you to leave the office of People's Songs in 1946. If I had had more sense, I would have drawn back, asked myself, 'What's wrong here?' But I have always been in too much of a hurry. . . .

"If you really don't want to sing four or five songs at Croton, I'll not try to force you. But I sure hope you change your mind. After all, this is Croton, where you live, breathe the air, drink the water, flush your toilet. . . ."

How could Lee refuse a Pete who manfully uncovered those old bleeding sores and took onto himself the blame?

They wouldn't call it a concert; they'd call it a rehearsal. Then if they muffed lines, well, they were *rehearsing*. For sure, they couldn't rehearse for the rehearsal. Between complex schedules (Pete's and Ronnie's and Fred's) and plain old feeling awful (Lee), they'd be lucky just to *be* at the Croton Festival in June.

Still, their scheduled appearance provided another opportunity for dissension and anger—the usual. Lee half promised Bob Sherman, WQXR's music director, who had played much Weavers music on his station, that he could record their performance. Fred, furious, declined to put "any recording of us with all our mistakes, tunings, fumblings, mumblings, coughs, groans, farts, etc." into any hands other than the Weavers'. Lee couldn't go back on his word to Sherman. Fred held his ground. How could Lee make such a decision unilaterally—who's in charge here? If the "rehearsal" is to be recorded by Sherman or anyone else, said Fred, "they can keep one microphone home. I will not appear." Fred prevailed. But someone in the audience taped them anyway, and that last, rather sloppy performance became what Fred had warned against—lousy underground tapes over which they had no control.

In July, Jim Brown and George Stoney moved the editing room up to Lee's house and invited the Weavers to a first screening. They'd edited the film to center it on Lee, the physical metaphor for survival with grace. Lee had protested, had asked Harold to urge them to find another approach. They'd followed their own vision. Now Lee wheeled himself into the kitchen, out of the line of fire.

On the first laugh, he rolled right back, remembered Jim Brown. "And everybody was laughing. They liked it a lot, and we liked it a lot. At that point, we knew we'd have no problems with it. We stayed up there a few days and refined some of Lee's voice-over lines. That was a month before he died. So he got to see the film."

Andy Perry, the boy next door, one of Lee's ex-kids, had died in a road accident in Florida, and the funeral was held on August 26. Lee sent over a beautiful eulogy he'd written. He was too upset to attend the service.

Lee's neighbors thought he'd deteriorated badly in the last several weeks, fading, shrinking, almost disappearing physically. They'd rigged up a horn, the kind boat owners use to signal a tender, so that Lee could blow out a warning if he needed help in the night.

Andy's parents, too exhausted to sleep after their harrowing day, heard Lee's horn. They rushed to his house and found him flailing for breath. Jim Callo was at his bedside, holding Lee. Herb Perry shouted at Carol to call the ambulance, call the police! Jim yelled, "Call Doctor Percy!" Police and ambulance quickly arrived and raced Lee to Phelps Memorial Hospital. Jim had leaped into the ambulance with Lee; the Perrys followed in their car. Dr. Brazil—

"Doctor Percy"—reached the hospital before the ambulance arrived.

Lee died that night. His Croton friends believed the immediate cause was his shock at Andy Perry's death. Lee's death certificate said diabetic cardiovascular disease.

"I knew a magical man once, a troubador. . . . He was a singer of songs. He used to sing them to my own young daughter, and he sang them to the big wide world," said Charles Kuralt, on his CBS-TV network television show, "Sunday Morning," two weeks after Lee's death.

"This was Lee Hays, who had started singing at church suppers and fish fries back home in Arkansas in the twenties; and sang with Will Geer and Woody Guthrie and Pete Seeger in the thirties, wandering the country. And sang on until last month, when he died. . . ."

Kuralt's opening words were followed by a long segment on the Weavers, Ronnie and Fred and Pete talking to the interviewer Charles Osgood, intercut with footage of the Weavers singing "Down for the Count," "Rock Island Line," "Wimoweh," "Let Me Go Home," and "Goodnight, Irene."

Finally, they'd broken through the network television blacklist. Too late.

Young Lee Hays wrote her college admission essay on her name. She'd hated it for years. Compared with names like Cynthia or Jennifer, it seemed too short. "This was not as bad as the fact that Lee is really a boy's name, and having to tell my friends that I was named after my great-uncle was embarrassing."

Then she'd learned more about her great-uncle, about his talent, about the blacklist, about his amputations, about the new life he made for himself in a small town in New York, about his humor, about the fact that he never stopped trying to learn.

"I hope that, when I am in my seventh decade," she wrote, "I will be able to look back and be proud of what I have done with my life. . . . I hope that I always will be able to laugh, to listen, to learn, and to care. In a way, I feel that my name is a legacy, but it has been left to me with one condition. I must make sure that the next Lee Hays is proud of the name and proud of the person for whom he or she is named. Perhaps I would be different if I had been named Cynthia or Jennifer. I am glad I was not."

When Lee's friends gathered to celebrate his life, it was Arlo who sang the words that Pete felt were most fitting, the verse of "Amazing Grace" that Lee had taught both of them:

> Shall I be wafted to the sky
> On flow'ry beds of ease,
> While others strive to win the prize,
> And sail through bloody seas?

Jim Callo waited for the go-ahead from Harold in regard to Lee's ashes. He knew where Lee had wanted them to be put—into his own compost pile. The idea rather unnerved Harold. But Toshi Seeger, who shared Lee's passion for organic gardening, assured Harold that Lee meant what he had so often made darkly funny remarks about. That settled it. Without further fuss, Jim did as Lee had wished. Some of Lee's friends and neighbors then took scoops of the compost to add to their own piles, hoping thus to have him with them forever.

Notes

Page

21 LEE WAS ALWAYS AN OLD MAN: Fred Hellerman, interview with DW, January 22, 1983.

21 TO PROVIDE EMERGENCY FINANCING: RFC Act, 1932.

21 PUCKISH . . . SENSE OF HUMOR: Joe Sedlak, letter to DW, March 18, 1983.

21 I'M PROUD TO BE HERE: LH, outtakes of recorded performances.

22 CLUNG TO OUR MISERABLE JOBS: Joe Sedlak, letter to DW, March 18, 1983.

22 ON THE BRINK OF A FASCIST REVOLUTION: LH, interview in *Sing Out!*, September/October 1980, 3.

23 AN AWFUL LOT OF MONEY: LH, taped memoirs.

23 EVERYTHING LEE DID SEEMED WRONG: Sue Brown Hays, interview with DW, November 3, 1983.

Chapter Three

25 IT TOOK BRAVE MEN: Willard Uphaus, *Commitment* (New York: McGraw-Hill, 1963), 44.

25 JESUS COME ALIVE: Willard Uphaus, interview with DW, May 2, 1983.

26 I GOT TO BE HIS CHIEF HELPER: LH, interview in *Sing Out!*, September/October 1980, 3.

26 WHAT CLAUDE HAS TRIED TO DO: LH, in *People's Songs Bulletin*, February–March 1948, 11.

26 BORN IN THE HILL COUNTRY: Cedric Belfrage, *South of God* (New York: Modern Age Books), 3ff.

28 CLAUDE WAS THE ONLY RADICAL: Myles Horton, interview with DW, November 27, 1983.

29 HE ISSUED AN ULTIMATUM: Myles Horton, interview with DW, November 27, 1983.

29 CLAUDE AND ZILPHIA DID MORE: LH, letter to Myles Horton, 1981.

29 LEE HAD AN INTUITIVE RAPPORT: Willard Uphaus, interview with DW, May 2, 1983.

30 LEE DID LIST AS NEAREST KIN: Transcript, College of the Ozarks, 1934.

30 THE OVER-RIDING THEME: College of the Ozarks Catalog, 1982–83, 1983–84.

31 THE DIRECTOR WAS ALWAYS CALLING IN: Belfrage, *South of God*, 244.

32 LEADERSHIP OF A PROPOSED STRIKE: Belfrage, *South of God*, 221ff.

33 I HAVE WORKED: House Un-American Activities Committee, *Communist Activity in the New York Area: Hearings*, 84th Cong., 1st sess., 1955, 2351.

34 WORKED AROUND FOR FOOD: Sue Brown Hays, interview with DW, November 4, 1983.

Chapter Four

37 A COMMUNITY SCHOOL: "Bill Moyers' Journal: An Interview with Myles Horton," June 5, 1981.

Page

38 CONCEPTS OF WHAT MIGHT BE DONE: LH, letter to Myles Horton, 1981.
39 IT CHALLENGED SOCIAL . . . POWER: *New York Times*, March 14, 1984.
39 THE SHARECROPPING SYSTEM HELPED PERPETUATE: LH, taped memoirs.
40 JUDSON CHURCH IS COMMITTED: *Judsonian*, April 1936.
41 TO PUT RELIGION INTO PRACTICE: Laurence T. Hosie, interview with DW, May 5, 1983.
41 AN EXOTIC: Seymour Hacker, interview with DW, April 12, 1983.
42 THE GREAT AMERICAN PHOTOGRAPHERS: LH, taped memoirs.
42 NO HOLLYWOOD PRODUCTION: Letter from the Sharecropper Film Committee to All Friends of the Sharecroppers of the South, dated 1936 and signed by Leon Rosser Land, Chairman; Rev. Hosie, Treasurer; Iva Wasson, Secretary.
43 IN 1936 I STUDIED BRIEFLY: LH, letter to Pare Lorentz, September 1980.
45 KIND OF A DISASTROUS EFFORT: LH, interview with Jim Capaldi, October 27, 1979.
45 HAVING TO EXPLAIN: Myles Horton, interview with DW, November 27, 1983.
45 A JUMBLE OF FILM: LH, interview with Jim Capaldi, October 27, 1979.
45 THE STORY OF THE SHARECROPPER: Script for *America's Disinherited*, 1936.
46 NEVER OWN MORE: Bill Hays Jr., interview with DW, November 4, 1983.
46 A NUMBER OF ELEGANT LADIES: Seymour Hacker, interview with DW, April 12, 1983.

Chapter Five

49 COMMONWEALTH COLLEGE: Raymond and Charlotte Koch, *Educational Commune* (New York: Schocken Books, 1972), and Charlotte and Raymond Koch Collection, Archives of Labor and Urban Affairs, Walter P. Reuther Library, Wayne State University.
50 BOLSHEVISM, SOVIETISM: Raymond and Charlotte Koch, *Educational Commune.*
52 WHEN LEE APPEARED AT COMMONWEALTH: Don Kobler, letter to DW, January 24, 1984.
52 LEE PROMISED A GREAT DEAL: *Commonwealth Fortnightly*, September 1, 1937.
53 AN EXPERIMENTAL PERFORMING GROUP: Raymond and Charlotte Koch, *Educational Commune.*
53 WE WROTE ZIPPER PLAYS: LH, in *People's Songs Bulletin*, February–March 1948, 11.
53 LEE WAS ABLE TO LEAD: Waldemar Hille, interview with DW, December 10, 1983.
54 IN THE EVENING: Don Kobler, letter to DW, January 24, 1984.
54 LEE LED ANOTHER KIND OF OUTING: Waldemar Hille, interview with DW, December 10, 1983.
54 THE CAR IN WHICH WE WERE RIDING: LH, in *People's Songs Bulletin*, February–March 1947, 15.

Page

56 Lee participated in meetings: Waldemar Hille, interview with DW, December 10, 1983.

57 so constructed: LH, in *People's Songs Bulletin*, February–March 1948, 11.

57 dubious luck: Raymond and Charlotte Koch, *Educational Commune*, 206.

57 When Claude was kicked out: Myles Horton, interview with DW, November 27, 1983.

57 an independent labor school: *Commonwealth Fortnightly*, September 1938.

58 sick all the time: Magda Fink, interview with DW, December 30, 1982.

59 big, disheveled: Hope Hale Davis, interview with DW, January 5, 1983.

Chapter Six

61 I do remember: LH, interview with Jim Capaldi, October 27, 1979.

62 It wasn't as easy: LH, in *People's Songs Bulletin*, February–March 1948, 11.

63 the kind of household: Angela Schwartz, interview with DW, October 24, 1983.

63 lots of music making: Angela Schwartz, interview with DW, October 24, 1983.

64 My dear boy: Lillian Lowenfels, letter to LH, undated.

64 sing worthily the songs: LH quoting Walt Whitman, "The Folk Song Bridge," from *The Elektra Folk Song Kit* (New York: Elektra Corporation, 1959).

64 Sometimes, reading this poem: LH, letter to DW, undated.

65 learn more from hitting the road: Pete Seeger, interview with DW, November 10, 1982.

66 hit it off pretty good: *Sing Out!*, September/October 1980, 4.

66 we got along well: Pete Seeger, interview with DW, November 10, 1982.

66 Pete gave the money to Lee: LH, in *People's Songs Bulletin*, November 1948, 9.

67 a real sassy song: Pete Seeger, interview with DW, November 10, 1982.

67 They were sentimental: LH, in *People's Songs Bulletin*, September 1948, 9.

67 A friend designed a beautiful table: Pete Seeger, interview with DW, November 10, 1982.

68 White purged himself: Kristin Baggelaar and Donald Milton, *Folk Music: More Than a Song* (New York: Crowell, 1976), 407.

68 a fine write-up: Pete Seeger, interview with DW, November 10, 1982.

68 It stunned 'em: LH, in *People's Songs Bulletin*, November 1948, 9.

68 still one of the best: Pete Seeger, interview with DW, November 10, 1982.

Page

68 ONE WEEKEND: Pete Seeger, interview with DW, November 10, 1982.
69 OUR WHOLE POLITICS: *Sing Out!*, September/October 1980, 5.
69 EIGHT-YEAR-OLD BUICK: Pete Seeger, interview with DW, November 10, 1982.
69 WE ROLLED THE GASOLINE HOSE: Woody Guthrie Archives, New York City.
71 ALMANAC HISTORY WILL PROBABLY NEVER BE WRITTEN: LH, in *People's Songs Bulletin*, December 1948, 9.
71 QUITE A SHIFTING PERSONNEL: *People's Songs Bulletin*, September 1948, 9.
71 NOT MUCH FURNITURE: Pete Seeger, interview with DW, November 10, 1982.
71 LADY, THE ALMANACS: LH, taped memoirs.
73 WE MADE UP SONGS: Woody Guthrie Archives, New York City.
73 ONE OF THE BIGGEST MISTAKES: Pete Seeger, interview with DW, November 10, 1982.
74 LOAFING AND INVITING THE SOUL: LH, letter to Pete Seeger, undated.
74 IT SEEMED TO ME THAT THE BEST THING: Pete Seeger, interview with DW, November 10, 1982.
74 I TOLD HIM: LH, letter to Pete Seeger, 1979, undated.
74 PETE REMEMBERED TALKING TO A FRIEND: Pete Seeger, interview with DW, November 10, 1982.
74 THE ALMANACS WERE MY OWN BROTHERS: LH, *People's Songs Bulletin*, December 1948, 9.

Chapter Seven

76 THE WAR PERIOD PASSED BY: *Sing Out!*, September/October 1980, 5.
77 BEETHOVEN, ET CETERA: Waldemar Hille, interview with DW, December 10, 1983.
77 READ WHATEVER HE PICKED UP: Co-worker who requested anonymity.
77 I THOUGHT IT WOULD BE A GOOD IDEA: Jean Karsavina, interview with DW, April 19, 1983.
77 I LEARNED A GREAT DEAL FROM HIM: Jean Karsavina, interview with DW, April 19, 1983.
78 THERE WASN'T ANYBODY AROUND: *Sing Out!*, September/October 1980, 5.
79 I HAD A FEELING THERE WERE PEOPLE: Pete Seeger, interview with DW, November 10, 1982.
79 PITCHING IN THEIR EFFORTS: Woody Guthrie Archives, New York City.
80 THE TWO MAIN FULL-TIME PEOPLE: Pete Seeger, interview with DW, November 10, 1982.
81 WE DON'T USE THAT TERM: Pete Seeger, interview with DW, November 10, 1982.
82 A TWO HUNDRED WORD COMMENT: LH, letter to Zilphia Horton, April 11, 1946.

Page

82 TRYING TO DO FOR PAC: LH, letter to Myles Horton, April 13, 1946.
82 THE ALL-PURPOSE FUCK-OFF THING: Fred Hellerman, interview with DW, January 22, 1983.
82 HE WAS AN EX-ALMANAC: Bernie Asbell, interview with DW, August 7, 1985.
86 LEE DIDN'T BELIEVE: A participant who does not want to be identified.
88 A LONG EXECUTIVE COMMITTEE MEETING: LH, taped memoirs.
89 THREE THINGS STAND OUT: Bernie Asbell, interview with DW, August 7, 1985.
90 IT SOUNDS LIKE: Pete Seeger interview with DW, November 10, 1982.

Chapter Eight

93 A NATIONAL MOVEMENT: Pete Seeger, letter to DW, June 28, 1985.
93 BEGINNING TO BE SUCCESSFUL: Pete Seeger, notes on his *People's Songs Bulletin*, collection.
94 I PROPOSE TO RUN A COLUMN: LH, in *People's Songs Bulletin*, January 1947, 11.
94 CLAUDE IS ONE OF THE PAPAS: LH, in *People's Songs Bulletin*, February–March 1948, 11.
94 WHEN ZILPHIA GOT UP AND SAID: LH, in *People's Songs Bulletin*, January 1947, 11.
95 FIRSTLY AND MOSTLY POETRY: LH, in *People's Songs Bulletin*, July–August, 1948, 17.
96 BEFORE TAPE RECORDERS: Fred Hellerman, interview with DW, August 1, 1985.
96 HOOT CALLS FOR THE BEST: LH, letter to Pete Seeger, 1948, undated.
96 THEN DURING BREAKS: Julian Roffman, letter to DW, May 31, 1982.
97 PISS-ASS DRUNK: Fred Hellerman, interview with DW, August 1, 1985.
97 OF THOSE YOUNG PEOPLE: Fred Hellerman, at the "Celebration of Lee Hays' Life," October 4, 1981.
97 LEE HAD A WAY: Fred Hellerman, interview with DW, August 1, 1985.
98 LEE ALWAYS NEEDED A COAUTHOR: Bernie Asbell, interview with DW, August 7, 1985.
98 LEE WAS A VERY CREATIVE FORCE: Pete Seeger, interview with DW, November 10, 1982.
98 WHICH, ACCORDING TO LEE: Pete Seeger, interview with DW, November 10, 1982.
98 A HAY-PITCHING GUEST: LH, in *People's Songs Bulletin*, November 1947, 11.
100 A GAL NAMED GERTRUDE: LH, in *People's Songs Bulletin*, July–August 1947, 19.
102 INTENSE CLASS CONFLICT: Ceplair and Englund, *The Inquisition in Hollywood* (Berkeley: University of California Press, 1979), 201–2.
104 THEATER PEOPLE: Fred Hellerman, interview with DW, August 1, 1985.

Page

106 THE END OF THE ENTHUSIASM: Fred Hellerman, interview with DW, August 1, 1985.

106 RIGHT AFTER ELECTION: Pete Seeger, notes on his *People's Songs Bulletins* collection.

Chapter Nine

109 A COUNTRY BOY GENIUS: LH, taped memoirs.

109 MARVELOUS TALENT FOR WRITING: Robert Mills, interview with DW, August 3, 1983.

110 TO COLONIZE: Ronnie Gilbert, interview with DW, January 28, 1986.

111 IN A WAY, WE THOUGHT: Pete Seeger, interview with DW, November 10, 1982.

111 IF WE SANG LOUD ENOUGH: Ronnie Gilbert, in *Wasn't That a Time!*

111 LEE HAD NOTHING: Fred Hellerman, interview with DW, August 1, 1985.

112 JUST EH: Fred Hellerman, interview with DW, August 1, 1985.

113 SIMON MCKEEVER AT PEEKSKILL: LH, in *Sunday Worker*, September 18, 1949.

116 A VERY TICKLISH SUBJECT: LH, interview with Jim Capaldi, October 27, 1979.

116 I DON'T KNOW WHETHER: *Sing Out!*, September/October 1980, 6.

Chapter Ten

118 LEE JOKED: Fred Hellerman, interview with DW, January 22, 1983.

118 THE GIRL SINGER: Ronnie Gilbert, interview with DW, January 28, 1986.

120 THE HELL WE WENT THROUGH: Fred Hellerman, interview with DW, January 22, 1983.

120 PETE TELLS A STORY: Pete Seeger, *The Incompleat Folksinger* (New York: Simon and Schuster, 1972), 461.

121 LONG BEFORE THE WEAVERS BECAME POPULAR: LH, taped memoirs.

121 SOMEHOW WRONG FOR OUR KIND OF MUSIC: LH, taped memoirs.

122 SMALL BUT INADEQUATE SALARY: LH, taped memoirs.

122 WE MAY HAVE TO TAKE THE BULL: Fred Hellerman, interview with DW, January 22, 1983.

123 I LEARNED A GREAT LESSON: LH, taped memoirs.

123 WHEN NEW SONGS CAME IN: LH, taped memoirs.

124 IN A MORE INNOCENT TIME: LH, taped memoirs.

125 WHO'S HANDLING YOU KIDS?: Fred Hellerman to DW, January 22, 1983.

125 I KNOW HIM: Pete Seeger, interview with DW, November 10, 1982.

125 WHEN I WENT BACKSTAGE: Harold Leventhal, interview with DW, August 10, 1983.

126 IN THE MONTH OF JUNE: Pete Seeger, interview with DW, November 10, 1982.

Page

126 THE RISE OF REPRESSIVE ACTION: Fred Hellerman, interview with DW, January 22, 1983.
126 NOW AT THIS POINT: Ronnie Gilbert, interview with DW, January 28, 1986.
126 THE WEAVERS REGRET: LH, letter to Van Camp, undated.
127 MUST HAVE WONDERED: Pete Seeger, interview with DW, November 10, 1982.
128 AFTER THE WAR THE FOUR MET: *Time*, September 25, 1950, 69.
129 SIMPLY SHOWED UP: Sue Brown Hays, interview with DW, November 3, 1983.
129 THE WEAVERS SEEM TO BE QUITE A HIT: Reuben Hays, letter to LH, September 12, 1951.
130 THE HELL WE WENT THROUGH: Fred Hellerman, interview with DW, January 22, 1983.
133 THEY CARPED THAT: Fred Hellerman, interview with DW, January 22, 1983.
133 PETE HEARD: David Dunaway, *How Can I Keep from Singing: Pete Seeger* (New York: McGraw-Hill, 1981), 149.
133 PERHAPS HE IS RIGHT: Pete Seeger, memo to the Weavers, undated.
133 OUR THEN MANAGER: Pete Seeger, *The Incompleat Folksinger*, 22.
134 PETE MADE US PAY DEARLY: Ronnie Gilbert, interview with DW, January 28, 1986.

Chapter Eleven

135 WE DISCUSSED THE CAREERS: Harvey Matusow, *False Witness* (New York: Cameron and Kahn, 1955), 51.
138 HARD NIGHT, OLD BOY?: Fred Hellerman, interview with DW, January 22, 1983.
141 LEE WOULD SOMETIMES WRITE: Sue Brown Hays, interview with DW, November 3, 1983.
142 BILLBOARD CHARTS SHOWED THREE WEAVER: *Billboard*, May 19, 1951.
142 AFTER COMMUNIST-INSPIRED RIOTS: *Columbus Citizen*, August 26, 1951.
142 THEY HAMMERED OUT A PRESS RELEASE: Harold Leventhal, interview with DW, August 10, 1983.
143 ALWAYS WHAT I WAS WEARING: Ronnie Gilbert, interview with DW, January 28, 1986.
143 A GEE-WHIZ PIECE: *Newsweek*, August 6, 1951.
144 WEAVERS BANNED AT FAIR: *Columbus Dispatch*, August 26, 1951.
145 AT THIS POINT: David Dunaway, *How Can I Keep from Singing: Pete Seeger* (New York: McGraw-Hill, 1981), 152.
145 FOR NEARLY TWO YEARS: LH, letter to Leonard Kapp of Decca Records, undated.
147 THE OWNER OF THE ICELANDIC RESTAURANT: *New York Journal American*, October 2, 1951.

Page

148 THAT KIND OF THING: Fred Hellerman, interview with DW, January 2, 1983.

148 LIFE BECAME HARD: Ronnie Gilbert, interview with DW, January 28, 1986.

Chapter Twelve

152 A CERTAIN KIND OF SELF-CENSORING: Fred Hellerman, interview with DW, January 2, 1983.

155 OCCASIONALLY, AN FBI AGENT: Earl Robinson, interview with DW, October 31, 1983.

156 HE REMEMBERED SHE WORE: LH, taped memoirs.

156 SHE'D DIED FOR HIM: Sue Brown Hays, interview with DW, November 3, 1983.

156 YES, IT USED TO BE: Walter Lowenfels, letter to LH, March 7, 1964.

158 I WAS FLUSHED OUT OF THE MOUNTAINS: Earl Robinson, interview with DW, October 31, 1983.

158 IN THE SAME WAY: LH, letter to Pete Seeger, undated.

158 A FRUSTRATED SOUTHERN LADY WRITER: LH, taped memoirs.

159 BANQUET AND A HALF: *Ellery Queen Mystery Magazine*, October 1954.

159 NOTES TO "BANQUET AND A HALF": LH, notes to Robert Mills, undated.

161 HE BEGAN TO WRITE "BAWDY STORIES": LH, taped memoirs.

161 NOR DID LEE SIGN HIS NAME: page found in stack of books on homosexuality in LH library.

161 OH YES, HE LIVES WITH ME: Bill Hays, Jr., interview with DW, November 4, 1983.

161 EMPLOYEE'S DISCOUNT PRIVILEGE CARD: B. F. Goodrich card dated January 3, 1955.

162 I HAVE BEEN GLUED TO THE RADIO: Minnie Frank Mosely, letter to LH, undated.

163 I AM NOT GOING TO ANSWER: Pete Seeger, *The Incompleat Folksinger* (New York: Simon and Schuster, 1972), 468.

163 CONGRESS HAS POWER: Larry Ceplair and Steven Englund, *The Inquisition in Hollywood* (Berkeley: University of California Press, 1979), 346.

163 I SIMPLY DID NOT FEEL: Pete Seeger, *The Incompleat Folksinger*, 468.

164 THE SONG THAT DEALS WITH VALLEY FORGE: House Un-American Activities Committee, *Communist Activity in the New York Area: Hearings*, 84th Cong., 1st sess., 1955, 2360ff.

164 WITHOUT HIS BANJO: HUAC, *Communist Activity*, 2451ff.

Chapter Thirteen

170 PETE KAMERON REAPPEARED: Fred Hellerman, interview with DW, January 22, 1983.

170 WHEN THE FILM WAS SCREENED: Earl Robinson, interview with DW, September 17, 1985.

Page

171 ALTHOUGH IT IS JUST A PAID JOB: LH, letter to Helen Robinson, undated.
171 WE ALWAYS TRIED: Harold Leventhal, interview with DW, August 10, 1983.
171 THE CONCERT, HELD ON MARCH 17: Joe Klein, *Woody Guthrie: A Life* (New York: Alfred A. Knopf, 1980), 411.
173 AFTER THE '55 CONCERT: Fred Hellerman, interview with DW, January 22, 1983.
173 A LOT OF EXTRA ATTENTION: Harold Leventhal, interview with DW, August 10, 1983.
174 AMAZINGLY LARGE CROWD: *Los Angeles Times*, April 15, 1957.
174 THEIR AUDIENCE: *San Diego Union*, April 8, 1957.
174 ONE OF THE SEASON'S MOST: *Salt Lake City Tribune*, April 5, 1957.
174 UNTIL LAST NIGHT: *Toronto Globe and Mail*, April 1, 1957.
175 A COMPLETELY DIFFERENT CROSS-SECTION: *San Francisco News*, April 22, 1957.
178 THE MATERIAL WAS NOT WORTHY: Maynard Solomon, interview with DW, January 18, 1983.

Chapter Fourteen

181 YOU MAY REMEMBER: LH, personal comment to DW, September 26, 1976.
181 BUT IT WAS A CIGARETTE COMMERCIAL: Fred Hellerman, interview with DW, January 22, 1983.
181 THE COMMERCIAL MAY HAVE BEEN: Pete Seeger, interview with DW, November 10, 1982.
182 PETE HAD SAID THERE'S SOMETHING: LH, taped memoirs.
182 IT'S MY THEORY: LH, taped memoirs.
183 WHEN PETE LEFT: Fred Hellerman, interview with DW, January 22, 1983.
183 GOOD NEW MATERIAL: Don McLean, interview with LH, talking together on tape about the Weavers over several sessions in March 1977.
184 MARVELOUS, ABSOLUTELY WONDERFUL: Fred Hellerman, interview with DW, January 22, 1983.
184 THE WEAVERS LIVED THE LIFE: Don McLean, interview with LH, March 1977.
184 I HAD NO STRONG OPPOSITION: LH, taped memoirs.
186 IT SEEMED SO RIDICULOUS: LH, taped memoirs.
186 THE NEXT NIGHT IT WAS ANNOUNCED: Don McLean, interview with LH, March 1977.
187 THIS IS LEE HAYS, ALL RIGHT: LH, letter to Maynard Solomon, undated.
188 THE KIDS CAN'T MAKE: LH, letter to Sue Brown Hays, undated.
188 ALL THE OLD WORRIES: Earl Robinson, interview with DW, October 31, 1983.
189 THE HOUSE WAS PACKED: *Billboard*, May 25, 1959.

Page

189 IT WILL BE A MUSICAL TRIP: LH, introd. to *The Weavers' Songbook* (New York: Harper, 1960).

190 HEADED FOR THE EIN GEV KIBBUTZ: LH, Newsletter No. 2, June 1959.

192 WE ARE DOING LOUSY PERFORMANCES: LH, Newsletter No. 4, July 1959.

192 A MARVELOUS, TRIUMPHANT TOUR: Fred Hellerman, interview with DW, January 22, 1983.

192 MY FIRST NEWS IS: LH, Newsletter No. 5, August 4, 1959.

193 WE DIDN'T SET THE COUNTRY ON FIRE: Fred Hellerman, interview with DW, January 22, 1983.

193 SO MUCH FUN TO OPERATE: LH, Newsletter No. 6, undated.

194 ONE THING I'LL SAY FOR PETE: Don McLean, interview with LH, March 1977.

194 THESE ARE LAUGHABLE THINGS: Fred Hellerman, interview with DW, January 22, 1983.

194 LIKE A PIECE OF FINE STEEL: Robert Shelton, in *High Fidelity*, December 1960.

196 EVERY BIT AS GOOD: Don McLean, interview with LH, March 1977.

198 HE JUST CAN'T HOLD AN AUDIENCE: David Dunaway, *How Can I Keep from Singing: Pete Seeger* (New York: McGraw-Hill, 1981), 217.

198 A STIRRING AND FABULOUS EVENT: Don McLean, interview with LH, March 1977.

Chapter Fifteen

200 SOME OF US WERE TOO BUSY: LH, letter to Harold Leventhal, November 6, 1963.

204 LEE LITERALLY LIVED OFF THE ROYALTIES: Harold Leventhal, interview with DW, August 10, 1983.

206 YOU CAUGHT ME AT A BAD TIME: Harold Leventhal, interview with DW, August 10, 1983.

207 IT WAS ALWAYS TO MY SORROW: LH, taped memoirs.

208 I WAS MORE THAN WILLING: Cisco tapes.

211 COULDN'T BELIEVE HIS GOOD LUCK: Bill Hays, Jr., interview with DW, November 3, 1983.

213 I COULD TALK TO LEE: Sue Brown Hays, interview with DW, November 3, 1983.

Chapter Sixteen

216 SUE WONDERED WHOM GOD HEARD: Sue Brown Hays, interview with DW, November 3, 1983.

217 MY BROTHER, I HAVE TREASURED: Reuben Hays, letter to LH, November 29, 1965.

220 AS A CHILD OF THE DEPRESSION: LH, letter to Harold Leventhal, April 14, 1973.

Page

221   YOU CAN'T GET BLOOD FROM A TURNIP: LH, letter to Lillian Lowenfels, undated.

222   JOE IS CYNICAL ALTOGETHER: LH, letter to Harold Leventhal, April 18, 1980.

223   WE ALL HAD COMMUNIST FRIENDS: LH, letter to Pete Seeger, October 23, 1979.

223   LEE'S HOUSE BECAME A HANGOUT: Jim Brown, interview with DW, December 29, 1985.

224   A COMPLETELY NONJUDGMENTAL ADULT PRESENCE: David Karpoff at LH memorial service, Oct. 4, 1981.

224   HE STRAIGHTENED OUT A LOT OF KIDS: Charlie Maguire, interview with DW, December 19, 1985.

224   I OFTEN THINK OF THE YEARS: Alan Arkin, letter to LH, undated.

225   THE STREET IS LIKE A COUNTRY LANE: LH, letter to Earl Robinson, undated.

228   I WAS BASICALLY YOUR AVERAGE KID: Arlo Guthrie, outtakes from *Wasn't That a Time!*

228   A VERY SOCIABLE, HUMOROUS, TALENTED BOY: LH, letter to Harold Leventhal, January 7, 1964.

228   HE STAYED FOR THE WEEKEND: LH, background notes for *Wasn't That a Time!*

229   NEVER MEANT TO SEND IT TO HIM: Harold Leventhal, interview with DW, August 10, 1983.

230   TWO VERY INSIDIOUS ILLNESSES: Dr. Percy Brazil, interview with DW, January 8, 1985.

Chapter Seventeen

233   WE CHAT LIKE TWO OLD COCKERS: LH, letter to Jim Brown, undated.

234   ENOUGH DARKNESS IN HIS PAST: Jim Brown, interview with DW, December 29, 1985.

235   A BIT OF A CHORE: George Stoney, interview with DW, December 29, 1985.

236   SUICIDAL ALMOST: Jim Brown, interview with DW, December 29, 1985.

237   ENERGY TO HER UNDERSTANDINGS: LH, background notes for *Wasn't That a Time!*

238   THE WHOLE THING COULD BE THOUGHT OF: Ronnie Gilbert, letter to LH, Fred Hellerman, and Pete Seeger, undated.

238   THE WORD THAT KEEPS POPPING UP: Fred Hellerman, letter to LH, January 24, 1980.

240   I BELIEVE THE WORK OF THE WEAVERS: LH, letter to Pete Seeger, March 18, 1977.

240   WE THOUGHT WE FAILED: Pete Seeger, interview with DW, November 10, 1982.

240   I DON'T THINK I CAN DO IT: George Stoney, interview with DW, December 29, 1985.

Page

241 IT WAS MAGICAL: Jim Brown, interview with DW, December 29, 1985.

241 LEE'S VOICE IS HALF SHOT: Pete Seeger, interview with DW, November 10, 1982.

242 CRACKER-BARREL HUMOR: Jim Brown, interview with DW, December 29, 1985.

242 A ONCE IN A LIFETIME EVENT: LH, letter to Jim Brown and George Stoney, May 17, 1980.

243 EACH OF US SHOULD ASK HIM/HERSELF: LH, letter to Ronnie Gilbert, Fred Hellerman, Pete Seeger, undated.

243 WHEN I WALKED INTO THE HEARING ROOM: Lee Hays (LH's great-niece), term paper May 1981.

244 BROWN-HAYS DESIGNER GENES: LH, postcard to Sue Brown Hays, June 8, 1981.

245 ONCE AGAIN, AND I REPEAT MYSELF: LH, letter to Sue Brown Hays, undated.

246 THANKS FOR YOUR CONSTANT ATTENTION: LH, letter to Sue Brown Hays and Reuben Hays, dictated to a nurse in Phelps Memorial Hospital, November 12, 1978.

246 ADOPTED EACH OTHER: Jim Callo, letter to DW, January 8, 1986.

247 EXPLOSIVE AND SUSTAINED LAUGHTER: Pete Seeger, letter to LH, undated.

247 SOMETIMES I GET THE FEELING: LH, letter to Pete Seeger, undated.

248 IT FELT LIKE A BASKETBALL TEAM: Pete Seeger, in *Wasn't That a Time!*

248 HOW WONDERFUL IT WAS: Ronnie Gilbert, in *Wasn't That a Time!*

249 THEN THINGS BEGAN TO MOUNT: Harold Leventhal, in *Wasn't That a Time!*

249 WE CAME OUT: Fred Hellerman, letter to LH, December 15, 1980.

249 CONSIDERING THE PROBLEMS: Ronnie Gilbert, interview with DW, January 28, 1986.

250 THE REUNION WAS ABOVE ALL A TRIUMPH: Harold Leventhal, letter to LH, December 3, 1980.

250 THE CHARACTERS WERE GREAT: Jim Brown, interview with DW, December 29, 1985.

250 I HAVE BEEN TELLING JIM BROWN: LH, postcard to Pete Seeger, undated.

252 WHAT'S THE CHAIN OF COMMAND: LH, letter to Fred Hellerman, dated "Going on 1981."

252 SOMEBODY HAS TO BE IN CHARGE: Fred Hellerman, letter to LH, January 5, 1981.

253 MY OWN VOICE: Pete Seeger, letter to LH, January 1981.

253 ANY RECORDING OF US: Fred Hellerman, letter to LH, May 27, 1981.

254 THEY CAN KEEP ONE MICROPHONE HOME: Fred Hellerman, letter to Harold Leventhal, May 20, 1981.

254 ON THE FIRST LAUGH: Jim Brown, interview with DW, December 29, 1985.

254 ANDY'S PARENTS: Carol Perry, interview with DW, January 1, 1986.

255 I KNEW A MAGICAL MAN ONCE: Charles Kuralt, on "Sunday Morning," CBS Television, September 13, 1981.

255 COMPARED WITH NAMES: Lee Hays (LH's great-niece), college application, autumn 1981.

Index